Contemporary
American Indian
Literatures &
the Oral Tradition

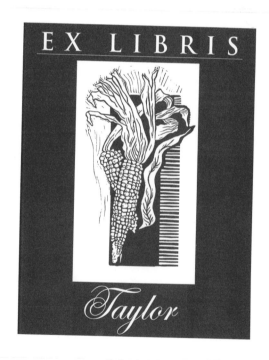

Contemporary American Indian Literatures & the Oral Tradition

SUSAN BERRY BRILL DE RAMÍREZ

The University of Arizona Press

Tucson

The University of Arizona Press

© 1999 The Arizona Board of Regents

First Printing

⊖ This book is printed on acid-free, archival-quality paper.

Manufactured in the United States of America

04 03 02 01 00 99   6 5 4 3 2 1

Library of Congress Cataloging-in-Publication Data

Brill de Ramírez, Susan Berry, 1955–

Contemporary American Indian literatures and

the oral tradition / Susan Berry Brill de Ramírez.

p. cm.

Includes bibliographical references and index.

ISBN 0-8165-1921-8 (cloth : alk. paper)

ISBN 0-8165-1957-9 (pbk. : alk. paper)

1. American literature—Indian authors—History and criticism.

2. American literature—20th century—History and criticism.

3. Oral tradition—United States.   4. Storytelling—United States.

5. Storytelling in literature.   6. Indians in literature.

I. Title.

PS153.I52 R35 1999   98-40233

810.9'897—dc21   CIP

British Cataloguing-in-Publication Data

A catalogue record for this book is available from the British Library.

Publication of this book is made possible in part by
the proceeds of a permanent endowment created with the
assistance of a Challenge Grant from the National
Endowment for the Humanities, a federal agency.

For my parents:

Dorothy Ann Retallack Brill
(1917–1979)
Robert M. Brill, M.D.
(1913–1981)

CONTENTS

ACKNOWLEDGMENTS

This volume is an offering of thanks to those whose guidance deepened my understandings of American Indian literatures; to those whose love and support nurtured the project in all its phases; to those of you who find in its pages some value in your own understandings of American Indian literatures and, concomitantly, of all literatures; and finally, and most importantly, to God and Bahá'u'lláh, for as a Bahá'í, I am taught that the origin of all knowledge is the knowledge of God.

Because the entirety of the volume was written during my tenure at Bradley University, I want to thank the university for providing an environment in which this work could come to fruition. Thanks are due the English Department, its chair, Dr. Margaret Carter, and the English majors and other students, all of whom enabled this project in diverse ways. In fact, the impetus for this volume came directly out of my American Indian literatures classes. Teaching non-Native students, I struggled with the incapacity of contemporary criticism and theory to open up American Indian literatures beyond the theories' critical boundaries. Wanting an approach that came out of the communities in which the literatures are crafted, I turned to their respective oral traditions to find a base for my students' approaches to, entries into, and engagements within these literatures and their stories.

I especially want to thank the Bradley students in my ENG 380.01 Southwest American Indian Writers course taught during the summer of 1996 on the Navajo reservation. As I watched my students conversively read themselves into the literatures studied in that class, I watched both their own transformations that came from those engagements and their own understandings of the literatures that were far deeper than is possible through a more disengaged approach. The learning that occurred in this class convinced me of the importance of a conversive approach for my own and student learning.

Grants from Bradley University's Provost's Office and the Office of Teaching Excellence and Faculty Development made the Southwest class (in many ways, an application of the work in this volume) and some of the research for the book possible, especially through the award of a summer stipend in 1995 to research and write one of the chapters. I have appreciated all of the support provided by the librarians, computing services staff, and English Department secretaries at Bradley University, most notably Willie Heberer, whose secretarial support has been invaluable throughout the project.

The staff at the University of Arizona Press has also been enormously helpful throughout the processes of review and publication. Joanne O'Hare (formerly senior editor at the press) supported the project in its early stages of review and revision. The Press's editor-in-chief, Christine Szuter, oversaw the later stages of review and revision. I cannot thank Dr. Szuter enough for her steadfast support of this project. Kathleen Ryan provided the thorough copyediting of the final manuscript, and Evelyn Vanden-Dolder, manuscript editor at the Press, guided me and the manuscript through the final stages of publication. I am grateful to these women for their conscientiousness and professionalism in bringing this work to fruition in book form.

A number of scholars have been strongly supportive of this project, providing their insights and encouragement (often, at times, when their words were sorely needed): Alanna Kathleen Brown, Kate Winona Shanley, David Moore, Carter Revard, Robin Fast, Sandra Sprayberry, Eric Anderson, Gloria Bird, Luci Tapahonso, Robert Parker, Phyllis Perrakis, Jim Sullivan, and Michael Fischer. This volume is built upon the work of the present and past generations of scholars of American Indian literatures. It would not have been possible without the work of scholars too many to note here, but whose words and insights are interwoven throughout these pages.

Special honor is due to the writers themselves whose novels, poems, and stories demanded of me new ways of reading and understanding beyond the bounds of contemporary critical practice. I especially want to honor those writers and storytellers whose stories grace this book: N. Scott Momaday, Nia Francisco, Luci Tapahonso, Esther G. Belin, Anna Lee Walters, Leslie Marmon Silko, Louis Owens, Lee Maracle, Sherman Alexie, and James Welch. This book really is my own retelling of their stories that, in part, form the larger story of American Indian literatures and, in turn, the even larger story of literary storytelling. It is, in many ways, a gift that I have received and retold in my own fashion. I thank everyone (writers, scholars, friends, and family) whose stories have found their ways, explicitly and implicitly, in this work. Special thanks are due to Simon J. Ortiz for permission to use sections from his poems for the epigraphs that begin each part of this book and to Luci Tapahonso for permission to quote liberally from her poetry in Chapter 3. Additional thanks are due to *The American Indian Quarterly* and the University of Nebraska Press for permission to reprint the article (*AIQ* 21.3 1998) that appears herein as Chapter 5, "Storytellers and Their Listener-Readers in Silko's 'Storytelling' and 'Storyteller.' "

To the two storytellers whose stories (told and lived) filled my childhood with awe and love, Dorothy Ann Retallack Brill and Dr. Robert M. Brill, I send my respect, love, and thanks. This book is my offering to you both. And to my husband, Antonio, whose own story continues to interweave my own in wondrous ways, whatever work I accomplish is very much the fruition of our lives together. Toño, for this and much more, I am thankful to you, and to God.

Contemporary
American Indian
Literatures &
the Oral Tradition

INTRODUCTION

Orality and Conversivity in Relation to American Indian Literatures

This book is an introduction to conversive literary and scholarly strategies. The term *conversive* conveys both senses of conversion and conversation in which literary scholarship becomes a transformative and intersubjective act of communication. Here the scholar becomes a listener-reader of literary works (like a listener participating in an oral storytelling event), and in turn becomes a storyteller-guide to assist others in becoming listener-readers of those literary works, not only in the classroom but also in one's written scholarship. After a visit to the Laguna elementary school, Simon J. Ortiz (Acoma) says, "Standing before the children, I realized that what I do as a writer, teacher, and storyteller is to demystify language, and I smiled. Making language familiar and accessible to others, bringing it within their grasp and comprehension, is what a writer, teacher, and storyteller does or tries to do" (*Woven* 4). In contrast to the apparent complexities of much contemporary literary criticism and theory, a conversive approach is a far simpler method that offers potentially deeper and more meaningful insights for scholars and their listener-readers.

My decision to approach American Indian literatures from an oral center comes from a conviction that oral storytelling is foundational to these literatures and, in fact, to all literatures. However, literary criticism has evolved into a largely textual endeavor overlooking the oral qualities of literature. Criticism as such reads and interprets literary texts in terms of specific theoretical frameworks against which they are understood and evaluated. Scholars of American Indian literatures have struggled with the extent to which contemporary literary theories and criticisms do more to obscure those literatures through (mis)readings that end up forcing works into interpretive frameworks that they do not necessarily fit. Literatures that are more textually informed and accordingly distanced from their oral roots will respond most effectively to those textually based criticisms and theories that are our twenty-five-hundred-year legacy of Western criticism extending back to Plato's written reconceptualizations and transformations of Socrates' oral teachings. Attempts to reclaim the oral within the textual (as in the case of Bakhtinian dialogism) do so, nevertheless, from a discursively textual and decidedly Western framework that privileges the textual at the expense of the oral.

For those literatures closer to their oral roots (as is the case for many works of American Indian literatures), scholarly reading strategies need to be based within the very traditions from which those literatures are based. Robert Allen Warrior (Osage) emphasizes the importance of "a mature Native cultural and literary criticism" that "ground[s] itself in its own history" and traditions (*Tribal* xiii, 2). I agree with Warrior in his criticism of "the preoccupation in American Indian Studies with oral traditions to the detriment of serious engagement with more theoretical work by Native intellectuals" ("Reading" 239). The problematic emphasis in Native studies on past oral traditions has perpetuated colonial romanticizations and, thereby, the continuing marginalization of American Indian literatures. This is what Greg Sarris (Coast Miwok/Pomo) points to when he writes, "Tradition is often considered as that which is unchanging in a culture, that which is canonical and which governs, or at least influences in significant ways, peoples' lives" (*Keeping* 179). Most discussions of past American Indian oral traditions have understood their significance within such canonical and static boundaries, but as Sarris continues, "tradition is not fixed, but an ongoing process" (180). Joseph Bruchac (Abenaki) criticizes "a lack of awareness" about American Indian stories, saying, "They are not 'myths and legends,' in the popular sense, stories which are untrue and belong to some distant past. They are, in fact, alive. . . . Stories are part of the life of the people" (*Roots* 91). The sorts of questionable scholarship that Warrior, Sarris, and Bruchac critique, rather than pointing to an avoidance altogether of discussions of orality, indicate the need for corrective work that reads American Indian literatures within their own dynamic and continuing oral traditions (written and performative), rather than through the externally imposed lenses of textually based Eurocentric traditions.

However, heeding Warrior's concern, it is crucial that we not interpret the orality of American Indian literatures solely in terms of a linear chronological narrative that posits orality as a prior, simpler form that then evolves into a more recent, more developed, and higher form of written literature. This was the sort of error made by scholars such as Walter J. Ong (*Orality*) and Albert B. Lord (*Singer*), who privileged the written form by virtue of the textual primacy of our times—a primacy that Ong and Lord very helpfully discuss, but which they do not then use to critique their own preconceptions. In contrast to the textuality which, William Clements reminds us, "continue[s] to be central to the study of Western literature" and in which "expression, verbal or otherwise" is frozen (6, 8), my understanding of American Indian literatures indicates that it is orality, not textuality, that is central to these literatures both in its presence and in its absence. Leslie Marmon Silko (Laguna Pueblo) tells us, "From the spoken word, or storytelling, comes the written word, as well as the visual image" (*Yellow Woman* 21). Ortiz explains, "The oral tradition of Native American people is based upon spoken language, but it is more than that. Oral tradition is inclusive; it is the actions, behavior, relationships, practices throughout the whole social, economic, and spiritual life process of people. In this respect, the oral tradition is the consciousness of the people" (*Woven* 7). Agnes Grant writes, "In order to fully appreciate Native literature, the reader must recognize the difference between oral and written literature. Oral literature is a special performance; it is unique. It is *one* moment of a tradition. Even when it is written down and becomes 'fixed', it is still oral" ("Native Literature" 61).

Of course, we cannot really draw strict and definitive lines between those literatures that are oral versus those that are textual, nor should we want to. Literature, unlike strictly textually based writings such as academic textbooks, manifests oral and textual elements to varying degrees. This is what differentiates literature from text. Kimberly M. Blaeser (Anishinabe) notes, "Most scholars agree that the oral can never be fully expressed in the written, experience cannot be duplicated in *text*" (*Gerald Vizenor* 15; emphasis added). Stephen A. Tyler comments on the differences between oral and textual representations when he notes, "Orality makes us think of many voices telling many tales in many tongues, in contrast to the inherent monologism of texts that only tell different versions of the one true tale, each version recapitulating—even unwittingly—the founding allegory of Q.E.D.,[1] which is its source, terminus, and standard" (136). The greater complexity of oral storytelling can be understood as an intricately woven tapestry or rug in contrast to the more simplistic productions of a single strand or thread of a monologue or the multiple strands or threads of a dialogue (as in a string or rope in which several threads are interwoven). This is why James Ruppert points out that "the multiple encoding that exists in oral transmission is almost impossible to duplicate" ("Uses" 107).

Arnold Krupat notes the critical dilemma when he writes, "And, of course, the texts of Native American literatures are not only theoretically but also in practice what we may call *oral texts*" ("Post-Structuralism" 124). Although such a reference to literatures that are largely orally informed as "texts" still privileges their textuality over their orality, Krupat clearly indicates that any literary approach to American Indian literatures must take into account their orality. This book does so through its articulation and demonstration of a conversively informed literary strategy that approaches the written in terms of its orality. Within such a framework, the written is understood as the vehicle for the transmission of the transformative power of oral storytelling.

Ortiz tells us about his own writing: "There is a certain power that is compelling in the oral narrative as spoken by a storyteller simply because the spoken work is so immediate and intimate. I wanted to show that the narrative style and technique could be expressed as written narrative and that it would have the same participatory force and validity as words spoken and listened to" ("Always" 66). Contrary to popular opinion (scholarly and nonscholarly), oral stories are no less sophisticated and complex than written literatures. In fact, I would hazard that it is the degree of conversivity and orality that gives literary works their power, depth, and vitality. Gretchen Bataille notes, "contemporary writers, although writing in English and in western genres—the novel and the poem—derive much of their power from the oral literary tradition" (17). Alanna Kathleen Brown goes even further in her assertion of the value of oral storytelling when she writes, "the stories evolve out of a richly textured oral tradition. Written words are merely the extension of that tradition, not a reflection of a higher form of culture and sophistication" (173). Rodney Simard (Cherokee) reminds us that oral literature "still is the basis for *all* literatures, and it is no less distinguished because of its orality" (247). In fact, storytelling in oral or written (literary) form is far more sophisticated and complex in its development of metaphor, symbolism, voice, timing, and effect than are those literatures and other writings that are more textually and discursively based (such as third-person voiced essays that are directed to no specific listener-reader). Stanley Diamond explains, "Writing was one of the original mysteries of civilization, and it reduced the complexities of experience to the written word" (4). Tullio Maranhão asks "whether the notion of text is inextricably associated with the technologies of literacy and writing" (269). It is, but as this chapter and book clarify, although textuality is the effect of a literate world, different works of writing reflect different degrees of textuality and orality, or discursivity and conversivity.

This book builds on the groundbreaking work of the past generations of scholars of American Indian literatures as I articulate, not only conversive ways to read American Indian literatures, but even more broadly, new ways to approach all other literatures. The discussion of orality is far from new, but what is new is my offering of an explicitly conversive approach. Ludwig Wittgenstein tells us that "A new word is like a fresh seed sown on the ground of the discussion" (*Culture and Value [CV]* 2e). What appears to be a minor shift in terminology from discourse or dialogism to conversive relations is actually a much deeper change. This change reflects a larger shift in orientation from a Western privileging of textuality that then approaches orality from an objectively and objectifying discursive framework to a focus that centers itself within the conversive relations of oral storytelling that takes an inherently intersubjective approach. June O'Connor advocates a similar shift in orientation in her field of anthropology: "It seems to me that it is much wiser to note from the start that we are subjects working to enter into the subjectivity of others. Objectivity is an unhelpful word in this context; . . . I myself see our work according to the model of a conversation" (8, 9). This volume is designed to be part of such a conversation and also to be a guide for others in their own participation in a transforming conversation that has been going on for as long as human persons have been telling stories.

For several decades, scholars of American Indian literatures have been emphasizing the importance of orality in storytelling traditions. More often than not, such discussions have centered around orally performative chants, songs, and stories, but a number of scholars have pointed to the importance of orality for written American Indian literatures as well. For example, John Purdy explicitly refers to American Indian fiction as "a hybrid fiction, derivative of spoken and written literatures" (372). And Elaine Jahner writes, "The journey toward decreased ethnocentrism in critical judgments can profitably begin with consideration of tribal aesthetics in relation to oral literature performance" ("Critical" 212). Jahner continues, pointing out "that oral forms reflect particular ways of knowing, that they are epistemological realities" (223). Andrew Wiget notes that "[t]oo frequently,

contemporary studies of Native American oral literature . . . remain en-
cumbered by a textual rather than a performative paradigm, ignoring char-
acteristics that set oral tradition apart from writing" ("Native" 16). The
value of a conversive approach is that the orality within American Indian
literatures (and other literatures) is foregrounded with its inherent emphasis on relationality and connectedness (*con*versive as distinct from the inherent separateness within *di*alectical, *dis*cursive, and *di*alogic frameworks).
Instead of approaching orality in American Indian literatures from a Western critical discourse that emphasizes the distanced objectification of texts—
thereby looking at orality as the object of a critical gaze—a conversive
approach places the scholar within the oral engagement as a "mutual participant" (Moore, "Myth" 371).

Conversive Structures and Strategies

Within American Indian traditions of oral storytelling, there is a power
that actually transforms the listener through her or his engagement with
the story. In fact, within the oral storytelling practice, the listener is an
active participant whose presence is necessary to the telling-creation of the
story. The storyteller and listener interact throughout the process in a
conversation that reflects the inherent interrelationality of storytelling. This
is also true of those literary works significantly informed in conversive ways
that enable the reader as listener-reader to participate more closely in the
written story than is possible in more strictly textual forms of writing in
which authorial control is a given. Within a scholarly framework, the
interactive relationship between the storyteller and listener is transformed
into the interactive and intersubjective relationship between the literary
work and the scholar (in the role of a listener-reader). This book specifically
delineates and discusses literary structures and strategies in a number of
works of American Indian literatures. These conversive structures and
strategies (such as the privileging of relationality over individuality, domains in which meaningfulness is defined relationally rather than semiotically, voice shifts that reflect the presence and necessity of participatory
listener-readers, and repetition for learning rather than for memorization)
are the literary manifestations of conversivity as represented in the oral
tradition. As noted earlier, I use the term *conversive* to describe the conjunctive reality of traditional storytelling through both its transformational
and regenerative power (conversion) and the intersubjective relationality

between the storyteller and listener (conversation). The ostensive strength of this method, insofar as this book is concerned, is its applicability for the reading and understanding of American Indian literatures; the method, however, is more broadly applicable for the study of all literatures.

As this book clarifies, a conversive literary scholarship engages with literary works, as scholars (1) learn to listen to voices previously silenced or otherwise critically altered through criticism's preconceived interpretive strategies, thereby gaining access in/to a range of literary works otherwise seemingly impenetrable; (2) serve as storyteller-guides teaching readers to listen to the words, worlds, realities, and histories within the literatures; and (3) demonstrate the transformative power of stories as manifested in the scholars' own interactions with particular literary works. Sarris writes that "certain kinds of pedagogies maintain chasms between home life, or lived experience, and school life. Such chasms make genuine critical involvement with texts impossible" (*Keeping* 175). However, when scholarship does become truly conversive, manifesting itself as a scholarly storytelling that brings stories, persons, and worlds together, then such scholarship, like storytelling, becomes transformative and a "tool for *changing* reality" (Kroeber, *Retelling* 13). This is what Sarris touches on when he advocates a literary scholarship that "move[s] closer to that which it studies" (*Keeping* 7).

To date, many literary critics who study American Indian literatures have been forced either to select among the array of literary criticisms available today (all of which bespeak, in some form or fashion, the Western tradition from which they derive) or to grapple with the inadequacy of these criticisms and theories for American Indian literatures, thereby using those theories provisionally, with a clear sense of that inadequacy. For over twenty years now, critics of American Indian literatures have consistently pointed to the deficiencies inherent in contemporary critical theories for understanding, interpreting, and evaluating Native texts. William Willard (Cherokee) notes, "Until recently, the vast majority of critical works about American Indian literature have focused on presenting introductory reviews of the field as a whole and legitimizing the literature to a non-Indian audience"—a process that served meaningful ends, but that also served, as Willard points out, to marginalize American Indian literatures (34). Elizabeth Cook-Lynn (Dakota) argues even more strongly when she writes, "The truth is, American Indian fiction and the American Indian novel, in particular, has been the captive of western literary theory" ("Literary" 51). She further explains,

> Because fiction in general and the novel, in particular, is thought to be imported from the nations of the West, and, therefore, concerning itself with originality, novelty, and worldview in celebration of the merchant bourgeoisie ideals of Europe, the criticism which has accompanied all novel writing, including the American Indian Novel, rests on these assumptions. . . . [Scholars] have focussed largely upon issues which concern the dominant culture, issues of identity, authenticity and purpose in the new stories called Native American Literature(s). ("Literary" 49, 47)

Grant writes, "And critics often apply criteria from the dominant culture while overlooking the unique qualities of Native literature" ("Content" 5). Penny Petrone points out, "Western readers are prone to view non-Western literatures in terms with which they are familiar, however irrelevant those may be to them" (4). Krupat states the problems that result from "projecting western interpretive categories on to Indian materials" ("Identity" 6). Yet he notes elsewhere, "what might be called an 'indigenous' criticism for Indian literatures remains to be worked out" (*Ethnocriticism* 44). Even within many discussions of orality in American Indian literatures, rather than centering the discussion within tribal oral traditions, the approach begins from a textually based framework that defines orality as "other" and "less than." Clements notes, "the standard of literary quality by which even the oral materials are measured is Western" (194).

Jeanne Perreault comments on the imposition of critical approaches that are directly informed by the same Eurocentric tradition that has wrought horrific real world effects upon Indian peoples. Perreault writes, "The activity of literary criticism itself has been called into question when the critic belongs to a group that is privileged over, indeed, oppressive of, the writer's community" ("Notes" 9). Ruth Finnegan asserts, "Thus to take as our yardstick the present circumstances of literature in Western Europe—or rather perhaps those of a generation or so ago—and assume that this is the standard by which we estimate all other literatures is to show a profound lack of historical and comparative perspective" ("Literacy versus Non-literacy" 143). Cook-Lynn explicitly calls into question criticism and literature in the extent to which both "successfully contribute to the politics of possession and dispossession" (*Why* 40). As Ortiz reminds us, "The European urge for domination, compounded by capitalism's quest for profit, overwhelmed and submerged everything and everyone not only with language, philosophy, behavior, economy, government but with violence and brute force when rhetorical persuasion failed" (*Woven* 19).

Perhaps the crucial concern of American Indian literatures scholars (and more broadly of indigenous literatures scholars around the world) is the silence of Native peoples' voices within contemporary critical methods. In relation to the study of African literature, Chinweizu writes, "African literature and scholarship ought to be written from the center of African experience and for the illumination of African life" (13). Analogously, scholarly methods for working with American Indian literatures need to be informed from the center of those Indian traditions. Moore explains, "The ways in which readers and writers conceive of culture, self and other, knowledge and experience, past and present, determine different relations between reader and text as well as different readings of literary elements" ("Decolonializing" 7). Although different readings in and of themselves are not necessarily a problem, Moore's point reflects the serious absence of scholarly strategies directly informed by non-Western traditions of literary interpretation and engagement. On this subject, Lee Irwin writes, "What is missing here is the indigenous participant, the voice of the cultural other who chooses to exercise self-expression in modes which are, in fact, less privileged in the academic environment. . . . For Native Americans, what is at risk is the constant loss of self-representation through the overwhelming appropriation of indigenous discourse into narrow modes of scholarly analysis" (15). In relation to African literatures, Mineke Schipper stresses "the power factor that erects barriers between their [scholars'] own perspectives and an understanding of the Other as an object of research in (white, colonial, and/or male) culture and history" (40). Grant writes, "We need a new theory of criticism, or at least new perceptions of existing critical theory as applied to Native American writers. What we do now as teachers and critics will largely determine what Native writers will be able to do or get credit for in the future" ("Content" 5).

The dilemma for scholars of American Indian literatures is to discover and develop strategies for working with those literatures in ways that are not definitionally hegemonic. Linda J. Krumholz asks, "[I]s it possible for white or non-Indian literary critics, or any critics in white academic institutions, to resist a reading practice that appropriates and diffuses Native American literature and its potentially subversive differences?" (109). Cook-Lynn argues, "It is important that the parameters of the discipline be defined, examined, redefined, and reexamined according to the experiences of American Indians themselves and in the context of a shifting and developing body of knowledge" (*Why* 108). A conversive strategy is an important step in this direction.

I mentioned in the acknowledgments that as a professor who teaches in the divergent areas of literary criticism and theory and American Indian literatures, I have struggled against the definitional boundaries of diverse contemporary critical methods and theories, finding myself continually frustrated with the inability of such methods to open up American Indian literatures to my students beyond the limited scope predetermined by specific critical methods.[2] What my students and I end up finding are little beyond the preconceived expectations of the theoretical approaches as applied to particular texts. Now, this isn't to say that these theories and methods are not useful. Of course, they can be. However, it struck me that an alternative methodology was needed, something that would help the students engage more closely and fully with the works of American Indian literatures that they were reading. It was clear that such a method would need to arise out of and be continually informed and reinforced by the respective traditions and cultures out of which the literatures arose. Therefore, I turned to American Indian storytelling traditions themselves in order to learn and develop such an alternative conversive strategy suitable for engaging with American Indian literatures. Through such a conversive methodology, the voices present within the literary works directly inform the scholarly process itself such that the process is not objectively critical, but rather cooperative and co-creative in a metastorytelling that in itself is a storytelling. The development of conversive literary strategies responds directly to the inadequacies of both modern and postmodern criticisms for the analysis of American Indian literatures. This work moves criticism and theory beyond the oppositional models of dialectical, discursive, or dialogic encounter to include a methodology in which diverse voices (both within and without texts) are seen to engage conversively with each other as equals—as we all do so often in our everyday lives and conversations.

Perhaps most importantly, a conversive strategy consciously approaches literary works as an intersubjectively relational engagement that resembles the interactions between a storyteller and her or his listeners. The literariness of the text is not given a primacy over the story's orality. A conversive approach responds to literary works through their orality. Such a method responds directly to the concerns of scholars and writers who continually emphasize the oral quality of American Indian literatures—hence Krupat's description of American Indian literatures as "oral texts" ("Post-Structuralism" 124). William Bright tells us, "the difference between speech and writing is not necessarily basic to a definition of literature" (171). In fact, Finnegan points out that such a mixing of the oral and literary is hardly a new phenomenon, but far more common than is generally recognized: "The basic point then, is the continuity of 'oral' and 'written' literature. There is no deep gulf between the two: they shade into each other both in the present and over many centuries of historical development, and there are innumerable cases of poetry which have both 'oral' and 'written' elements. The idea of pure and uncontaminated 'oral culture' as the primary reference point for the discussion of oral poetry is a myth" (*Literacy and Orality* 24). My discussions within this volume are focused on the domain of North American Indian literatures, but, as Finnegan notes, the presence of the oral in written literatures is far more widespread and significant than most literary critics have acknowledged. Silko explicitly notes that her book *Storyteller* "is for people who are interested in that relationship between the spoken and the written" (Interview by Kim Barnes 84). She explains that she consciously played with oral storytelling techniques in her transformation of the oral into her written tellings: "I like seeing how I can translate this sort of feeling or flavor or sense of a story that's told and heard onto the page" (87). The Canadian writer Louise Profeit-LeBlanc (Tutchone) states about herself, "I don't call myself a writer, I call myself a speaker" (111). But Joel Sherzer and Anthony C. Woodbury point out, "Understanding the nature of oral discourse requires an examination and analysis of the ways in which individuals employ these features and others, the varied and complicated ways they structure their performances. . . . It is by studying the ways in which the different properties and features of oral discourse relate to one another, intersect one another, and play off against one another that we can come to terms with the true complexity of this discourse" (10).

What this means for literary scholars is the necessity of studying those aspects of literary works that have previously been considered the domain of folklorists, linguists, and anthropologists. Far from irrelevant, such work will meaningfully inform literary studies into the future with a depth previously unavailable to most literature scholars. This is one of the best kept secrets among the practitioners in those fields whose "texts" are often oral. The linguist Livia Polanyi tells us,

The emphasis, however, has remained on the "literary," with no real attention being paid to the nature and construction of meaning in the oral non-literary narrative texts (i.e. "stories") which we routinely produce and interpret in the course of conversations everyday. My belief is that careful, informed attention to the constraints on talk that regulate the orderly flow of non-literary discourse can be, potentially, a source of insight for those concerned with literariness and specifically with questions of communication and meaning in literary texts. Such awareness should not, in any way diminish one's appreciation of the accomplishments of literary artists, but may well help to clarify precisely the nature of that accomplishment. ("Nature" 63)

Of course, this necessitates additional knowledge on the part of scholars (e.g., "shared intentions based upon prior knowledge, the context of the utterance, and habitual patterns of interaction" [Olson 261]), but as this book demonstrates, an orally informed conversive strategy, in fact, facilitates insights into written stories by virtue of the collaborative nature of conversivity. This is especially important for scholarly approaches to American Indian, Alaskan Native, and Canadian First Nations literatures which, as Barbara Godard points out, are "reviving traditional storytelling techniques in new forms. . . . [And in so doing, the literature] posits the word as a process of knowing, provisional and partial, rather than as revealed knowledge itself, and aims to produce texts in performance that would create truth as interpretations rather than those in the Western mimetic tradition that reveal truth as pre-established knowledge" ("Politics" 184).

Godard explains elsewhere, "What characterizes the oral text is its interactive, communal nature, which transgresses the author(ity) in the written text. For the bounded nature of this latter is exploded as the text embraces the shifting relations of author to listener, listener to context and both to extratextual history" ("Voicing" 91). The shifting relations that Godard notes reflect the transformative realities of storyteller-writer, story-text-context, and listener-reader. Each of these three elements is inextricably interwoven through the process of a conversive relationality that informs and transforms each of these intersubjective elements. Jeannie Ludlow calls for "a critical stance that would allow for politically active, mobile subjectivities" (38). While I might quibble with Ludlow's term *stance*, which signifies the sort of positionality that is more the domain of discursively oppositional scholarship, her emphasis on the importance of a scholarly method that includes "active, mobile subjectivities" points us toward a scholarship that is, in turn, interactive and intersubjective. To achieve this, a methodology is needed that emphasizes the relational process of knowing that is at the heart of all oral storytelling traditions.

Oral storytelling is a process not a theory. Conversive literary structures within written literature enable the reader to assume her or his interactive listening role. Blaeser explains, "Oral culture thus owes its vitality, at least in part, to the relational contexts of language" (*Gerald Vizenor* 27). David Bleich has correctly pointed out that "intersubjective readings are growing things" ("Intersubjective" 419), even if he does not note the transformative effects on the persons involved as well. It is not just the reading that is transformed. All involved are transformed through the conversive process. As Gerald Vizenor (Anishinabe) says, "It's engagement, in the simple way people talk together or they confront each other.... It's communal.... It's life, it's juice, it's energy.... But it's not a theory, it's not a monologue" (qtd. in Blaeser, *Gerald Vizenor* 162).

The responsibilities for conversive readers are manifold. Most important is the active role that transcends the more bounded role of the textual reader. The conversive listener-reader interacts intersubjectively with and within literatures, with the outward text being the vehicle through the telling that is below the surface level of text. Again, this process transforms all involved. This can be clearly seen in my writing of this book. Initially, I intended to delineate several aspects of conversive literary structures and discuss those elements discretely in separate chapters with examples from specific literary "texts." At that point, I did not fully realize the transformative power of conversive engagements nor how they would change my relationships with the literary works in my scholarship and in my teaching. The first chapter to be fully written was Chapter 3, which looked at the work of several Navajo women poets. Three events occurred during the writing of this chapter that taught me that my preconceived plans would have to (1) be thrown out altogether; (2) respond conversively with the literatures and be open to a possibly radical change in the direction of the project; or (3) remain fixed and thereby be in conflict with the method and structures in the literatures. Obviously, my choice was the second, but not without some struggle.

For Chapter 3, I had planned to discuss several poems by Luci Tapahonso along with two or three other poems by other Navajo writers. I had selected the different poems ahead of time, choosing those that demonstrate the conversive elements I intended to discuss. I began by looking at two poems, Tapahonso's "Blue Horses Rush In" and Nia Francisco's "Naabeeho Women with Blue Horses," in relation to each other. But in the process of discussing those poems, the direction of the chapter started to change. I ended up centering much of the paper, not around the poems I had previously chosen, but rather around various stories of childbirth, including poems that I had not intended to discuss.

The second event involved real world changes in my own life as I, too, entered into the conversation about childbirth with the poems. Although the power of literature to affect readers is well known, the distancing involved in much literary scholarship mitigates the conversive effect of literary works on the scholar during the critical endeavor. A conversive scholarship necessitates an intimate and transformational relationship between the scholar and the story world of the literary works.

The third event that caused me to take especial notice about the process of conversive scholarship involved a brief conversation with a former colleague of mine, Jim Sullivan. He had graciously read over an early draft of the chapter, and he noted that my voice and writing style changed and became less theoretical and more engaging as I engaged with the poems. His comment immediately struck me, for I had noted the transformative aspect of conversivity, but I had not realized the extent to which I would be a part of that transformative experience. This was not part of my design. But the transformation in my writing in the course of the one chapter was exciting. It demonstrated exactly what I had understood to be the case; I had just not fully realized that I (and my writing) would be transformed in the process. Ortiz emphasizes that language needs to be "regarded not only as expression but . . . realized as experience as well" (*Song* 3). Helen Jaskoski writes, "Conversely, just as texts explain life, life glosses texts" (57). The transformative process of conversive scholarship is analogous to what John Attinasi and Paul Friedrich refer to as "conversion conversations" or "the phenomenon of life-changing dialogue" (43, 50).[3] June O'Connor explains, "The dialogical, conversational nature of the inquiry makes possible the expansion of my horizons, affections, valuations and therefore understanding"—what O'Connor explicitly refers to as "a process of moral conversion and reformation" (9, 10). And Gloria Bird (Spokane) writes, "I suspect that once we come to an awareness of the 'word' as a creative force and, with that knowledge, that language has the potential to 'create' or 'make happen' that we have discovered much—maybe everything" ("Towards" 7).

The entire process involved in working on this book followed along these lines, although not always quite so dramatically (and I might add, mercifully so). Chapters changed directions. One literary work that I had intended to discuss only briefly in one chapter evolved into the chapter's primary developed example, and two stories I had planned to discuss at length in that chapter ended up with brief discussions—only to be greatly expanded and placed at the center of a subsequent chapter where they are put to greater use.[4] Outside references useful in certain contexts and discussions proved useful in different ways and in different contexts and discussions than I had expected. Even the quotations themselves are transformed as their respective significances mold within their use. Gabriele Schwab writes, "The text as other can be perceived as a virtual life-form (in the Wittgensteinian sense of a 'language game' as a life form), as a complex and dynamic pattern (of signifiers) that forms part of the self-shaping process of a living cultural system" (111). In the dynamic interrelationship of the oral storytelling event, all elements involved in the telling are part of the changing story. O'Connor points out, "In this respect, too, our work is like a conversation which always carries the potential of continuing in another time and place, always carries the potential of being resumed and sustained. While we recognize the necessary pauses and breaks and silences, we also recognize that there is always more to be said for there is always more to be learned and there are always more angles from which to see and understand and judge" (10). This is what Jaskoski refers to as "the personal engagement with the material and the process of understanding it that contrasts with much of the students' other educational experience" ("Teaching" 60). This process of conversive reading and listening strategies contrasts markedly with standard scholarly practice through the conversive elements of repetition (considered redundant within a literarily informed mode), voice shifts, an interrelationality that speaks with literary works and worlds rather than about them, a changing writing style, and personal reminiscences (neither "objective" nor sufficiently formal).

Chapter Summaries

The book is divided into three parts, with each chapter introducing and delineating specific aspects of conversive criticism and demonstrating their effectiveness for reading American Indian texts. Please note that in each section, first references to American Indian and Canadian First Nations persons identify their respective tribal affiliations.

Part 1, "Conversive Beginnings: Wittgenstein, Semiotics, and American Indian Literatures," which includes the first two chapters, is transitional, providing a bridge between contemporary literary critical practice and the development of a more orally and indigenously based, conversive literary scholarship. Even the style of these chapters straddles worlds and approaches that, at times, are openly conversive and that, at other times, are decidedly discursive.

Chapter 1, "The Emergence of Conversive Literary Relations: Wittgenstein, Descriptive Criticism, and American Indian Literatures," emphasizes the importance for a literary scholarship substantively informed by the respective 'language games' evident in American Indian literary works. Wittgenstein explains that he chose this term "to bring into prominence the fact that the *speaking* of language is part of an activity, or of a form of life" (*Philosophical Investigations [PI]* 23). Throughout this book, all mentions of 'language games' refer to this notion—especially important in light of the fact that literature and storytelling (like any speech) are parts of an activity, forms of life. In Wittgenstein's notion of participatory 'language games', literature and storytelling are 'language games' in which their listener-readers are invited to co-create and participate.

Chapter 2, "Semiotic Significance, Conversive Meaning, and N. Scott Momaday's *House Made of Dawn*," turns to the ways in which meaning is conveyed within conversively informed literatures. In this chapter, I explain the differences between semiotic significance and conversive meaning. Within a semiotically based literary criticism (which includes most contemporary criticism, implicitly or explicitly), significance is defined in terms of differentiable signs, objects, and interpretants, or signifiers and signifieds, or even subjects and objects. However, within American Indian literatures, meaningfulness is defined in relational terms with signs and objects not meaningfully differentiated from each other. Here the division of elements in the world into discrete signs and objects constitutes the absence of meaning. Because meaningfulness within a conversive framework is found in the intersubjective relationships between diverse persons (human, animal, plant, rock, planet), everything in creation is understood to possess subjective status as persons (a status attribution) in the world. Where semiotic significance depends upon a prior division of elements into signs and objects with a reconnective interpretive linkage, conversive meaningfulness exists within the interrelationships throughout all of creation. To gain knowledge about various aspects of the world means one's coming into relationship with those aspects. The difference between semiotic significance and conversive meaningfulness is clarified in this chapter through a conversive approach into *House Made of Dawn* by Momaday (Kiowa), in which, for example, the discursive significance that Tosamah achieves is contrasted with the conversive meaningfulness Abel finds in his relationships with his grandfather, brother, Angela, and Ben.

Part 2, "Conversive Relations with and within American Indian Literatures," consists of Chapters 3 through 6 and presents more closely developed engagements with specific works of American Indian literatures. These chapters move into an even more conversive mode as the writing and discussion interacts more closely with specific stories, poems, and novels.

Chapter 3, "Conversive Storytelling in Literary Scholarship: Interweaving the Navajo Voices of Nia Francisco, Luci Tapahonso, and Esther G. Belin," has previously appeared in a slightly different form as "Discovering the Order and Structure of Things: A Conversive Approach to Contemporary Navajo Poetry," *Studies in American Indian Literatures* 7.3 (1995). This chapter further introduces and demonstrates a conversive scholarly method through a conversive engagement with the poetry of several Navajo women writers. In this chapter, I converse with the poems individually and collectively, noting meaningful 'family resemblances' and interrelationships that exist between the writers and their work. This chapter also provides a conversive model demonstrating a method by which other literary scholars can begin to approach a broader range of American Indian and other literatures, both oral and written.

Chapter 4, "Relationality in Depictions of the Sacred and Personhood in the Work of Anna Lee Walters, Leslie Marmon Silko, and Luci Tapahonso," emphasizes the importance of relationality in any conversive communication, arguing that relationality is the element that makes communication transformative. Relationality is contrasted with the oppositional strategies of Western critical method (be they dialectical, discursive, or dialogic) as a means of demonstrating the categorical differences between (inter)relational and (op)positional language use. In this chapter, relationality is discussed in relation to (1) diverse presentations of the sacred (focusing on Leslie Marmon Silko's *Ceremony* and the short story, "The Devil and Sister Lena," by Anna Lee Walters [Pawnee/Otoe-Missouria]); (2) status attributions of personhood (here, interweaving stories from Luci Tapa-honso's poetry, the Bible, and my own life); and (3) the extent to which connections with the sacred and with other persons are transformative or not. The chapter notes that at the heart of all storytelling always remains the sacred, whether it be in its presence or even in its absence.

Chapter 5, "Storytellers and Their Listener-Readers in Silko's 'Story-telling' and 'Storyteller,'" which appeared in *American Indian Quarterly* 21.3 (1998), discusses a number of conversive literary strategies directly in-formed by their oral storytelling roots. These strategies (e.g., voice shifts, repetition, intersubjectivity between teller and listener-reader, and conver-gences of mythic and historic time) are noted in relation to two specific works from Silko's volume, *Storyteller*. The chapter specifically focuses on the relationship between the stories and their listener-readers and notes the extent to which this relationship is explicitly elicited by the stories' literary structures. "Storytelling," which focuses on the process of storytelling, is more orally or conversively informed and elicits a very direct and active interrelationship with its listener-readers. In contrast, "Storyteller," which focuses on several storytellers and the extent to which their roles as story-tellers are impeded, presents a text that is more discursively based and fol-lows a more Western narrative pattern. Robert M. Nelson writes that throughout Silko's volume *Storyteller*, "the development is concentric rather than linear, associational rather than chronologically determined" (43). These distinctions can be further noted even in the differences between some of the pieces within *Storyteller*, with "Storytelling" representing the elements of concentric and associational development and "Storyteller" demonstrating the more linear and chronological form of Western literary texts.

Chapter 6, "The Conversive-Discursive Continuum in the Work of Louis Owens, Lee Maracle, and Sherman Alexie," turns to three very differ-ent writers and investigates the ways in which their writing manifests varying degrees of conversivity and discursivity. I have deliberately chosen three writers of diverse backgrounds in order to discuss the fact that in the works of each of these writers, we see conversive and discursive literary strategies converging, at times clashing, and coalescing into orally informed written literatures. My discussion of these writers' works also notes the ways by which this straddling and intermingling of worlds (literary, mythic, and lived) differs from writer to writer and even within one writer's own work.

The book ends with Part 3, "Transforming Literary Relations," consisting of the Epilogue and three appendices, in which I suggest new directions for broader conversive studies. In the Epilogue, "Conversive Literary Relations and James Welch's *Winter in the Blood,*" I explicitly advocate a shift for literary studies away from literary criticism and toward conversive literary scholarship. The Epilogue concludes with a discussion of the importance of conversive literary strategies, pointing out their usefulness even for those works rooted more firmly in the Western literary tradition. A brief look at James Welch's (Blackfeet/Gros Ventre) *Winter in the Blood* provides the final example in the volume.

Appendix 1, "Conversive Literary Structures," lists a number of conversive literary structures, some of which are discussed at greater length in this book. This list provides a handy framework for scholars interested in exploring conversive literary strategies in American Indian literatures (and other literatures as well) and the conversive engagement between literary scholars and the written story worlds with which they interact. Appendix 2, "Grammatical Rules for Literary Scholarship," encompasses both textually and orally informed systems of signification and meaning. Appendix 3, "Circular and Spherical Realities," gives a brief descriptive sketch in geometric terms of the 'language game' of conversive relations. This provides a geometric heuristic with which to conceptualize the differences between discursive and conversive communication.

The book introduces a conversive method for reading, understanding, and interacting with American Indian (and other) literatures. I offer this method as a means of re-membering the dynamic and conversive interactions between storyteller-writers and their listener-readers. This conversive strategy is based upon the underlying thesis that literary scholarship must respond to and be informed by the literary works themselves, and that this process needs to manifest itself in a deliberate and intentional conversation between the scholar and the literary works as the scholar actually enters the storied worlds and comes to be in relationship with the work, the teller-writer, and the persons/characters within the stories. Here literary knowledge comes from being in relation with the story rather than by looking at it from without. The power of a conversive approach is in the relational quality of that engagement through which scholars discover various pathways in/to stories that other listener-readers may also traverse, and thereby enter, the story worlds of those literatures. As Carter Revard (Osage) ends "A Giveaway Special" (the introduction to *An Eagle Nation*), "You are welcome in my books at any time, and if you are going home now, or wherever you are going, I hope you have a safe journey and a good life, and you live into the happy days, ho^n-ba tha-gthi^n" (xix). This volume is a guidepost along the way, pointing scholars and other readers in the direction of conversive listening-reading so that we may, in fact, enter Carter Revard's book, other works of American Indian literatures, and other literary works. With Revard, I, too, wish my readers well. I offer you this book as a step toward a radical revisioning of literary studies in which storytelling is returned to its rightful place at the center of literary studies. After all, as Karl Kroeber states, "storytelling may be the best use to which we can put any language" (*Retelling* 193).

PART ONE

CONVERSIVE BEGINNINGS
Wittgenstein, Semiotics, and American Indian Literatures

The stories. The words in the stories. . . .
They go on in some way, leading away
from a start, even away from me, and then
finding their own road, getting lost
at times until they discover the way
there is to go.

—Simon Ortiz, *After and Before the Lightning*

CHAPTER I

THE EMERGENCE OF
CONVERSIVE LITERARY RELATIONS

*Wittgenstein, Descriptive Criticism, and American
Indian Literatures*

KIM BARNES: "Has there been a single novelist or poet whose work
you find particularly inspirational or informational?"

LESLIE MARMON SILKO: "Well, lately, the one person that's meant
a lot to me is Wittgenstein. I think his remarks on color[1] turn
into some of the most beautiful poetry I've ever read. People
call Wittgenstein a philosopher and I call him a poet. I really
like reading Wittgenstein right now."

—Barnes interview, 102

Ludwig Wittgenstein, a Viennese philosopher who lived during the first
half of the twentieth century, turned his back on the past twenty-five-
hundred-year tradition of Western philosophy and transformed philosophy
back into the poetry it had been within the orally based cultures of the
world. Silko's (Laguna Pueblo) description of Wittgenstein's philosophy as
poetry is right on target. During 1933–1934, Wittgenstein explicitly wrote,
"I think I summed up my attitude to philosophy when I said: philosophy

ought really to be written as a *poetic composition*" (*CV* 24e). Wittgenstein's work is transitional, directing us away from the constricting confines of a twenty-five-hundred-year literary history of increasing textuality and discursivity and decreasing orality and conversivity. Conversivity in relation to literary critical practice (again, combining both senses of conversation and conversion) reflects the orality of American Indian (and other) literatures through the conversational engagement between listener-reader and story as manifested through the transformative power of language. So, in a book that moves the development and articulation of new strategies for reading and understanding American Indian literatures (and other literatures significantly informed by their oral traditions) even more fully down the road of orality and conversivity, I want to begin at the beginning as all stories are supposed to begin. And this story begins with Ludwig Wittgenstein's pioneering work in philosophy.

This first chapter introduces the notion of conversive approaches to literature in light of its Wittgensteinian legacy from my earlier work. As such, this chapter serves as a means of providing the needed bridge beyond the Western critical interpretive communities in which most contemporary literature scholars participate and into the world of a conversively informed and inscribed model for reading American Indian literatures. The work of Wittgenstein, a poet-philosopher who pointed the way beyond the Western tradition of objectively distanced observation and abstract philosophy, points scholars in the direction of potentially new and deeper readings of all literature. For literary scholars interested in reading, studying, and teaching American Indian literatures, a relationally conversive strategy informed by Wittgenstein's own philosophical investigations can enable non-Native critics to gain such a deeper critical entry into seemingly resistant texts.

As a scholar who must cross the divide between the Western tradition and American Indian cultures on a regular basis, I find Wittgenstein's work an invaluable guidepost to help me move more easily beyond the frontiers of the Western literary tradition and into the oral territory of storytelling. And as a scholar trained in critical theory and American Indian literatures, I find Wittgenstein's discussions of the limits of theory especially intriguing, challenging, and, in the end, convincing. He explained that any theory brings to its applications the worldviews within which the specific theory was developed. Wittgenstein did not throw theory out willy-nilly. In fact, he noted the value of theories, especially in relation to the physical sciences.

But his clearly defined and delineated explanation of the boundaries that circumscribe any theory helped me to understand the problems inherent in the application of any Eurocentrically derived literary theory or criticism toward non-Western literatures as a whole, including American Indian literatures.

Wittgenstein provides clear explanations about the dangers that accrue when we approach any aspect of the world (in this case, American Indian literatures) from the objective distance of preconceived interpretive categories—what he refers to as 'theory'. Although I have come to see the critical orientation of literary studies as misdirected, I would not throw out the entire history of literary criticism. Many of the tools of the trade have proven enormously useful in our articulations of what we see in texts, and many of these same tools can also be applied within a conversive approach to literatures. Here I disagree in part with Audre Lorde's statement, "For the master's tools will never dismantle the master's house" (99). Screwdrivers that were used to screw in the screws can also be used to unscrew them, but they need to be used differently in the dismantling process. But then this is the deconstructive work of postmodern critics (if I may use the term *deconstruction* more broadly than in the stricter Derridean sense).

Insofar as a conversive approach into American Indian literatures is concerned, some of the finely honed tools of literary criticism and theory (especially the recent work of cultural critics and the close reading skills of the New Critics) could be usefully applied in conversive listening-reading engagements that enable the interpersonal and intersubjective relationships between listener-readers and written stories. This is an ever changing constructive and co-creative process that begins again and again yet never ends. Unlike the more fixed boundaries of narrative texts, stories always begin at the beginning even though there never is a fixed ending. Each told story continues in the lives and tellings of each participant. Within the domain of a conversive approach to literatures, literary scholars, too, become part of the written stories through their own writing, teaching, and living.

Implicit throughout this book is the questioning of the critical endeavor itself, even beyond its relative usefulness for opening up American Indian literatures to readers. Central to the practice of criticism is the objectification of literary works as texts for critical consumption and discourse. Within this framework, literatures become objects for critique and analysis, rather than stories for engagement and co-creative participation. Instead of approaching literary works from without via a theoretical or critical measure against which particular works are critiqued, a conversive approach transforms the scholar into a listener-reader who engages with the work from within. The distancing inherent within literary critical theory and its application to specific works prevents readers from becoming listener-readers who actually step within the stories behind the texts and engage with those works as participants in the story. Wittgenstein's rejection of a priori theoretical interpretations of the world and his methodology of descriptive investigations provided the base for the development of a conversive literary method that would engage with American Indian literatures in ways that enable (1) those works to speak their own worlds, realities, and histories; (2) scholars to hear voices (literary and lived) that have been previously silenced or otherwise critically altered through critics' preconceived interpretive strategies; and (3) readers to gain access in/to[2] a range of literary works otherwise seemingly impenetrable.

Toward the development of such engagements, this first chapter brings together the voices of a range of scholars, particularly those who have pioneered the study of American Indian literatures. These scholars' insights and concerns are interwoven with Wittgenstein's guidance for a scholarship that is not constrained by the limiting boundaries of any set of preconceived literary interpretive expectations—those which he states tell us more about ourselves and our own worldviews than about that which we attempt to understand. I am sure that there are writers other than Wittgenstein whose work could serve analogously mediating roles between discursive and conversive reading practices, but it was Wittgenstein whose guiding hand greatly enabled this project, and so it is in conversation with his work that this book begins.

An explicitly Wittgensteinian informed approach proves particularly helpful in delineating those boundaries that have defined the canon of Native American literature—boundaries that have served to introduce important writers and texts to scholars and other readers, but that have also served to further marginalize and silence those other works of Native literature that do not fall within the critically accepted boundaries. Such a conscious recognition of the boundaries that circumscribe our critical and philosophical orientations toward the world and toward texts is a crucial first step in moving beyond those boundaries or, perhaps, in redefining them. It is only through our recognition of those critical boundaries that have constrained our appreciation of and access into the diverse range of literatures throughout the world that we will be able to step beyond those boundaries and discover new ways of engaging with those literatures.

The extent to which critical theories and methods are externally contrived and preconceived can result in the sort of forced interpretations that Wittgenstein argues against. Too often, the critical imposition of theoretical approaches upon various texts is a forced entry, generally by virtue of the fact that critics have not taken the time to ascertain the actual pathways in/to texts already accessible to critical approach. This is an especial concern for those critical approaches that are largely Eurocentrically derived, yet applied toward literary works from significantly divergent cultures and traditions. As Wittgenstein continually reminds his readers, "don't think, but look!" (*PI* 31e): "But how is it possible to *see* an object according to an *interpretation?*—The question represents it as a queer fact; as if something were being forced into a form it did not really fit. . . . [W]hat is at issue is the fixing of concepts. A *concept* forces itself on one" (*PI* 200e, 204e). In some cases, such "forcing" results in problematic misreadings, and in other cases, the "forcing" or lack of "fit"[3] results in the utter absence of readings of those different texts defined as "other." This is particularly true for the burgeoning canon of American Indian literatures, whose works are still largely unread outside of courses explicitly delineated to focus on "ethnic" literatures or "Native American" literatures.

Objectification and Wittgenstein's Remarks on Colour

One specific example from Wittgenstein's *Remarks on Colour* will help to clarify the degree to which our perceptions are informed by our respective worldviews and how those perceptions serve to impede and skew our understandings of realities outside the purview of our own lives and worlds. In his investigation, Wittgenstein discusses how we perceive and differentiate between colors and how we determine normative categories of color—all of which serve as metaphors for how we perceive and evaluate the world, ourselves, and other people. Here he makes clear that discriminations concerning different colors do not reflect absolute or essential distinctions in the world, but rather perceptual judgments that are granted a normative status within particular groups of people.

For Wittgenstein, the fact that a majority of people in the world may recognize the color red as red and that this same majority may agree on this particular concept does not constitute the fact that this perception is necessarily more correct or less correct than an alternative perception by people we might define as "color-blind." Of course, this is a complex issue involving the related processes of perception, understanding, interpretation, evaluation, and description, topics further discussed by Wittgenstein in the two-volume set of his *Remarks on the Philosophy of Psychology*. A more involved treatment of the process of perception is beyond the bounds of this chapter. However, what is important here is the fact that our recognition and delineation of different colors does not reflect essentially correct discriminations and evaluations, but merely agreed upon sets of distinctions by certain peoples. Wittgenstein clarifies this when he writes, "There are people who behave like you and me, and not like that man over there, the blind one" (*Remarks on Colour [RC]*, 334). In this one sentence, Wittgenstein points out that we objectify and, thereby, define as inferior and "other" those whom we recognize as different from ourselves. In the case of the individuals whom we describe as "blind," we define them in terms of their difference from us and name them accordingly: "that man over there, the blind one."

One problem that Wittgenstein notes here is our readiness to define "others" in terms of aspects that we might not consider noticeably significant in ourselves. We take for granted that we, as humans, can see, and we do not define ourselves in terms of our sightedness. However, when we encounter others who differ from us in some respect, because we perceive ourselves as normative, we then define those others in terms of their differences from ourselves. Therefore, that one quality (sightedness) becomes magnified in its significance solely in light of its divergence from the norm that we have defined in terms of ourselves. As Wittgenstein pointedly asks, "And how can it be meaningless to say 'there are humans who see,' if it is not meaningless to say there are humans who are blind?" (*RC*, 331).

There are two issues here that Wittgenstein is alluding to that have direct bearing on the concerns of cultural criticism. The first is the crucial acknowledgement that two different 'language games'[4] are going on here (perception with eyesight and perception without eyesight), or at the very least, one 'language game' being played differently (perception)—NOT one 'language game' being played correctly and well by those with sight and the same 'language game' (sightedness) being played inadequately by those who are blind. Yes, there are differences, and, yes, there are difficulties that blind people have within the bounds of a seeing person's world, but this is not to say that the blind people are by definition inferior to seeing people merely by virtue of this difference.

The second issue here is the ascription of a subjective status to those like ourselves and the relegation of those different from us as objectified "others." This situation can be seen in Wittgenstein's example of color-blind people. He stresses over and over again that what is different is not necessarily less than the norm. Of course, this is not to say that what is different is never "less than"; in some situations, it might be "less than," but this is not necessarily the case and remains to be demonstrated in specific cases. As Wittgenstein writes, "We speak of 'colour-blindness' and call it a *defect*. But there could easily be several differing abilities, none of which is clearly inferior to the others" (*RC* 31). In other words, "not every deviation from the norm must be a blindness, a defect" (*RC* 9). The importance Wittgenstein gives to this is underscored by the fact that throughout most of his writings, he repeatedly emphasizes that many of our conceptual confusions (philosophical, psychological, aesthetic, mathematical) are due to our inabilities or unwillingness to recognize different realities as alternative 'language games' or as acceptable alternative ways of playing our 'language games'. Wittgenstein exemplifies this in his discussion of a community of color-blind people: "Imagine a *tribe* of colour-blind people, and there could easily be one. They would not have the same colour concepts as we do. For even assuming they speak, e.g. English, and thus have all the English colour words, they would still use them differently than we do and would *learn* their use differently. Or if they have a foreign language, it would be difficult for us to translate their colour words into ours" (*RC* 13).

Our ascription of difference as a defect is by virtue of *our* incapacity to understand a different language or reality. As Wittgenstein writes, "Someone who describes the phenomena of colour-blindness in a book describes them in the concepts of the sighted" (*RC* 55). The writer of the book misunderstands, misinterprets, and misevaluates the color-blind people in his or her assumption that a normative condition and capacity within one society is definitional for all societies and peoples. For the tribe of "color-blind" people, the members of the tribe function successfully within the bounds of their own world. Wittgenstein hypothesizes, "There could very easily be a tribe of people who are all colour-blind and who nonetheless live very well" (*RC* 128). It is only through their interaction with peoples who see differently (e.g., those like us) that they learn that their sight, perhaps perfectly adequate for their own lives, is inferior within our evaluative framework because they do not see colors as we do.

What if, in fact, their sight is superior to ours and they see colors that we do not? Because our knowledge *and* perceptions are bounded by our learning, what is beyond the limits of our 'language games' is invisible to our sight and understanding. If, as Wittgenstein conjectures, there are people who know "colours which our people with normal vision do not know" (*RC* 42), then our capacity to learn those new colors is contingent upon our learning the other 'language game' of those other people (thereby making that 'game' and those people no longer "other") and playing that other 'game', or redefining our own 'language game' to include those new colors. The members of this tribe might also see combinations of colors or intermediary colors that we do not recognize as primary. "Even if green is not an intermediary colour between yellow and blue, couldn't there be people for whom there is bluish-yellow, reddish-green? I.e., people whose colour concepts deviate from ours—because, after all, the colour concepts of colour-blind people too deviate from those of normal people, and not every deviation from the norm must be a blindness, a defect" (*RC* 9). One case that speaks directly to Wittgenstein's concern is the Navajo color, *dootł'izh*. This color is a bluish-green, frequently mistranslated as turquoise—*dootł'izh* is a much broader concept than our word, *turquoise*. Sky, grass, leaves, turquoise stones, and water could all be described as dootł'izh. Does this mean that Navajo people are incapable of differentiating between the colors of a blue sky and green grass? Of course not. These differences reflect societal valuations of how to delineate and describe the world. And, again, as Wittgenstein makes clear, such differences do not necessarily signify superior and inferior capacities and ways of seeing, but rather perceptual and descriptive differences for different groups of people.

If our desire is to understand peoples, worlds, and stories that are different from our own frame of reference, we can either understand them in terms of our own conceptual framework (which in all likelihood will result in misunderstandings), or we can attempt to understand them in terms of their own descriptive and interpretive criteria. All too often, our understandings and explanations of the world gain their legitimacy not because of their accuracy but because they "appeal to an inclination in ourselves" (*Remarks on Frazer's* Golden Bough [RFGB] 6e). Wittgenstein notes elsewhere, "That it seems so to men is their criterion for its *being* so" (*RC* 98).

But he further emphasizes, "Because it seems so to me—or to everybody—it does not follow that it *is* so" (*RC* 96). Krupat comments on this sort of interpretive problem in relation to the criticism of American Indian texts: "Once more we have the assumption of what needs to be demonstrated; but once the assumption has been made, it consequently serves to legitimize 'our customary procedures' as adequate to understanding" ("Identity" 7). Krupat further asserts, "Too many Westerners have played carelessly in the realms of Otherness, taking what they wanted—a little of this, a little of that—and blithely moving on, 'savagizing' or 'orientalizing' the Other" (*Ethnocriticism* 36). In order for scholars to avoid such objectification of peoples and cultures, scholars ought to learn about those peoples and cultures through an interactive and relational model in which scholars and their subjects of study conversively engage each other in a collaborative process of perception, description, interpretation, and evaluation. As Kenneth M. Morrison points out, the underlying issue involved in learning about diverse peoples and cultures is "the integrity of interpersonal discourse as constituted in a real give-and-take between equals" (12).

Orality in American Indian Literatures

In approaching any literary work conversively, a reader is committed to engaging the multiplicity of voices within the work in the sense of a Bakhtinian heteroglossia. Insofar as the domain of American Indian literatures is concerned, these works themselves elicit such a response on the part of their listener-readers. Most American Indian writers have been varyingly influenced by their respective tribal oral traditions—particularly within the framework of oral storytelling. This storytelling practice in which the audience or listeners are present while the story is being told demonstrates a conversive interaction that continually, cyclically, and repetitively turns its focus from storyteller to story to listener to ancestors to descendants to other relatives and other persons, peoples, animals, things; and in this process, the listener's relationship to these "others" is emphasized such that the listener becomes a part of the story herself.[5]

American Indian literatures straddle the worlds and words of their respective tribal oral storytelling traditions and literary heritages. Orality and textuality are interwoven within the fabric of these (and other) literatures that varyingly demonstrate conversive stories and discursive positions. Bruchac (Abenaki) explains, "Not only are they [Native American writers] able now to draw upon the wealth of world literature, . . . but they also are able to refer to and draw from a variety of oral traditions" ("Contemporary" 311). Accordingly, any meaningful approach in/to these literatures requires navigation that brings together critical tools from these divergent yet intertwined traditions. Wittgenstein's philosophical methodology has significant value for literary scholars interested in moving beyond the bounds of the Eurocentric and textually driven criticisms of contemporary theory. In the development of new strategies for listening to and reading the oral behind the textual, the storytellings within the writing, and the experiential inside the literary, Wittgenstein dismantled the foundations of the blind colonialism and hegemony of scholarly traditions that have impeded our appreciations and understandings of anything outside the bounds of those traditions. As Wittgenstein tells us about his work, "What we are destroying is nothing but houses of cards and we are clearing up the ground of language on which they stand" (*PI* 48e). Wittgenstein gives the call ending the imperialism of inappropriately applied Eurocentric understandings of the world. Straddling many worlds in his own life (e.g., affluence and poverty, Vienna and rural Austria, Cambridge University as a renowned lecturer and remote rural schools as a country schoolteacher, Christian faith and Jewish ancestry, and the reality of being a veteran who served as a soldier in WWI), Wittgenstein understood the living diversity of the world and the implications of that diversity for our own understandings of and responses to the world around us.

Wittgenstein's philosophical work is enormously important for the study of literature and particularly for the study of literatures on the margins (or beyond the bounds) of the Western tradition. Contemporary postmodern criticisms question the critical constructs by which literature had been previously studied and evaluated. However, postmodern and poststructural criticisms do not fully let go of the past which, on the one hand, they question and reject, and which, on the other hand, they hold onto in a continual backward referentiality through which they define themselves in terms of what they critique. The power of Wittgenstein's philosophy is that he articulates a method that brackets out what he rejects, sets it aside within its own theoretical boundaries, and thereby makes room for new ways of approaching the world. As he questions in the *Philosophical Investigations,* "Where does our investigation get its importance from, since it seems only to destroy everything interesting, that is, all that is great and important? (As it were all the buildings, leaving behind only bits of stone and rubble.)"

(48e). For literary criticism, this is crucial as a means of clearing the space necessary in order to foreground new and different texts and to read, understand, interpret, and evaluate those texts in new and different ways. In fact, Wittgenstein even states that the interpretive categories and theories we have inherited and been told are "great and important [are] nothing but houses of cards," which, as noted earlier, he sees himself as destroying and clearing away (*PI* 118e).

Scholars of American Indian literatures are continually presented with a body of works (oral and written) that categorically resist the imposition of Western strategies of reading and interpretation. Even the multiplicity of postmodern critical approaches that purport to give voice to those texts previously silenced by the metanarratives of an earlier traditionalist criticism is incapable of providing sufficient, meaningful, and useful pathways in/to the diverse range of American Indian literatures. The explicit difficulty is in the application of Western categories of oppositional discursive structures upon conversively informed non-Western texts. Even contemporary postmodern assertions of difference obscure the very real diversity of literatures, cultures, and peoples in the world through their globalizing assumptions that a discursive oppositionality is foundational to any people's and person's voiced subjectivity (literary or lived). In Ludwig Wittgenstein's *Remarks on Frazer's* Golden Bough, he makes it very clear that our difficulties in understanding diverse peoples are largely due to our own preconceived notions about the world—notions that generally reflect our own limited understandings of our own world, which we then impose on "other" worlds and "other" peoples whose realities may not fit our preconceived categories and theories. Wittgenstein repeatedly counsels his readers to question, and question again, their assumptions about how the world is, because all too often the assumptions are what impede our clear vision. As Wittgenstein writes, "I must plunge again and again in the water of doubt" (*RFGB* 1e).

Only once we let go of our own preconceived notions of how people and texts ought to be, can we then begin to approach diverse peoples and literatures on their own terms and through their own voices. Kenneth Lincoln advocated this shift a decade ago: "If we could begin recognizing our own biases, we might correct them. If we listened and looked more carefully, as 'word senders' all, we might hear and see native structures of thought and language" (116). Wittgenstein reminds us, "We must always be prepared to learn something totally new" (*RC,* 15 and 45). This advice resonates even more powerfully today as the canon of literature in the English language expands at ever increasing rates to reflect the breadth and depth that have been obscured for far too long. Rodney Simard (Cherokee) points out, "Literature not only does not transcend social issues; it is the *text* of society, the body of verbal artifacts offered up in support of the current sociopolitical 'reality' or, perhaps more appropriately, 'fiction'" (243). Although I would not refer to literature as "text" (hence the shifting orientation of this volume away from more strictly textualized readings of literature), Simard's larger point about the centrality of literary works as representations of their respective worlds is crucial. Michael Dorris recommended, "To investigate any Native American literature one must examine its evolution and development through time; one must know something of the language—its rules, its implied worldview—of its creation; one must know something of the culture's history of contacts with other peoples, both Native American and Euro-American; and one must know something of the modern social setting of the culture" (157). Warrior (Osage) more specifically states, "American Indian intellectual production from this century needs to be read with a critical eye toward both the historical circumstances from which it emerges and the political associations of its producers" ("Reading" 239). This is what Wittgenstein told us over half a century ago. He very clearly argued that we must understand diverse peoples' worlds, behaviors, and words, on their own terms, within their own frameworks, based on the underlying grammatical rules of their own 'language games', not ours.

Wittgenstein criticizes the notion of objective interpretation, arguing that we can only understand those 'language games' in which we participate or, at the very least, have a sufficient familiarity with their rules and play in order to speak about them in a meaningful way. He argues against externally imposed interpretive categories, which he refers to as "sinister": "What is sinister, deep, does not lie in the fact that is how the history of [a particular] practice went, for perhaps it did not go that way; nor in the fact that perhaps or probably it was that, but in what it is that gives me reason to assume it" (*RFGB* 16e). Karl Kroeber tells us, "Narratives, like conversations, are infinitely diverse. In theorizing about universal principles of narrative we risk forgetting the historical, localized, facts that determine the final character of every particular storytelling" (*Retelling* 22). In the fields of linguistics and anthropology, certain scholars have been raising the same concerns. Linguist Polanyi emphasizes that all linguistic texts invariably "bear the marks of the culture of their producers" ("What Stories" 110). She further stresses, "One must understand the culture of the inside speakers in order to really 'understand' the texts which native speakers produce" (110). In relation to the field of anthropology, folklorist Lee Irwin explains, "For Native Americans, what is at risk is the constant loss of self-representation through the overwhelming appropriation of indigenous discourse into narrow modes of scholarly analysis. The dialogue with other cultural and religious practitioners must allow for the widest arena of participant self-expression" (15). It is this very issue of familiarity that points us toward a participative conversive strategy and away from a more distanced and objective critical imposition upon passively objective texts defined as "other than" or "different from."

Arnold Krupat criticizes both "traditional Western disciplinary theory and practice" and "postmodernist orientations for criticism" as viable methods for approaching American Indian literatures (*Ethnocriticism* 7); Paula Gunn Allen (Laguna Pueblo) rejects Western strategies of reading that "tend to see alien literature in terms that are familiar to [Western readers], however irrelevant those terms may be to the literature under consideration" (*Sacred* 54); and Louis Owens (Choctaw/Cherokee) rejects a postmodernism that "celebrates the fragmentation and chaos of experience" as useful in reading Native literature that "places humanity within a carefully, cyclically ordered cosmos and gives humankind irreducible responsibility for the maintenance of that delicate equilibrium" (*Other Destinies* 20). Krupat writes, "an adequate ethnocriticism for Native American culture, history, and literature . . . which does not yet exist . . . will only be achieved by means of complex interactions between a variety of Western discursive and analytic modes and a variety of non-Western modes of knowing and understanding" (*Ethnocriticism* 43–44). Greg Sarris (Coast Miwok/Pomo) echoes this concern in his explanation of his own method of reading Native texts. Sarris points out that these diverse "methods and modes [need not be seen] as dichotomous and oppositional, but as interrelated and relational, as different voices capable of communicating with and informing one another" (*Keeping* 7). And Jeannie Ludlow argues for "a critical stance that would allow for politically active, mobile subjectivities" (38).

What underlies the concerns of American Indian literatures scholars is the inevitable silence of Native peoples themselves within critical approaches informed by the Western tradition. Some Native writers and critics, such as Gerald Vizenor (Anishinabe), have reinforced such strategies to fit their work—Vizenor, for example, using poststructural criticism in his discussion of the post-Indian trickster figures common in some contemporary Native literatures. Sarris moves in the direction of a conversive criticism in his struggle to arrive at a criticism that is more relational and informed by both Western and Native traditions. However, the absence of Native voices within the critical endeavor bespeaks the struggle of scholars who study Native texts. Krupat forthrightly acknowledges, "the danger *I* run as an ethnocritic is the danger of leaving the Indian silent entirely in my discourse. I don't know of any way securely to avoid this danger" (*Ethnocriticism* 30). As this chapter suggests, a conversive method informed by Wittgenstein's philosophical method points the way in/to American Indian literatures through conversive engagements with those literary works.

Conversive Approaches to American Indian Literatures

Such a methodology that centers the relationship between the listener-reader and the literary work as story is not entirely new. Although Wittgenstein's emphasis on avoiding externally imposed theoretical interpretations and understanding realities from within their worlds moves us closer to conversive relations, a number of feminist scholars have explicitly argued the value of intersubjective relationality within the scholarly endeavor. Nel Noddings critiques the lack of relationality in nonfeminist discussions of ethics and moral autonomy, noting that a caring, ethical self "can emerge only from a caring for others" (14). Winnie Tomm argues for an "interpersonal dialogical space" in which the "mutual respect of interacting subjects is expressed" (104, 105), and Seyla Benhabib advocates a "communicative ethic" by which "moral agents communicate with one another . . . [as in] an *actual* dialogue situation" (93). Benhabib explains that through such a "relational-interactive theory of identity," individual selves ("I's") relate to "other subjects" as other selves or I's (94). More recently, Margaret A. Farley and June O'Connor have emphasized the importance of relating to others as equals. Farley points out that such relationality involves the recognition of the "unconditional value of persons" (195). "If relationships among persons are to incorporate respect, there must be a way to address otherness without devaluing whoever is the other" (195). O'Connor echoes these concerns in her work in religious studies. She advocates a model of scholarship that takes the form of "a conversation [in which] 'The Other' is seen as partner to and participant in the process" (9). Irwin concurs, specifically in relation to American Indian studies, adding that "the reconstruction of interactive relations between mutual participants, each maintaining the integrity of their own cultural views, requires a recognition of the 'integrity' of the other" (15).

Of course, the primary difficulty underlying these concerns is their methodological and theoretical origins within an essentially discursive scholarly framework. Even in the desire to equalize the relations between a self and other, between the subjective scholar and subjective other, the other is still viewed as "other"—even if that other takes on subjective status through the self/other, scholar/subject relationship. Alterity raised up from the subaltern is alterity nonetheless. A conjoint reliance on Wittgenstein's philosophy and American Indian literatures with their interwoven oral and written traditions moves us closer to a truly conversive model of literary scholarship. Here relationality is intersubjective and takes the form of a circular conversivity (as distinct from the linear oppositionality of dialectic, discursive, and dialogic models). Such a model provides a strategy in which peoples, cultures, persons, and texts interrelationally inform and reform literary scholarship, thereby leading to new readings and insights otherwise not possible.

Wittgenstein's emphasis on descriptive investigations and his rejection of preconceived theoretical approaches move us away from contemporary critical practice that perpetuates the colonialist scholarly endeavor that invariably imposes Eurocentrically derived interpretive categories upon literary works whose stories struggle against that imposition. Rather than observing the world from the vantage point of an outside distanced observer, Wittgenstein chooses to place himself within that world and understand it within its own rules and grammar. For Wittgenstein, it is through our interactive observations of the world that our knowledge gains its significance since that significance is, by definition, in relation to our orientations and is thereby informed by those observations and descriptions. As Wittgenstein writes, "We distinguish between a person who knows what he is talking about and a person who doesn't. If a person is to admire English poetry, he must know English" (*Lectures and Conversations [L&C]* 6).

Susan Hegeman argues the importance of a "de-emphasis on standards derived from the academy or western conceptions of 'high art'" for the study of American Indian literatures (282); Lincoln criticizes "academic methodologies reflexive of our own epistemologies" (116); and Joshua A. Fishman states, "The antidote to ethnocentrism . . . is thus comparative cross-ethnic knowledge and experience, transcending the limits of one's own usual exposure to life and values" (306). Here we see the value of Wittgenstein's descriptive philosophical method as applied to literary study. Within a descriptive critical method, before attempting to apply a particular critical approach toward a work, the critic would first work to discover the various 'language games' that are involved in the work. This initial descriptive stage is designed to help literary scholars ascertain the range of possible pathways in/to texts. As Wittgenstein writes, "Language is a labyrinth of paths" (*PI* 203). So too is literature. Maracle (Métis/Cree-Salish) explains this: "All of our stories are kind of like that in that a number of people tell them, and they tell them from a number of different directions from where they're standing; they see the story in a certain way and they tell it to you. You go to another person and they're standing here. And they tell it to you. Pretty soon you have a full-fledged story" (qtd. in Kelly 86). Hence the importance of contemporary critical pluralism, which recognizes the benefit in a multiplicity of critical methods and theories. Hegeman rightly recommends a "plurality of approaches to native [*sic*] American texts" (282), but even so, there is still the problem of critical boundaries constraining texts.

By means of a Wittgensteinian orientation, the role of the critic is transformed to become that of a storyteller-guide (or sign-post),[6] describing literary worlds and pointing out the various pathways of approach and entry from which other readers may choose. Wittgenstein reminds his readers, "A multitude of familiar paths lead off from these words in every direction" (*PI* 143e). Through a conversive approach, the multiplicity of paths in/to Native literatures is discovered and made accessible to diverse readers. Poet and storyteller Luci Tapahonso (Navajo) explains one origin of such complexity in relation to her own writing: "This writing, then, is not 'mine,' but a collection of many voices that range from centuries ago and continue into the future" (*Sáanii* xii). Rather than the simpler discursive polyphony of a Bakhtinian heteroglossia, the unified (not unitary) voice of Tapahonso's writing is a conversively informed voice reflecting and interweaving the diverse voices of her worlds into a sophisticated tapestry that reflects the highly developed complexities of storytelling. Jahner points out, "most [American Indian writers] have established and depend on an especially close relation between the writer, work, and the traditional community—a relation that determines the contextual semantics of the work and therefore shapes the author's options regarding text structure" ("Indian

Literature" 3). For writers, the traditional community of the storytelling event is broadened to include the greater and more diverse spectrum of possible listener-readers. Owens explains that American Indian literatures reflect "a collaboration of sorts as well as a reorientation [conscious or unconscious] from the paradigmatic world of oral tradition to the syntagmatic reality of written language" (*Other Destinies* 6). Owens is completely correct in his recognition of the complex interrelationship between the oral and textual within American Indian literatures. This relationship does not necessarily reflect a "reorientation" away from the oral, but rather its manifestation within a written form. The extent to which American Indian literatures demonstrate such a conversively informed manifestation or a discursively constructed reorientation will vary from writer to writer and writing to writing.

A conversive strategy, informed by Wittgenstein's method of descriptive investigations, provides a means by which literary scholars can engage with American Indian literatures through an intersubjectively collaborative process that defines neither side of that engagement as "other." This is where a conversive strategy proves most useful. Insofar as literary works are concerned, through a descriptive approach, the scholar first works to become fairly familiar with the 'language games' and 'family resemblances'[7] in which the literary work participates. Once the scholar has achieved a sufficient degree of familiarity with those 'language games' in order to communicate with/in the story, the scholar must discover and traverse particular descriptive and interpretive pathways in/to the literary work. Within a conversive mode, this twofold process from start to finish is co-creative, with each move mutually transforming the work and its listener-reader (in this case, the literary scholar). O'Connor argues for such a process in her call for a "dialogical, *conversational* nature" of inquiry involving "the exchange of intuitions and insights, hard questions and mutual critiques," which thereby effects an interactive process of "moral *conversion* and reformation" (9, 10; emphasis added).

The power of a conversive methodology is in the relational quality of that engagement by which scholars, literary works, and writers work together to discover various pathways that other listener-readers can also traverse and enter the diverse worlds of American Indian literatures. As Silko writes, "Many worlds may coexist here" (*Yellow Woman* 61). Wittgenstein's philosophical storytelling segues from past critical theories and practices into conversively informed engagements. As a philosopher strictly trained in the traditions of Western scholarship, Wittgenstein was intimately aware of the limiting boundaries of that tradition—hence his warnings about the blindness of narrow interpretations of the world, its peoples, cultures, and words. The next chapter moves this discussion even more closely into the world of conversive relations. Wittgenstein emphasized the importance of avoiding externally imposed theoretical approaches and of knowing aspects of the world by being in relationship to them. Chapter 2 takes the next step and explores the Western tradition of semiotics, noting that field's limitations for describing signification within orally conversive cultures. The chapter then moves to an articulation of ways to engage and illustrate meaning that is conversively engendered. After this discussion, the chapter provides a preliminary example from N. Scott Momaday's novel *House Made of Dawn* to show how meaning within a conversive domain differs from signification within discursive texts.

SEMIOTIC SIGNIFICANCE, CONVERSIVE MEANING, AND N. SCOTT MOMADAY'S *HOUSE MADE OF DAWN*

In the foreword to *Native Women of Western Canada: Writing the Circle—An Anthology,* editors Jeanne Perreault and Sylvia Vance write that "readers will discover the limitations of their own reading practices as they encounter the emotional and intellectual demands of this collection" (xi). This statement resonated powerfully with my experiences teaching American Indian literatures to non-Native students. The range of critical theories and methods available to us today gave my students a choice of interpretive strategies for approaching those literatures, but those tools did not help them to enter the stories behind the texts. The limitations of their/our reading practices are the limitations of our own Western interpretive categories—interpretive categories that obscure the storytelling below the surface levels of literary texts. Those writers whose works are more informed by their respective oral traditions produce writing that reflects the sort of conversive meaningfulness that is at the heart of all storytelling traditions. In contrast, critical strategies that have been developed within the textually based tradition of Western literature seek to discern significance within literary works through the application of those theories and through the recognition of the signifying aspects of the texts. Of course, what is defined as significant here is determined within the framework of the applied theory, and such textually derived theories can only access significance in terms of their respective signifying systems.

Although the textually driven orientation of interpretive semiotics has proven to be an enormously powerful means of describing signification within texts (hence Saussure's distinction between *parole* [speech] and *langue* [written language]), noting signification is a categorically different endeavor than the accession of meaning within stories. The former approaches a text from without as an object of study; the latter involves entering the story and discovering meaning within it through one's engagements as part of the story. Within a conversive domain, meaning exists and is created through relational experience.[1] If scholars are interested not only in approaching American Indian literatures as texts for critical analysis, but also in engaging with them on their own terms as stories, then the more superficial reading of textual signs will need to be deepened into the transformative realm of conversive relations. Only when we approach American Indian literatures through their conversive pathways will we be able to enter those storytelling worlds otherwise impenetrable via the interpretive strategies of a textually and Eurocentrically derived and driven criticism and theory.

Wittgenstein ended his *Tractatus* noting our incapacity to move beyond our conceptual boundaries. He pointed out that "what we cannot speak about we must pass over in silence" (*Tractatus Logico-Philosophicus [TLP]* 7). Without appropriate methods for entering and engaging with American Indian literatures on their own terms, we are reduced to speaking about them through our own conceptual frameworks. But if we seek new words and language for speaking about these literatures in their own terms, then it is essential that we learn the limits of our own conceptions and begin to step beyond them. In this chapter, through a reliance on American Indian storytelling traditions, the boundaries of semiotics and literary criticism are delineated, challenged, crossed, and expanded to redefine the very foundations upon which semiotic signification rests. Appendix 2 provides a listing of a number of underlying grammatical rules for the 'language game' of literary scholarship, rules that help to describe an expanded approach to literatures that applies to both textually and orally informed traditions of signification and meaning. Please note that this is not a comprehensive list, but I think that such an outline of some of the ground rules for this work will be helpful for some readers.

Both in this chapter and in Appendix 2, we will see that new pathways into American Indian literatures can provide the means of distinguishing the boundaries of semiotics (and, even more broadly, literary criticism as a whole) in ways otherwise impossible. The importance of this delineation is twofold: (1) it provides a means of recognizing those limits beyond which a Peircean semiotics does not apply; and (2) it provides a means of broadening the very foundations of literary study to include diverse spaces of meaning previously outside the bounds of contemporary semiotic inquiry (for example, those cases in which signs and objects are not differentiated from each other, but, in fact, are essentially conjoined—a situation that is especially the case within the domain of oral cultures). What is particularly new here is that the presymbolicity of the oral tradition is redefined as a symbolic world of meaning with boundaries that are other than those defined by a Peircean semiotics.

Within American Indian storytelling traditions, the fact that any element or aspect of a story might have many levels of meaning in no wise signifies that to access that meaning one must objectify those elements or aspects and then read them in terms of some interpretive theory or method. Meaning within conversive storytelling is inherently relational, and one discovers the meanings (literal and symbolic) through one's personal engagement with those elements and aspects (persons, places, times, events). In contrast to the Western scholarly tradition that purports to know something through its differentiation from other things (the endeavor that produces the definitions that describe a thing's distinctiveness), knowledge within oral storytelling traditions comes from those interconnections and relationships that permeate all of creation. Within such a framework, one knows something by knowing its interrelationships. Whereas signification looks at objects and signs, conversive meaningfulness looks at the connective links between those elements and then understands those elements through those connections. The second half of this chapter will look at how such an approach to N. Scott Momaday's (Kiowa) *House Made of Dawn* opens up new ways of understanding Abel and other parts of that novel.

For instance, within the bounds of conversive meaning in which signs and objects are indifferentiable, the limits of the Western Euclidean figurations of Peircean triadic semiotics become manifest. The textually based Eurocentric foundations of Western semiotics bespeak an essential privileging of a domain in which symbolicity can be abstracted from those objects in the world to which they refer. Such abstraction represents the categorization and differentiation inherent within written cultures. Once words are written down, the writing itself can be abstracted from its origin; the words and statements of that text can be understood and interpreted within diverse interpretive frameworks that may have varying degrees of relation to the text's origins; and the text itself, thereby freed from its original boundaries of signification, emerges into a poststructural interpretive world that grants to the reader/critic absolute power of signification.

Within a conversive framework, a sign in and of itself is meaningless. An object in and of itself also is meaningless. But within a semiotic framework, both sign and object gain their significance, conjunctive in nature, only through the recognition, determination, and imposition of interpretive significance via some external point of interpretation. Without a responding interpreter, significance is insignificant. However, within conversive relations, signification is not contingent upon an external point of interpretation. Where objects in the world also possess subjective, and therefore signifying, status, a relationship between two signifying objects (which are also simultaneously objective signifiers because there is no meaningful separation between any element's objective and subjective or signifying status) is sufficient to define meaningful space—without the necessity of any external point of interpretation. This removes the need for the outside critic to interpret a work for others. The conversive literary scholar may serve as a storyteller-guide, indicating pathways in/to the work for others to traverse, but each individual must make her or his own way into and through the story.

This chapter discusses the fundamental distinctions between semiotic significance and conversive meaning. Although each is valuable in its own domain (signification in texts and meaning in stories), literary scholars interested in opening up American Indian literatures beyond the more superficial levels of discourse and critique must recognize the boundaries that circumscribe the critical endeavor as a means toward stepping beyond those boundaries and into the world of conversive storytelling. The irony here is that in order to discern the limits of our critical concepts, we must first step outside those boundaries. In his early work, the *Tractatus,* Wittgenstein explains that "in order to be able to draw a limit to thought, we should have to find both sides of the limit thinkable (i.e. we should have to be able to think what cannot be thought)" (3). As a young philosopher, Wittgenstein believed that it was impossible to step beyond our conceptual limits—a crossing over that the later Wittgenstein strongly advocated. Through a conversive engagement with N. Scott Momaday's novel *House Made of Dawn,* we will be able to cross over to the other side and into the domain of what Western semiotics defines as presymbolic, a domain in which signs and objects are not meaningfully differentiated from each other but exist as different aspects of lived experiences in the world.

Western Semiotics and American Indian Literatures

The primary problem with Western semiotics, for our purposes, is the fact that significance is, by definition, an experience that is mediated through the dissociation of signs and objects. As Thomas A. Sebeok explains, "the central preoccupation of semiotics is an illimitable array of concordant illusions; its main mission to mediate between reality and illusion—to reveal the substratal illusion underlying reality and to search to the reality that may, after all, lurk behind that illusion" (129). John Deely writes, "Precisely as signs, ideas are separated from rather than identified with the objects they signify, and objects signified that in turn become signs do so by themselves becoming differentiated from what they signify" (53). Signs represent aspects of reality, but they represent what they are not. Deely continues, "To be a sign, it is necessary to represent something other than the self. Being a sign is a form of bondage to another, to the signified, the object that the sign is not but that the sign nevertheless stands for and represents" (35). Tyler points out, "This is the contradiction at the heart of the idea of the sign—that it has a meaning that is other than itself" (133). The intersubjectively informed storytelling of American Indian writers in which meaningful experience is defined in relational terms differs significantly from the mediated experience of the dissociated text in which, as Richard Handler notes, "we act upon objects, but do not interact with them" (172).

Within Western semiotics, relational experience as abstracted in terms of language is definitionally disjunctive. Signs and objects are differentiated and then reconnected through semiotic interpretation. Here, through the textualized experience, by virtue of its abstraction from direct relational experience, the dissociated objective text is reconnected (represented) through the process of external interpretation linking dissociated signs and object. Deely further explains that traditional semiotics works under the assumption that all meaning is textual: "Texts are not only literary. They can be any physical structure at all made to embody ideas in the semiotic sense. Indeed, the whole of culture, in this radical sense, is a text" (64).

However, if semiotic sense is achieved through direct conversive and

interrelational experience (as is the case in much of American Indian literatures, even in written form), then the mediated process of interpretation
and reconnection is unnecessary. If, as Deely tells us, "Semiosis is a process
of revelation, and every process of revelation involves in its very nature the
possibility of deceit or betrayal" (11), then this signifying process is the
betrayal of meaningful experience that is not in need of an objective process
of mediated interpretation. Dennis Tedlock writes,

> If, on the other hand, we are to free semiotics from its subordination
> to linguistics—a movement which requires a balanced approach to
> the relationship between signals and signs, one in which the demands
> of codification are denied any claim to finality—we may allow our-
> selves to realize that in exploring the region on and around the "lower
> threshold" of an established code, we have inadvertently discovered
> that the code itself does not occupy quite as remote a layer of heaven
> as we thought it did and may even be suspected of having inescapable
> connections to the ground, given that even the semantic field of its
> morphemes (to say nothing of its lexemes) is inhabited by gross acous-
> tical features that resist final reduction to the status of perfect signs.
> (*Spoken Word* 214)

Tedlock's use of the term *reduction* is very important here, for all too often
the words and worlds of Indian people are reduced to the point of insignificance because of the incapacity of Eurocentrically informed and textually
based systems of semiotics to find meaning beyond their own conceptual
boundaries. In some cases, those boundaries are useful for delineating semiotic codes of meaning, but in other cases, those boundaries prove to be
reductive, merely delineating the limits of those boundaries because of the
incapacity to go beyond them. Wittgenstein writes, "One thinks that one is
tracing the outline of the thing's nature over and over again, and one is
merely tracing round the frame through which we look at it" (*PI* 114).

The difference is between a semiotic model in which signs and objects
are dissociated and then relinked through the linear connections of Peirce's
semiotic triangle and an alternative conversive model in which interconnected subjects (as distinct from passive objects) in the world and in words
reflect their own meaningfulness through their intersubjective relationships with other subjects (human and nonhuman). On oral communication,
Gumperz writes, "Conversational inference, then, is more than simply a
matter of sentence decoding; it is also a matter of being able to produce an

appropriate response, that is, following lines of thematic progression which take the form of linguistically and culturally sanctioned relationships between utterances. . . . Meaning in conversations is usually jointly produced" (194–5). As Jack Goody and Ian Watt explain, "Instead [of dictionary definitions], the meaning of each word is ratified in a succession of concrete situations, . . . and as a result the totality of symbol-referent relationships is more immediately experienced by the individual in an exclusively oral culture, and is thus more deeply socialised" (306). Scholarly readings of American Indian literatures must take into account the definitional boundaries that circumscribe conversive writing; otherwise our readings of these literatures will continue to force textually driven strategies upon works whose literary structures reflect varying combinations of discursively abstracted written patterns and conversively relational oral traditions.

As a means of moving beyond the more linear dyadic Saussurean and Derridean and triadic Peircean and Lacanian semiotic models, in this chapter, I suggest the value of circular and spherical models to demonstrate (1) a new conversive grammar for understanding and interpreting signs, objects, objective signs, signifying objects, and their relationships; and (2) a theory, grammar, and model for broadening the boundaries or limits of semiotics to facilitate our perceptions, understandings, and interpretations of those aspects of the world that we currently ignore, devalue, or otherwise define as insignificant by virtue of the incapacity of interpretive schema to recognize any sign outside their signifying boundaries as significant. Wittgenstein writes, "what lies on the other side of the limit will simply be nonsense" (*TLP* 3). The distinctions between Western critical semiotics (structural or poststructural) and conversive storytelling relations will serve to delineate the boundaries of semiotic inquiry as a means of assisting our redefinitions, our reconceptualizations, and our reconstructions of literary study. This is especially crucial now in light of the growing interest in American Indian and other indigenous literatures and storytelling traditions.

The previous chapter explained the importance of a shift from externally imposed theoretical approaches to conversive relations in literary scholarship. Building on that framework, this chapter delineates the underlying distinctions between those criticisms based in Western semiotic traditions (in which one searches for significance in texts) and a conversive approach to American Indian (and other) literatures. For a geometric model that describes these differences, see Appendix 3. Because this appendix is a fairly technical, albeit brief, discussion of a conversive framework and will only be of interest to some readers, it is placed outside the bounds of this immediate discussion. At this juncture, I include a brief description of the underlying grammar of the 'language game' of semiotics to clarify the need for an alternative approach to more orally informed literatures.

The problematic limitations of the more narrow linear models of semiotic inquiry have been well noted by a range of poststructuralist critics. Derrida forced us to recognize our collusion in the construction of the very structures we had previously ignored as constructs, Foucault unveiled the underlying discursive structures of historical "fact," and Lacan reread psychoanalytic myths in terms of their semiotic relations. Each of these moves questioned, and in certain cases expanded, the boundaries circumscribing our analytic worldviews. However, these models are all dependent upon the binary and triadic linear relations they struggle against. Bakhtin went further in his privileging of a dialogic heteroglossia that is indeterminate, evolving, and unfinished, which in its novelistic fullness reflects reality more completely than do more limited models; but even this approach is based on the oppositional linearity of a discourse in which language is "represented precisely as a living mix of varied and opposing voices" (49). Bakhtin explicitly defines his notion of dialogism upon a grammar of oppositionality: "one point of view opposed to another, one evaluation opposed to another, one accent opposed to another" (314).

Two more recent writers, Jean Baudrillard and Yuri Lotman, have also critiqued the narrow boundaries of a linear semiotics. Baudrillard critiques our devaluation of objects by asserting the actual control objects have over our perceptions, interpretations, and evaluations of those objects. The objects seduce us, so that the hierarchy between our interpretive subjectivity and the interpreted objectivity of the object and sign is inverted (Bakhtin 111). Nevertheless, Bakhtin and Baudrillard, as well as other poststructuralist critics, acknowledge the foundation of the linear oppositions upon which our critical interpretive schema are based. To use a Wittgensteinian metaphor, the 'language game' of linear oppositionality is not changed; the basic rules are the same. What is different is that we are reading those rules differently and playing the 'game' by means of new interpretations of those initial rules. Even Lotman's important discussion of heterogeneous and asymmetrical semiospheres merely plays the old 'game' in a slightly different way: "It has been established that a minimally functioning semiotic structure consists of not one artificially isolated language or text in that language, but of a parallel pair of mutually untranslatable languages which are, however, connected by a 'pulley,' which is translation. . . . Thus culture is (as a minimum) a binary semiotic structure" (2). Although Lotman's semiospheres, like Bakhtin's dialogic heteroglossia, do expand the boundaries of earlier semiotic structures, the 'game' is fundamentally unchanged. Oppositional relations between subjects and objects, differentiation between signs and objects, and distinctions between language and speech, synchrony and diachrony, and center and periphery demonstrate the discourse that structuralists encourage and poststructuralists struggle to reread and subvert.

Dell Hymes writes, "Despite the general meanings given the term, however, semiotics and its congeners, such as semiology, continue to suggest most readily logical analysis, and the study of systems of signs as codes alone" (*Ethnographies* 9). Hymes explains that logically based systems of traditional semiotics are inadequate as a means of describing the diverse communication events that are extant within divergent cultures and contexts. He explains that even within the semiotically informed tradition of anthropology, "the fundamental anthropological contribution to any semiotic discipline or theory, the empirical field study of systems of signs in systems of use, seems lost from sight" (9).

After a brief discussion of the historicity behind critical approaches to American Indian literatures, I will turn to a number of specific stories (written, oral, and performative) to see how conversive systems of meaning diverge from the semiotic signifying traditions of Western textuality. This turn to conversive relations as represented in American Indian literatures provides us with a means of determining and selecting between discursive and conversive literary methods. In some cases, it may be useful to use a linear and oppositional discourse to describe a text or aspect of the world. In other cases, it may be more useful to rely upon the more inclusive circular model of conversive relations.

The question arises concerning the fact that literary study has largely ignored the conversive orality of American Indian (and other) literatures, privileging textually derived theories and methods. Of course, the larger and more obvious reasons are those involving issues of racism, colonization, objectification, and marginalization. But a subtler problem has arisen that has served to obscure the reason; ironically, the recent emergence of Native American literatures as a legitimized canon for literary analysis has revealed the interpretive difficulties while concomitantly obscuring the immediate needs for alternative strategies. Within this new literary canon of

Native American novels, stories, drama, and poetry, those works that have been valorized by literary critics have tended to be those texts most accessible to Western interpretive strategies. Other works, particularly those that participate more fully in orally based or conversive storytelling traditions, have tended to be ignored, whereas those texts that are more widely read continue to be read primarily in terms of our Western semiotic capacities—thereby ignoring crucial aspects of these works that are less accessible, or even inaccessible, by Western critical approaches.

The past three decades have seen the emergence and development of the canon of Native American literature. Writers such as Leslie Marmon Silko (Laguna Pueblo), N. Scott Momaday (Kiowa), and Louise Erdrich (Ojibwa) are widely taught and read, not only in the United States and Canada but also abroad. The status of Native American literature is assured in the larger canon of American literature as attested by the growing inclusion of Native-authored texts in American literature anthologies. And yet, this growing literary diversity obscures an actual underlying reification of objectified sameness that bespeaks more the modern and postmodern demographic metaphors of the melting pot or a salad rather than the more appropriate living and organic image of a garden.[2]

The problems inherent in the canon of Native American literature prove to be nothing less than the very limits against which the various fields of critical inquiry abut. How do we approach, enter, interpret, and evaluate peoples, cultures, and literatures that communicate through the assumably presymbolic and pretextual 'language games' of the oral tradition? The answer historically given to this question has been the very same answer that centuries of Eurocentric colonization and objectification have given to indigenous peoples around the world. What is beyond the bounds of one's interpretive experience either cannot exist or is interpretively insignificant by virtue of being "sign-less." We can only interpret the meaningful relationships between signs and objects where signs and objects can be differentiated from each other. But where such differentiation does not meaningfully exist, signs can only be (mis)read through a forced imposition of Western semiotic sense that destroys the undifferentiated subject (person) that is conjointly both sign and object (as in the case of the orally informed literatures of American Indian peoples). Where signification is defined in terms of the relationships between persons (human, animal, plant, rock), a semiotic framework that interprets "persons" as objects or signs and that finds meaning in individuated signs and objects, in turn, can only find meaning in terms of its own definitional grammar. Accordingly, many literatures, cultures, and lives become inaccessible to a semiotic approach. Yet as Kevin Dwyer points out, such an approach betrays the underlying relationality inherent in any interpretation, what he refers to as "the inevitable tie between what is studied—the 'Object'—and who studies it—the 'Subject': neither can remain unaffected by changes in the other" ("Dialogic of Ethnology" 205). As noted from Wittgenstein's *Tractatus,* we are the limits of our (the) world, but we cannot draw the boundary of our world by virtue of being within it (5.6–5.641). In the next section of this chapter, an initial presentation of a conversive approach to American Indian literatures is offered to demonstrate how such a listening-reading method deepens our entries into the literatures and can suggest new understandings of the works. Insofar as semiotically driven critical readings are concerned, this presentation will also help to demonstrate the limitations of externally imposed objectifying readings of stories as texts.

N. Scott Momaday's House Made of Dawn

Within the domain of oral storytelling, we are told that stories are always to begin at the beginning because each part of the story meaningfully informs what comes later, and without the needed foundation, we would be likely to misunderstand the later events. So, to tell the story of conversive relations with American Indian literatures, it seems important to begin at the beginning of the development of this canon. N. Scott Momaday's Pulitzer-Prize-winning novel, *House Made of Dawn,* really heralded the legitimization of American Indian literatures beyond the divergent domains of Indian communities, in which storytelling has always been valued, and the field of anthropology, in which Native America has been objectified as a privileged area of study for over a hundred years. Beyond these two areas, American Indian stories (oral and written) received little attention prior to the entry of Momaday's novel as a work that commanded serious attention by American literature scholars. As a means of honoring Momaday and his novel, the first presentation of conversive literary relations begins with *House Made of Dawn.* And as that novel began to shift the boundaries of the canon of American literature to include works by American Indian writers and storytellers, my turn to this work serves the analogous purpose of shifting the boundaries of scholarly approaches to American Indian literatures to include conversively informed storytelling strategies.

In Momaday's *House Made of Dawn,* discursive positions and conversive relations reflect the contrast between temporal and relative significance on the one hand, and essential and relational meaningfulness on the other. In his character Abel, Momaday represents the very conflict that arises when outside forces (such as the dominant white legal system or urban mixed-bloods like Tosamah) interpret and respond to Abel as the object of their preconceived prejudices concerning reservation Indian peoples. The inter-actions and relationships in the novel provide the contrasting models of discursive oppositionality and conversive relationality. The practice of lit-erary criticism generally takes a discursively objectifying stance toward the literatures it critiques (notwithstanding the objections of scholars who ar-gue for greater subjectivity in scholarship, a position that I would argue participates nonetheless in the 'language game' of academic discourse). But such an orientation places the reader in the same discursive space as Tosamah, a character who rails against historical injustices, but who, in his own assertions of personal subjectivity, disempowers Abel and those "oth-ers" he relegates to the subaltern of his own worldview. Alternatively, readers may choose to engage with the novel by means of a conversive approach that enables the reader as listener-reader to also engage with Abel within his own world—the story world of the novel. In so doing, we see the novel's protagonist, Abel, as he struggles to find, assert, and maintain his own personhood in a world that continually denies his personhood.

Throughout the novel, Abel is objectified by those who refuse to recog-nize his personhood and who, thereby, only interact with him in a discur-sively oppositional manner; and he is defined as an outsider (a mixedblood within the pueblo community, an Indian within the dominant culture, and a marginal figure in the pueblo, on his job in Los Angeles, and in the urban Indian community). Abel's struggle for wholeness in a world that reduces him to an objective status represents the inherently oppositional struggle faced by the mixedblood Indian—what Susan Scarberry-García refers to as "the clash of cultural values and identity problems that Abel experiences" (2). The novel presents Abel's struggle against his discursive disempower-ment and, more importantly, his eventual rejection of the Anglo world that can only offer him relative and temporary significance at the expense of his own meaningfulness as defined in terms of his relationship to the sacred, his fellow tribal members, and his homeland.

Abel grows up in his pueblo community participating in the ceremonial rituals and events, as had his grandfather before him. Like that of his mixedblood grandfather (fathered by the priest Fray Nicolás), Abel's ancestry is even more complex in its straddling of worlds. Whereas the grandfather, Francisco, is primarily torn between the two worlds of the colonial church and the colonized pueblo—worlds that the pueblo people have struggled to integrate in ways that do not fully rob them of their own ancient heritage and traditions—Abel's wholeness is threatened more seriously by his own ignorance of his background. His mother is Francisco's daughter, a member of the tribe; his father is Indian, but it is unclear exactly who he is. Weight seems to be given to a Navajo man who was somewhat involved with Abel's mother, but even this fact is questionable: "He did not know who his father was. His father was a Navajo, they said, or a Sia, or an Isleta, an *outsider* anyway, which made him and his mother and Vidal somehow foreign and strange" (15; emphasis added). This doubt ascribed to Abel's father casts an even greater doubt about the condition of a mother who is portrayed as promiscuous and who either does not know or, for whatever reasons, refuses to name the father of her son. Nevertheless, Abel is a member of his pueblo, albeit marginally so—his strongest connections being those to his older brother Vidal and his grandfather. In these relationships, we see Abel as a person in the world interacting intersubjectively with his grandfather and brother. These relationships are mutually transforming and give meaning to all of their lives. But beyond the safe boundaries of these familial connections, Abel's personhood is continually challenged and called into question. His very lineage back to Fray Nicolás serves as the sign of his objectification as the descendant of objectifying (and possibly violent) colonial carnal relations. The premature death of Abel's brother Vidal makes Abel's already marginal status and identity that much more fragile and tenuous, like a web of life whose few remaining strands are being torn apart.

The sections of the novel that present Abel as most fully in possession of his life and its direction are those that show his early years with his brother, his participation as a young man in the traditional ceremonies of the tribe, and the final scenes in which he prepares his grandfather's body for burial (with both pueblo and Catholic traditions, recognizing his grandfather's dual lineage) and participates with the other runners of his tribe as he runs himself back into the tribe. These parts of the novel provide a holistic contrast with the rest of the novel (in fact the greater part of the novel), which presents Abel in his incapacity, confusion, and dissolution/disillusion. The meaning that defines Abel as a person in the world comes through those conversive relationships that connect him to all of creation. His difficulty lies in the fact that he gradually loses sight of that interconnectedness as the worldview of his people is obscured by the glitter and glare of the dominant culture that surrounds him ever more completely—even as manifested in the silencing discourse of Tosamah.

Within the discursive or dialogic oppositionality evidenced throughout much of the novel, individuals struggle to gain and assert their own significance in the world as signifying subjects rather than as passive, and therefore less significant, objects. We see this embattling approach in the character of Tosamah, who incessantly asserts his own subjective status in the world through a concomitant reactive objectification of white people and Indian people unlike himself (e.g., reservation Indians like Abel). Such dichotomized hierarchies that differentiate and privilege subjects over objects represent a Western code of separation and ranking that is alien to conversively informed traditions, such as those of the pueblo and Navajo peoples, two Indian traditions that have strongly influenced Momaday's novel. As Owens (Choctaw/Cherokee) explains, Momaday's novel reflects "a sophistication of 'otherness,' a discourse requiring that readers pass through an 'alien conceptual horizon' and engage a 'reality' unfamiliar to most readers" (*Other Destinies* 92). In the persons of Abel and Tosamah, as well as the other characters in the novel, we see conflicting approaches to language and discourse that manifest themselves in the various characters' degrees of silence and vocalization.

Through a discursively informed lens, we see Abel's continuing silence and inaction as disturbing signs of his disempowerment. This perceived inertia is contrasted with his actions at the end of the novel (taking care of his grandfather and running in the very same ceremony that his grandfather had run in many years before), which are presented as symbolic of his return to life and to the tribe. This successful return may, in fact, be a fairly standard reading given to the novel, but this interpretation is circumscribed by a Western semiotic that forces a text straddling divergent semiotic discourse and conversive meaning into a predominantly Western interpretive framework. Although such a method might very well yield valuable insights into the novel, it is incapable of accessing meaning that lies beyond the bounds of its own signifying interpretive framework. Hence the importance of new ways of approaching the novel and the range of American Indian literatures from within the bounds of a conversively informed approach.

Instead of looking at Abel's situation largely in terms of oppositional struggles, a listener-reader enters the novel's story world and responds to Abel and his world by noting his very real struggles, but also by noting, perhaps even more importantly, his moments of interpersonal strength and wholeness, which appear not only at the end of the novel, but also throughout Momaday's depictions of Abel's life. In fact, because of their own discursive biases, many of the characters in the novel cannot fully recognize the reality that Abel is much more able than they imagine. We see Abel's strength in the stories that depict his times with his brother and grandfather, in his experiences as the mythic bear of Angela St. John's story and time near his pueblo, and throughout his powerful moments of silence, when words would only destroy the tenuous personhood that he desperately holds on to.

In Abel's conjoining of worlds, tribal traditions, and sacred rituals, he demonstrates the conversive power of oral storytelling in which individuals and events are transformed through the co-creative relationships of those involved. Through his conversive relationships with his grandfather, brother, Angela, Millie, and "Ben" Benally, we see Abel and those others in their own transformations and growth at different points in the novel. In contrast, we see those who interact with Abel in discursively oppositional manners continually reminding him of his second-class objective existence: most notably in the behaviors of the albino; the attorneys at court; the social workers with their questionnaires; Tosamah, whose words take up so much space that there is no room for anyone else's; and the foreman at the construction job. But in all of his interpersonal interactions, we see Abel as a person, albeit wounded and conflicted, but a person nonetheless. In his interactions with those who objectify him, for the most part, Abel chooses not to engage with them at all, refuses to "play" a discursive 'language game' that he cannot win. We see this during his trial for killing the albino. We are told, "When he had told his story once, simply, Abel refused to speak. He sat like a rock in his chair, and after a while no one expected or even wanted him to speak. That was good, for he should not have known what more to say. Word by word by word these men were disposing of him in language, their language" (102). Abel tells his story, but within the discursive domain of the courtroom, what is wanted is not a conversively told story that requires a depth of engagement. The lawyers want facts that require little more than the superficial interpretation of textual analysis. Here I simply want to note that the discursive positions of the attorneys as

well as Tosamah and the priests serve as powerful metaphors for the practice of literary criticism. This will be discussed more completely throughout
the course of this chapter, but for now it is important to get to know Abel
more closely, because he serves as a model for the sort of conversive meaning that is a part of his life and that is at the heart of all true storytelling.

Ironically, it is only when Abel fights back against those who seek to
disempower him (as in his murder of the albino) that his own personhood
and freedom are compromised. Moore suggests that "personhood" reflects
"the interaction of relationality and agency" ("Myth" 389), both of which
are varyingly absent in Abel's life throughout much of the novel. However,
there are also many scenes that present Abel as a man in control of his own
power and sense of self—even before those external forces that seek to
destroy his power (externally and internally). We certainly see this in his
silence in court. He tells his story about his murder of the albino fully and
completely, and then he remains silent throughout the rest of the proceed-
ings. As Jaskoski explains in relation to Momaday's *Way to Rainy Mountain,*
"But silence is the necessary condition for meaningful language. In any
conversation, only one can talk; the other must know how to receive, in
silence, if words are not to be mere noise" ("Image" 69). In both his story
and his silence, we see Abel's strength, assurance, and focus, which represent a worldview categorically divergent from the world of the courtroom.

It is far too easy to interpret Abel simply as a passive object with no
control over his life, who finds his own salvation and healing in the final
scenes through his return to the pueblo and tribal traditions. This return is
significant, but it is hardly the successful healing struggle of Silko's Tayo.
Although it would be wonderful to have a conclusively happy ending for
Abel, it would be unrealistic. The novel ends with Abel back home, but his
struggles follow him just as painfully as he follows the other runners. Yes,
the running represents him as an active participant, but it is a Western
interpretive framework that privileges behavioral activity as representative
of strength and devalues silence and inactivity as weakness. Clearly, in
many instances in the novel, it is Abel's silence (like the silence of the
Eskimo woman in Silko's story "Storyteller") that represents his strength
and subjective determination in the face of those who would mold him
after their own likenesses. As Elizabeth Cook-Lynn (Dakota) comments in
relation to the high dropout rates of Indian students, "My work has turned
out to be unabashedly based on the idea that there is probably nothing
unhealthy in Indians dropping out of racist and damaging school systems to

which they are routinely subjected" (*Why* x). Of course, this is not to say that Abel's silence always represents his strength and presence in the world. In Los Angeles, Abel's silence is clearly disabling—in fact, we see Abel dissolve into an abyss of alcoholism, poverty, unemployment, and finally physical abuse. Abel's presence within the bounds of a white world is portrayed as a failure. He is expected to "play" a discursive 'language game' that is not the conversive one he is familiar with. As his friend Benally explains, "They have a lot of *words,* and you know they mean something, but you don't know what, and your own words are no good because they're not the same; they're different, and you don't know how to get used to it. . . . You've got to take it easy and get drunk once in a while and just forget about who you are" (158–59). Abel has an even harder time than Ben getting used to a world in which he knows he will never really succeed.

Tosamah is one of the few Indian characters who appears to successfully integrate the two worlds of Indian and white America, and yet the trickster figure of Tosamah is a problematic one. Tosamah is a mixedblood urban Indian con man who preaches in a ministry devoted to the Indian community. He is a wizard with words, interweaving worlds and traditions in ways that, at times, help the urban Indians in their straddling of worlds; but, more often than not, Tosamah's discursive power surrounds them like a snake around their necks, threatening to choke them with each word. Ben and Abel resist Tosamah's power simply by refusing to get caught up in the discursive power struggles that pervade white America and Tosamah's church. As Ben explains, "He's always going on like that, Tosamah, talking crazy and showing off, but he doesn't understand. . . . He's educated. . . . But he doesn't come from the reservation" (150). Ben and Abel look at the world conversively as a storied place that gives meaning to one's life. But the discursive reality of Los Angeles is a place filled with words but bereft of the meaningfulness and purpose of stories. Tosamah, with all of his words, struggles to find meaning within them underneath the deadening layers of his seemingly endless sermons. With all of his words, Tosamah never finds the depth of meaning that is at the heart of Abel's life.

For Tosamah, language is a discursive text capable of giving those who wield it subjective power and discursive significance in the world. In his sermon on "The Gospel According to John," Tosamah takes the most textual and least storied of the biblical Gospels to note how the living Word of God is made text. "The white man takes such things as words and literatures for granted. . . . He has diluted and multiplied the Word, and words have begun to close in upon him. . . . It may be that he will perish by the Word" (95). Here Tosamah tells us how discourse has destroyed story, meaning, and those who become lost in discursive black holes. Yet, like the attorneys at Abel's trial, Tosamah sees myth and story, the sacred and faith, as dead relics of the past. Even Ben loses his own perspective after his years in Los Angeles: "You go up there on the hill and you hear the singing and the talk and you think about going home. But the next day you know it's no use; you know that if you went home there would be nothing there, just the empty land and a lot of old people, going no-place and dying off" (159). But unlike Ben and Tosamah, Abel never loses so completely his own conversive sense of where meaning lies in the world and in his own life.

Immediately following Tosamah's lecture on "The Word," Momaday moves us back to the courtroom scene, where the lawyers are disposing of Abel. Abel's perceptions of the attorneys' words in court also ring true for Tosamah's words: "Word by word these men were disposing of him in language, their language, and they were making a bad job of it. They were strangely uneasy, full of hesitation, reluctance. He wanted to help them. He could understand, however imperfectly, what they were doing to him, but he could not understand what they were doing to each other" (102). Abel understood the lawyers' desires to dispose of him, but he couldn't understand why they were disposing of each other and, thereby, themselves. Ironically, Tosamah, too, in his sermon about the dangers of language, destroys himself with each word that he uses to assert his own discursive presence in the world. As Momaday comments about his character Tosamah, "I think of him as being in some ways pathetic, too. He's very displaced" (qtd. in Owens, "N. Scott Momaday," in Crawford, et al. 65).

Like Tosamah, most of the characters in the novel seem to be caught between worlds. Father Olguin, Angela St. John, and Ben all achieve varying degrees of integration between the two worlds; but in each of these cases, the more successful integration occurs when the person returns to his or her own world, having learned and kept something from the "other" world. Angela, back in Los Angeles, is seen as more assured and confident than she was at the pueblo, but she has learned from her time there. Ben, Father Olguin, and Milly straddle worlds, but in their respective displacements from their own homelands, they appear out of place, confused, and, at times, ridiculous. Abel, on the other hand, may seem lost and confused, but he never seems ridiculous. As Owens very interestingly points out,

"Abel is alienated, but unlike many protagonists of postmodern fiction, Abel is not schizophrenic" (*Other Destinies* 99).

Because Abel's identity is that of the mixedblood, it is his nature to straddle worlds. His difficulties arise when he attempts to live in only one world, thereby denying the other parts of who he is. Unlike a schizophrenic character whose individual identity is split apart, Abel's condition is the obverse—a mixedblood man whose identity is essentially one that reflects difference. For Abel, his divergent selves do not represent a pathological condition, but instead, simply his own mixedblood self. As many critics have noted, the novel ends where it begins. Abel is not healed, but he finally accepts himself, the mixedblood son of a pueblo mother and an unknown, and possibly Navajo, Indian father. In some ways, it seems that *House Made of Dawn* ends where Silko's *Ceremony* begins. Abel's acceptance of his self places him in a position to begin his own healing ceremony reflected in his running and his prayer. He is not healed, but the novel ends with that promise, albeit not with the sort of complete resolution one might like to find. Momaday's novel clearly portrays Abel as a man who represents the angst and alienation of the modernist novel (such as Saul Bellow's *Dangling Man*), while at the same time bespeaking a decidedly Indian worldview. Scholarly reading methods that represent traditions that are more literarily informed (Western literary critical approaches) and/or more orally informed (conversively relational approaches) will both shed light on a novel that, like Abel, straddles worlds. And like Abel, whose confusion stems from his attempts to live in one world or the other, more successful readings of the novel will need to take on a range of strategies that can approach the text from critically discursive orientations and the story from relationally conversive means.

Within the critical discourse that perpetuates a hierarchized privileging of subjective activity over objective passivity, Abel's silence and inactivity are interpreted as indicative of a pathological condition, and his resumed participation in tribal traditions is seen as indicative of his healing. But such an interpretive semiotic defines human significance in terms of progress and change as manifested in outer behavioral signs. It is true that Abel's connections to the sacred represent a crucial connective force in his life. But for Abel, the sacred is manifested in many ways. He is a full and complex person; thus, any critical analysis that reduces him to the more limited representation as a "character" in the novel denies him his essential humanity and personhood. The question is whether we read the novel as a literary text accessible through critical analysis or as a story inviting its listener-readers into its worlds. Insofar as the sacred is concerned, a Western and colonial interpretation that privileges the sacred as manifested within ancient tribal traditions (Abel's participation in his pueblo's traditional ceremonies), while concomitantly devaluing those "other" spiritual connections (such as Ben's drunken prayer or Angela St. John's story about the bear[3]), reduces Abel and his experiences to preconceived cultural categories that only give Abel significance to the degree that he fits into romanticized categories of a tribally integrated reservation Indian. But the history that is Abel's life is far more complex than any nostalgized and romanticized tribal history that would deny him his own *mestizo* or mixedblood experience, which defines his struggles and his "otherness" as well as his strengths and his personhood.

Luci Tapahonso (Navajo) notes the especial strengths in mixedblood Indians in her story, "White Bead Girl," about a Navajo girl whose father is from one of the Pueblo tribes. In the story, she receives a blessing ceremony from a Navajo medicine man, who tells her, " 'This,' he said, 'represents Changing Woman. This represents you. It shows us that young girls like yourself are strong because you're Navajo. You have extra help, too, because of your Pueblo side' " (*Blue Horses* 69). On the one hand, we could see Abel's running at the end of the novel as a reintegration for him as a member of his tribe; on the other hand, we could see it as another sign of his complex positionality as a mixedblood member of his tribe. But such choices are the domain of literary criticism and the need to fit literary texts into certain discursive categories. Yes, Abel is running with the other runners, but he is apart from them and hardly in sufficient condition or with the expected preparations to successfully complete the ceremony. Yes, he participates in it, but he does so partially and painfully. Abel's participation in the ceremony at the end of the novel presents him as we have seen him throughout the novel, as he continues to struggle to assert his own mixedblood and idiosyncratic self in the world. What he does, he does in his own way. If his participation in the running ritual is a fractured participation, it reflects Abel's own fractured self (literally due to his beating, familially in his parentage and more distant lineage, tribally in his marginal status in his tribe, and historically from centuries of racist colonization and genocide). Much like the narrator of James Welch's (Blackfeet/Gros Ventre) *Winter in the Blood,* in Abel, we see a man who is caught between worlds and who struggles to find some sort of balance between them. We never see him fully achieve that balance in the novel. Rather, we see his continued struggle throughout, whether that struggle is manifested within the pueblo world or within the outside world of dominant culture.

Rather than interpreting the final scenes in either positive or negative ways (reductive interpretations that reduce the story to the simplistic interpretive confines of a text), using a conversive approach would respond to the fullness of the story from start to finish, fleshing out aspects and details and understanding the story through one's own participation in it. In such a manner, Abel is seen as the complete and complex person all persons, in fact, are——whether in real life or in story. It is our objectifying readings that rob Abel of his personhood, leaving him beat up and confused. But in his stronger moments, he knows who he is and sees his strength—in his silence, in his intimate relationships (with his grandfather, his brother, Angela, and Ben), and in his participation in tribal ceremonies. In a conversive listening-reading, there is no expectation of a linear narrative that culminates in some final resolution. That is not how life really is. It is much more complex than that, and stories, like life, are lived realities. When a reader steps into the role of a listener-reader, far greater complexity and also greater simplicity are found within the story as connections, otherwise missed, are made, and depths, otherwise attenuated, are discovered, explored, and experienced. Within a conversive approach, we see Abel in the final scenes as we have come to know him throughout the novel, as a man who has survived some unbelievably horrific experiences and who has also made some very tender and meaningful relationships. All of these inform who he is at the end of the novel, as he runs with no voice of his own but with the words of a Navajo song/prayer given to him by his friend Benally.

Within the general expectations of the novel form, there is either the modernist desire to see linear progress with a final resolution that is satisfying or postmodern desires for the deconstructive rupturing of such linear resolutions that are understood to be the illusory constructs of our past assumptions about the world and about texts. In both cases, however, such expectations impose unrealistic burdens upon a novel that straddles the domains of open-ended and episodic storytelling and upon a seemingly progressive and directed, yet existentially disturbed, novel. Although a literary critical approach will open up the novel, finding significance according to the preconceived boundaries of that criticism, such a method is incapable of accessing, engaging, and entering the novel as story, and of finding meaning—as meaning can only be found—through the conversive relationships possible between persons (human and nonhuman) in the world (be that world actual and/or storied).

Part of the difficulty in a critical interpretation of Momaday's novel lies in the novel's heteroglossic straddling of worlds. Momaday presents Western semiotic distinctions that differentiate and nostalgize traditional pueblo traditions and conversely devalue a dominant culture world (insofar as that world is an appropriate home for Abel or the other reservation Indian characters in the novel). However, such a cultural or regional dichotomy overlooks the greater complexity of Abel, the man. Largely due to his marginal status in the pueblo as a mixedblood Indian whose parentage is not completely clear, Abel is not presented as fundamentally healthy nor in control of his life when on pueblo land. When *House Made of Dawn* is approached as story, Abel cannot be reduced to the more limited textual constructs of either an object or a sign, nor can Abel's reservation be reduced to the sign of his integration. For Abel, it is not solely the pueblo land that provides his grounding.

Abel's reality is that of the mixedblood whose heritage combines at least three cultures and traditions (pueblo Indian, Spanish, and other Indian). This contrasts with Ben, who is fully Navajo and whose alienation in Los Angeles is clearly described as largely due to his distance from his Navajo homeland. As Owens notes about the ending of the novel, "It would *seem* that Abel has recovered his place in an Indian world, moving outside of the entropic, historical consciousness of Eurocentric America, with its voracious linear temporality" (*Other Destinies* 117; emphasis added). Momaday gives Abel the *appearance* of recovery, but in fact, Abel remains a character who straddles worlds and who may never become a full participant in the world of his pueblo community and its traditions. Even the land and Abel's relationship with it and his other surroundings are much more complex and dynamic than can be communicated through any textual interpretation.

The novel ends with Abel singing the Navajo prayer he learned from Benally—a prayer that signifies Abel's acceptance of his mixed ancestry—but even in this prayer, we hear more than simply his sense of identity (personal or tribal). Here Abel vocalizes without his own voice his place and interconnectedness with all of creation. And he does so in his own way and after his own fashion. He participates in the tribal ceremony of the dawn runners. Even though he is not fully a part of that ceremony, he participates nonetheless. Abel creates his own ceremonies and prayers that reflect his straddling of worlds and tribes, just as Angela St. John's bear story and Tosamah's Native American church sermon straddle their respective worlds and experiences. In contrast to Tosamah's discourse, Abel, like Angela, creates his own story through his prayer, and through the conversivity of his prayers, his words (unvocalized yet uttered) have the transformative power that is always a part of true storytelling. We see his power here and in the courtroom; also in his speech and in his silence. But in order for us to really hear these stories, we must make the effort to engage with them from within their own worlds and words.

In the writings of American Indian authors such as N. Scott Momaday, literary scholars are faced with the limits of critical inquiry. This is not to say that contemporary modern and postmodern strategies are incapable of opening up these literatures, but in order to do so, the boundaries of literary criticism need to be redescribed. In a discussion of the limitations of contemporary poetics for approaching the oral storytelling tradition, Tedlock writes, "In the same move in which we open our visible text to the phenomena of practical poetics, we begin to extend our poetics into a region where linguistics—or a semiotics that models itself on linguistics—begins to lose its power to provide us with a paradigm" (*Spoken Word* 9). By broadening our conceptual definitions of semiotics, we will see the development of a more diverse literary grammar capable of perceiving, describing, comprehending, interpreting, and evaluating stories (written, told, and lived), which are currently outside the bounds of a contemporary critical interpretation that is largely Eurocentrically, literarily, and textually based. Such an expansion will not only redefine and reinfuse discussions of literary signification and meaning, but also address the postmodern concerns of exclusion, silence, devaluation, trivialization, and marginalization. In so doing, cultures, literatures, and lives previously ignored and relegated to subaltern domains of definitional insignificance and marginalization become reevaluated in conversive terms that include without a correspondent exclusion. This is especially necessary in relation to Native American and Native Canadian literatures, which Godard notes as "dis/placing and hybridizing conventions" through their "intersemiotic 'translation'" from oral traditions to "written genres" ("Politics" 184).

When diverse systems and frameworks of signification and meaning clash, there can be serious real world and literary effects. This clash generally results in the imposition of the dominant system over the other. In the case of a Western discursive semiotics, this involves assertions of interpretation over interaction, differentiation over relationality, linearity over circularity, objectification over intersubjectivity, and discursive structures over conversive relations. The subjugated meaning system is unrecognized as semiotically significant, particularly when the dominant semiotic 'language game' functions with a categorically different underlying 'language game' than that of the [other] meaning system. Wittgenstein writes, "We also say of some people that they are transparent to us. It is, however, important as regards this observation that one human being can be a complete enigma to another. We learn this when we come into a strange country with entirely strange traditions; and, what is more, even given a mastery of the country's language. We do not *understand* the people. (And not because of not knowing what they are saying to themselves.) We cannot find our feet with them" (*PI* 223e). This also holds true for those people and places we meet within the realm of storytelling. As a discursively interpretable character, Abel the storied man is reduced to the status of a sign. To the degree that this reduction fits within our critical scopes, Abel becomes interpretable and "transparent" to us. But, per Wittgenstein's example, this does not mean that we *understand* Abel. Wittgenstein further recommends, "We must do away with all *explanation,* and description alone must take its place" despite our "urge" to misunderstand (*PI* 109). In the chapters that follow, through investigations into the respective 'language games' involved in the works of various other Indian writers, we will be able to better determine how meaning is constituted within those texts and what reading methods will help open up the worlds within those texts most effectively.

In a discussion about the future, Wittgenstein says that "we always mean the destination it [the world] will reach if it keeps going in the direction we can see it going in now; it does not occur to us that its path is not a straight line but a curve, constantly changing direction" (*CV* 3e). In regards to the future of literary study, investigations surrounding orally based relational meaning systems indicate that words (written and spoken) and worlds (lived and storied) also change form, and that circular and spherical models can best describe the conversive structures necessary to perceive, recognize, interpret, and evaluate the depth, holism, and inclusivity of a diverse and interconnected world. Tyler explains, "In the history of Western thought, speech, not writing, has rightly been associated with the 'lively' aspects of kinesis, and it is worth remembering that it was this changeable, impermanent character of speech that led Saussure to reject speech (*parole*) as the basis of semiology" (134).

Simon J. Ortiz (Acoma) reminds us of the necessity of such a shift away from the textually based system of semiotic analysis when he writes, "Coyote as animal and motif is not enough" (review of Reed and Blue Cloud 599). Silko says, "we don't think of words as being isolated from the speaker, which, of course, is one element of the oral tradition. Moreover, we don't think of words as being alone: words are always with other words, and the other words are almost always in a story of some sort" ("Language" 55). Within a conversive domain, meaning is always relational. The abstracted or objective significance of semiotic analysis is valuable within a more strictly textual domain, but within a more orally informed realm, the disconnections that are inherent within critical discourse constitute the rupture of meaning, resulting in partial meaning or the absence of meaning altogether. This is what Tyler means when he writes, "Paradoxically, orality is also the name of the counter discourse that resists the hegemony of the written word by recuperating the past, by reminding us that speech and communication ground all representation, not in the sign's alienation of the world, but in commonsense practices when word and world meet in will and deed" (132). James Ruppert tells us, "Once the distinctions that separate oral literature from written literature are banished, new fields of discourse increase the possibilities of mediation, of new insight, and of experiencing new world views" (*Mediation* 37).

The conversive reorientation of literary study to include *parole* provides us with a language and a methodology for engaging with literatures substantively informed by their oral traditions on their own terms and after their own fashions. In this case, this means approaching and entering the storied worlds of American Indian literatures and listening to those stories as would a person listening to a storytelling elder. Although there will be certain commonalities in each listener's remembering of a story, there will also be meaningful differences in each of our scholarly retellings (e.g., literary scholarship) of that story. In both our similarities and our differences, there are meaning and value; for here, literary study is conversively alive, taking on the "changeable, impermanent character of speech" that Saussure rejected and that we are now reclaiming (Tyler 134). We now turn to the second section of this book, in which several elements of oral storytelling are discussed in relation to the work of diverse American Indian writers. The next chapter takes a conversive approach to the work of several Navajo women writers, looking at how such a listening-reading strategy can open up the various conversations within and between their writing.

PART TWO

CONVERSIVE RELATIONS WITH AND WITHIN AMERICAN INDIAN LITERATURES

Story has its own life, its very own,
and we are the voice carried with it.

—Simon Ortiz, *After and Before the Lightning*

CHAPTER 3

CONVERSIVE STORYTELLING IN LITERARY SCHOLARSHIP

Interweaving the Navajo Voices of Nia Francisco,
Luci Tapahonso, and Esther G. Belin

Contemporary literary analysis provides a range of theories and methods by which critics can interpret, analyze, and evaluate diverse texts. Notwithstanding the plethora of critical approaches in current use, the oppositional linearity upon which these methods and theories are based indicates potential problems in their actual applications toward the literary works of a number of American Indian authors. It is true that particular strategies have proven more useful than others in critical readings of American Indian literatures. The new historicism and cultural criticisms have critiqued earlier methods by which peoples and their histories and literatures have been ignored, marginalized, or even erased from scholarly analysis. Feminist criticism has directed attention to particular American Indian literatures and worldviews insofar as they evidence varying degrees of matrifocality, which are seen as important contrasts to the predominant phallocentricity of most non-Native cultures. And Bakhtinian-informed criticisms have applied notions of dialogism and heteroglossia in explications of the oppositional vocality evident in much contemporary Native writing. However, regardless of the well-intentioned efforts of literary scholars, critical strategies turned toward American Indian literatures have all too often distorted or silenced the Native voices within and behind the literatures they intend to illuminate.

Critical methods perpetuate the institutionalization of Native peoples' silence in two serious ways. The first is through a critical privileging that gives precedence to the voice of the critics at the expense of the objectified Native voices present in the literature. To avoid this problem, a conversive critical strategy can enable the critic to work in concert, rather than in competition, with the voices of Native peoples and literatures. In noting this sort of difficulty, Jahner writes, "Critics need to be aware that conventional approaches and vocabulary are as likely to obscure as to illuminate the ways in which a specific tribal tradition can provide a writer with a set of optional approaches to the form and content of original creative work" ("Critical" 212). This necessitates that literary scholars develop new strategies of literary analysis that will enable their voices to intermingle with the voices in and of American Indian literatures, thereby yielding scholarship that is more informed by the voices of the literary works themselves than by the critical voices of scholars. Krupat writes, "the Euramerican attempt to think a Native American 'literature' has always been marked by the problem of Identity and Difference, a problem that—as we shall see—marks as well the attempt to develop a written criticism of this 'literature'" ("Identity" 3). He concludes that the substantial differences between critical and Native voices are unavoidable in our critical readings: "While we cannot avoid the explanatory categories of western culture, we can at least be aware of them and beware of them as we approach the 'literature' of other cultures" (10).

The second way in which Native voices are silenced by contemporary criticism is in the imposition of critical strategies and theoretical approaches that force particular readings upon texts regardless of whether that critical orientation is appropriate for the specific text. The underlying grammatical problem (using the term 'grammatical' in the Wittgensteinian sense of 'language game' rules) for such endeavors is that both modern and postmodern criticisms are based upon models of linear oppositionality. From the New Critical clashes of opposites reconciled in an eventual forced "harmony" to Marxist informed criticisms that posited the dialectical class struggles of society as manifested in literary works, the modern period explicitly sought in literature the oppositional linearity that modernists erroneously assumed and that we now understand to have been the spurious and problematic assertions of an earlier critical absolutism. As scholars and readers of American Indian literatures know all too well, all literary texts do not manifest the oppositional struggles posited by Western critical strategies—a condition that has functioned to ignore and accordingly devalue those texts that do not fit critical demands. American Indian literatures garnered scant attention by literary critics until a number of Native writers of mestiza/o background produced literatures more accessible to Western critical strategies than had been the earlier narratives, stories, chants, and prayers from the oral traditions, which had been available to critics for generations.[1] Carol Hunter notes, "Contemporary Indian fiction, the novel and poetry, is perhaps more popular among a general audience. It appears to some readers less complex because it conforms with contemporary literary forms and conventions" (84). Of course, the ease with which many readers and critics approach such literary works obscures the actual complexity within those texts.

Postmodern criticisms and theories have attempted to remedy some of the problematic exclusionary effects of modern criticism by offering methods that expand the literary canon through the acknowledgement and privileging of literatures by women, working class, and ethnically diverse writers. Foucault and Lacan pushed the boundaries of earlier historical and psychoanalytic interpretations of texts and of the world and shifted the notion of dialectical class struggles to the more individualized emphasis on discursive analyses that demonstrate the objectification of those individuals denied full subjectivity within the world and within texts. Such analyses also described the processes by which individuals move from subaltern positions of objectivity and into subjective placement. But both dialectical and discursive approaches are based upon a linear oppositionality that assumes inclusion necessarily at the expense of exclusion. Subjectivity, within such a hierarchy, demands a concomitant object against which one's subjectivity is defined. Jeannie Ludlow explains that within a discursive framework, "subjectivity is defined as a (series of) position(s) into and out of which a subject can move, . . . [therefore] a critic should be able to move into and out of subjectivity in order to provide a space within the criticism for the subjectivity of the poet(s)" (26–27). Although such a jockeying for and from position can make critical room for Native voices, it does not facilitate the sort of relational conversivity that is evident within the practice of storytelling and which this book demonstrates is possible within the practice of literary scholarship.

Points of emphasis in this chapter and in the following chapters include

  1. an intersubjective relationality that privileges relationality and thereby problematizes the self-focused individual;

2. the realization that signs and objects are not divorced from one another (or in other words, a recognition of the presence of signifying objects and objective signifiers);

3. the recognition of subjects and objects in relation to various centering forces (a fact that shifts geometric descriptions away from Euclidean linearity, as in the case of semiotic triangles, and toward non-Euclidean elliptic geometries);

4. the written as an extension of the oral (with varying degrees of orality or conversiveness reflected in any [Native or non-Native] work of literature);

5. the very real transformative power of conversivity;

6. the recognition of individuality and that significance as manifested in varying degrees of relationality;

7. authorial presence asserted through an intentional marginalization that emphasizes the center and privileges self in relation to that center; and

8. the presence and importance of a participatory [audience]—placed in brackets by virtue of the listener-reader's active participation.

Building on the introductory groundwork of the first two chapters, which discuss the limitations of literary criticism for opening up the conversive aspects of American Indian literatures, this chapter turns to the work of several Navajo women writers: Della Frank, Nia Francisco, Luci Tapahonso, Gertrude Walters, and Esther G. Belin. A conversive approach to several poems by these women places them in conversation with each other and with me and my words in this chapter. Accordingly, this chapter continues the stories of the poems while it becomes, in its own right, a new story birthed from the conversive parentage of the poems and my scholarship. After a brief look at contemporary postmodern criticisms to see the ways in which a conversive method takes us in new scholarly directions, the remainder of the chapter interweaves the poems and voices of these women writers as each informs and reinforms itself and the others anew. In the storytelling fashion in which each retelling is both a reiteration as well as a new story in and of itself, this chapter is a retelling of some of the poems' stories, as well as its own new story. And this new story moves us even more firmly beyond the bounds of contemporary literary criticism as we step into the oral storytelling worlds of these Navajo women writers.

Although some scholars have found Mikhail Bakhtin's recognition of the diverse voices within a literary dialogism useful for critical readings of

American Indian literary texts, the development of this chapter goes beyond the capacity of a dialogic textual analysis to engage with the stories that lie behind the more superficial level of textuality. Insofar as the recognition of multiple and diverse subjectivities is concerned, Bakhtin's work moved narrative theory forward through his emphasis on the dialogic heteroglossia extant in human discourse and in the range of discursive structures evident within prose fiction; however, even the greater inclusivity of diverse voices within a Bakhtinian interpretive framework is, nevertheless, based upon the oppositional linearity inherent to discursive structures. Moore points out, "dialogic survival, unlike dialectic synthesis, maintains difference within the dynamics of opposition" ("Decolonializing" 17). The points of opposition are more numerous and more diverse, thereby insuring the inclusion of more and diverse voices, but this inclusion is still at the expense of those voices seen to be silent, less significant, or absent—still largely the case for American Indian voices (literary and lived). Moore is quite correct in noting that "a dialogic moves toward relationality" (18). Bakhtin's work has moved literary scholarship closer to the relational intersubjectivity achievable through a conversive literary method. But a heteroglossia in which distinct voices assert their own subjectivities and presences alternately through dialogue is a substantially different reality than the conversive interweaving of voices and persons that co-create and transform their own stories and each other through their relational storytelling communication.

Other critics have responded to the possibilities within postmodern criticisms for reading Native American literatures. Whereas Vizenor (Anishinabe) hails the arrival of postmodernity, seeing it as a fitting critical position for contemporary mixedblood trickster writers whom he refers to as "postindian warriors of survivance" (*Manifest Manners* ch. 1), Owens (Choctaw/Cherokee) points out significant distinctions between a postmodern agenda and the aims of Native writers: "Ultimately, whereas postmodernism celebrates the fragmentation and chaos of experience, literature by Native American authors tends to seek transcendence of such ephemerality and the recovery of 'eternal and immutable' elements represented by a spiritual tradition that escapes historical fixation, that places humanity within a carefully, cyclically ordered cosmos and gives humankind irreducible responsibility for the maintenance of that delicate equilibrium" (*Other Destinies* 20). Owens's point is well taken, even though a number of contemporary American Indian writers such as Vizenor have experimented with avant-garde postmodern literary styles and aims in order to convey their own mixed backgrounds and multiplicitous perspectives. Vizenor's volume, *Manifest Manners: Postindian Warriors of Survivance,* ostensibly postmodern and poststructural, nevertheless demonstrates conversive literary structures in his fluid movements between creative fiction, literary essay, and literary criticism. Throughout the work, diverse voices are interwoven (sometimes comfortably; at other times startlingly, and thereby effectively) in a remarkable postindian trickster discourse.

Relevant to this discussion is Wittgenstein's concern about philosophical methods. He writes, "In philosophy it is not enough to learn in every case, *what* is to be said about a subject, but also *how* one must speak about it" (*RC* 23e). In other words, rather than focusing on the content of our analyses, often the problem is more deeply rooted within our scholarly methodologies. As noted earlier, Wittgenstein goes on to point out, "One must always be prepared to learn something *totally* new" (*RC* 23e). The notion of conversivity as introduced in this volume emphasizes both the orality of American Indian literatures (and which I believe is a part of all literatures, albeit to varying degrees) and the transformative power of language (in the very real sense of conversion, change, a turning from and toward). What is notably new here is that this method is developed through a conversation with the literary works and their storytelling traditions. The development and the practice of this method is inherently consultative in that its origins are to be found in a conjunctive effort of Western and Native voices—not the forced imposition of Western critical strategies upon American Indian literatures. The method is directly informed by the method and practice of the oral storytelling tradition.

This chapter demonstrates how literary scholars can move to engage literary works through a conversive method that shifts the critic away from a critical hegemony over literary texts and toward the humbler role of a storyteller-guide who enables other readers to find their ways to, into, and within the literatures discussed.[2] In such a fashion, the literary scholar serves very much the same role as a storyteller who relates a story which s/he feels is significant for her or his audience. With each telling, the story changes to maintain its significance for the listener(s). Certain basics, however, do not change. This could be described through Wittgenstein's 'language game' image in which fundamental grammatical rules cannot be changed without altering the 'game' itself; however, on the surface level of play, one can move quite freely and flexibly (albeit within the bounds of the base rules). Insofar as literary criticism is concerned, what this signifies is that one does not alter the essential story, the literary work. One does not misrepresent the story, but rather one must relate it accurately, honestly, and completely. But how we tell that story through a scholarly retelling can take many forms based on our intended audiences, our intentions behind telling our scholarly stories, and our own engagements with the literatures (engagements that reflect our intersubjective relations with the voices and persons in the literatures).

The conversiveness of Native literatures reflects the oral traditions of the writers' particular tribal backgrounds. Anna Lee Walters (Pawnee/Otoe-Missouria) notes that "the points of reference in oral tradition from which [Navajo writers write] . . . are not recently contrived inventions or devices incorporated into the works here simply for literary purposes or effects" (*Neon* viii). An example Walters notes is from Della Frank's poem "T'aa Diné Nishli." Although a literal translation of the title and ending line of the poem would read, "I am Navajo," the English translation cannot possibly convey the depth and history signified in the Navajo statement, *"T'aa Diné nishli."* First of all, the prioritized subjectivity in the English sentence that begins with the first-person referent "I" is absent in the Navajo sentence. Rather than first emphasizing herself and then describing herself in terms of her tribal affiliation, Frank's Navajo sentence emphasizes the reality of the tribe and *then* identifies her in terms of the tribe. The reality of the speaker of the sentence is contingent upon her relationship to the tribe, the "sh" first-person marker being evident only within the connective relationship noted in the verb. Even in this simple, yet profound, statement, we see the conversive interaction between individual and tribe—the individual speaking her reality as a Navajo, yet that very speech being informed by the reality of the tribe, a reality that in turn is realized and informed through Frank's utterance and inscription. On this intertwining of individual and tribe, Jahner comments, "most of [today's Native American] writers have established and depend on an especially close relation between the writer, the work, and the traditional community—a relation that determines the contextual semantics of the work and therefore shapes the author's options regarding text structure" ("Indian Literature" 7).

A closer look at several poems by Navajo women writers will demonstrate how they convey within the bounds of the English language (at times switching to the Navajo language where there is no adequate English equivalent) their own worldviews and realities. These writers do not present their perspectives to their readers as outsiders reading and critiquing the poems as poetic objects. Instead, through a conversive engagement between and across events, times, and persons (including the writers of the poems, the persons in the poems, and the readers of the poems), these writers invite their readers into the Navajo worlds of their poems much as a friend would be invited into one's home. The conversive reading of these poems involves a responsibility on the part of the reader, much as any person would have certain responsibilities as a guest in someone else's home (and analogously as the listener of a story would have responsibilities as a participant in a storytelling event).

Nia Francisco and Luci Tapahonso

Conversive structures are not only evident within works of literature. Conversive structural relationships also exist between the different literary works of one writer, between one literary work and its writer and audience, and between different writers and their literary works. This last conversive relationship can be seen through a pairing of Nia Francisco's poem, "Naabeeho Women with Blue Horses," and Luci Tapahonso's poem, "Blue Horses Rush In." Tapahonso and Francisco grew up together in Shiprock, New Mexico, and were friends. Each is familiar with the other's work, and it was Tapahonso who gave the introduction for Francisco when she gave a reading of her poetry at the University of New Mexico in 1988. Regardless of the interpersonal history of Tapahonso and Francisco, the interliterary historicity of their writing is evident within the conversive structures of these two poems. Francisco's poem is the earlier of the two, having appeared in her 1988 volume, *Blue Horses for Navajo Women*.

In the poem, "Naabeeho Women with Blue Horses" (27–29), the image and reality of blue horses are inextricably linked to the capacity of Navajo women to successfully traverse the changes of the world and of their own lives. As Francisco writes, "Devotees of Holy Ones [say] . . . that we Naabeeho women with blue horses must be ready / for the great storms to pass thru our lives during our middle ages / . . . to be the protectors of the younger generations." The blue horses signify the Navajo women's connection with the sacred, their connection with older ways ("the great secret of old women   medicinal ways of knowing") as a means of preparing and empowering them to live in the present and into the future worlds. The second stanza of the poem focuses on the physical, mental, emotional, and spiritual destruction of alcohol. Francisco immediately responds to this stanza with a direct question to other Navajo women and to herself (and, as well, directly to her readers) as she asks, "Are we preparing? getting decorated dressing up young Naabeeho women / for the passing of age no one warned us of." As in the oral tradition of storytelling, Francisco's question invites her reader into an imagined listener's vocalized response, "Yes, yes," "Ah yaa ah." Here we see Francisco's openly engaging conversive style that speaks directly to her readers, and in the open-ended and inclusive first-person plural pronoun "we," Francisco graciously includes them with herself and with other Navajo women. In such wise, Francisco offers and expects the same responsibility for the future—of herself, of other Navajo women, and of any reader of this poem. As Silko (Laguna Pueblo) reminds us, it is not an omniscient storyteller-narrator who relates the story, but rather the storyteller who serves "to draw the story out of the listeners" or, in a written domain, the readers ("Language" 57).

The fourth stanza continues the conversive structure of the poem in its direct parallel with the previous stanza's beginning query: "Are we preparing?" The fourth stanza begins, "Must we talk about our tasks   or our fastings." (27). At this point, the poem, as in the earlier stanza, responds and converses with itself, with Francisco, with the reader: "let's talk about the tiny piñon nuts [mythically and historically significant for the Navajo with important roles in a number of stories] . . . tell our stories until White Dawn yellow corn meal for female / white corn meal for male in prayer" (27–28). Traditional oral stories and ceremony conversively engage with the complexities of contemporary poetry and the real world concerns of alcoholism, sexual relationships, conflicts between Christian doctrine and traditional Navajo beliefs about the sacred, and the changing needs of the younger generations. For Francisco, the changes of the world need not be seen in an inevitably discursive, or at the least an inharmonious, relationship. The difficulties and complexities of the world are one-half of a reality that necessarily involves both good *and* evil, both health and disease. The balance of these elements, like the balance between day and night, is crucial to the functioning of societies, peoples, and persons. Francisco notes the non-Navajo oppositionality in her contrast between "fleshy desires or christian woes" (29). But "Naabeeho women with blue horses," women who straddle worlds and who work to conversively interweave those worlds through telling their stories, are those who sleep a "sleep that rested" (29).

Throughout the final stanza, Francisco conversively interweaves these worlds, referring to the mythical and traditional blue horses in the first line, then referring to a woman birthing a new life (her own or that of her child or both)—an image and reality that equally applies to all time (knitting past, present, and future together through a reference that also points to mythic births and mother figures). The third line of this stanza refers to "every woman who selfishly took from her lover's hand"—a reference and diction ("lover's") that plant us firmly in the present—but this clause is conversively continued in the subsequent and final line that clarifies that what is taken from the lover's hand is a "brand new / turquoise necklace" (29). In the poem's ending, we've come full circle, with the traditional and mythical significance of turquoise interwoven with a contemporary (and/or myth-ical) lover and his necklace—an image and story that equally applies today, yesterday, and tomorrow. In the woman's desire for the turquoise necklace, we see her misplaced longing for the turquoise or blue horses of myth transferred to the materiality of a necklace—the necklace serving as the divorced object of her desire and the sign of her discursive longing for subjective status in relation to the objectified turquoise. Although it is not clear that the woman locates her desire for the necklace within the realm of myth, Francisco makes it so for her readers by conversively intertwining the material desire with the larger and more profound lack of blue horses.

Francisco's conversive tone and structure make it clear that the domain of the sacred, which is foundational to the traditional and everyday em-powerment of the Navajo (and, insofar as the Navajo are concerned, of any human being in the world since all human persons are understood to be fundamentally spiritual beings), is as real and concrete as a turquoise neck-lace and blue horses. As one would expect in a conversational style, the ending is not the linear conclusion of a narrative that begins with a title and first line and extends directly toward its concluding statement or image. Instead the last line of this poem points beyond its literary boundaries to a reality and worldview that posits the essential connections between the future and past, both of which necessarily inform the present and which, for the Navajo, are as real as the present is for more linear Western narra-tives. The poem circles back on itself showing us the nonlinearity, holism, and welcoming inclusivity of Francisco's Navajo worldview.

Tapahonso's poem, "Blue Horses Rush In," the first poem in her volume, *Sáanii Dahataał: The Women Are Singing,* and also the last poem (slightly modified) in her most recent collection, *Blue Horses Rush In,* demonstrates this conversive style in her poem's continuation of the themes, images, and

hopes raised in Francisco's poem and in other nonliterary oral stories. Both
Tapahonso and Francisco emphasize the importance of the interwoven images of blue horses and women: Francisco in titling her book *Blue Horses for
Navajo Women,* and Tapahonso in beginning her book of singing women
with the poem "Blue Horses Rush In," in entitling her new collection *Blue
Horses Rush In,* and in ending that volume with this poem. The poem is
dedicated to Tapahonso's granddaughter, "Chamisa Bah Edmo who was
born March 6, 1991" (*Sáanii* 1). Throughout the poem, the image of "horses
running: / the thundering of hooves on the desert floor" represents the
power and strength of women as they travel through their lives. The
"thundering of hooves" and the "sound of horses running" are the prenatal
sounds of the little girl's "heart pound[ing] quickly" as "she moved and
pushed inside her mother." In a discussion of the conflict between "Christianity and tribal religious practices," Blaeser (Anishinabe) points out that
Native writers "appropriate" Western practices, thereby "investing [them]
with a new interpretation" ("Pagans" 13, 14). Although I do not believe that
the verb *appropriate* conveys the adaptive and, at times, welcoming conversive realities of Native transformations of Western traditions, the interpretive newness of American Indian systems of meaning that Blaeser alludes to
is paramount. We see this sort of transformation as Tapahonso takes the
mechanical sounds of a fetal monitor and transforms the sounds into the
"thundering of hooves" heralding the arrival of Chamisa Bah Edmo into
this world—the world of a hospital room transformed into a world of
mythic significance.

The "thundering of hooves," immediately followed by the lines, "Her
mother clenched her fists and gasped. / She moans ageless pain and pushes:
This is it!" emphasizes that the image of blue horses also represents the
power and strength of the mother birthing her baby (*Sáanii* 1; *Blue* 103).
The reference to her pain as "ageless" communicates to the reader that this
pain is real *and* mythic—a conjunction that serves to underscore the profound significance of her pain, her strength as she pushes through pain, and
her/their success, mother, baby daughter, family, tribal community. Tapahonso's conversive style shares this success and joy with her readers. Silko
points out that in storytelling, there is a "kind of shared experience [that]
grows out of a strong community base" ("Language" 57). Although the
community base within the Navajo tribal community is understandable,
storyteller-poets like Luci Tapahonso speak and write to a broader audience, with no less commitment to the storytellers' responsibilities toward

their readers' accessibility in/to their poems and stories. As the mother pushes, we read, "This is it!" as the excitement of success is communicated by Tapahonso and directly shared with us all.

In the next stanza, "Chamisa slips out, glistening wet and takes her first breath" (*Sáanii* 1; *Blue* 103). This first breath, for the Navajo, signifies the beginnings of her spirit in this world, entering the baby as she inhales for the first time. Tapahonso shares this very personal and sacred experience with her listener-readers in the conversive style of a sharing between friends.

> Her father's eyes are wet with gratitude.
> He prays and watches both mother and baby—stunned.
>
> This baby arrived amid a herd of horses,
>   horses of different colors.
>   (*Sáanii* 1; *Blue* 103)

Tapahonso shares with her readers a father's tears, concerns, and thanks, and also his responsibilities to his wife and daughter as he prays—assisting and watching Chamisa's arrival into this world. This "herd of horses, / horses of different colors" represents the power of all the individuals involved, including the good wishes of family and friends. The different colors point to the different directions, and each color is connected with a particular gender. East and yellow represent woman (as evidenced in Francisco's poem, "yellow corn meal for female"); west and white represent man ("white corn meal for male in prayer"). In Tapahonso's poem, we see the father in prayer, and we read about different horses "thundering" assistance (mechanical, medical, human, familial, mythic, sacred) for the birth. From the father and other men, "White horses ride in on the breath of the wind"—this breath that brings life and spirit to Chamisa (*Sáanii* 1; *Blue* 103).

Tapahonso tells us that horses arrive from each of the four sacred directions, demonstrating the wholeness and sacredness of this birth—a sacredness that is the domain of any birth, but here we see the circle complete with horses arriving from each direction. Each of the directions represents one gender. South and the color blue represent the female: "Blue horses rush in, snorting from the desert in the south. / . . . Bah, from here your grandmothers went to war long ago" (*Sáanii* 1); and "Blue horses enter from the south / bringing the scent of prairie grasses / from the small hills outside" (*Blue* 104). Nia Francisco asks in her poem, "Are we preparing?" Tapahonso answers Francisco's question in this poem in which we see the preparations and tasks performed for the baby's first change of life in this world; we hear the baby's pounding heart, her mother's moans and father's prayers; we watch their efforts to insure the strength of Chamisa's beginning. After describing the arrival of the horses from each direction, Tapahonso ends the poem:

> Chamisa, Chamisa Bah. It is all this that you are.
> You will grow: laughing, crying,
> and we will celebrate each change you live.
>
> You will grow strong like the horses of your past.
> You will grow strong like the horses of your birth.
>   (*Sáanii* 2; *Blue* 104)

This strength that is and will be Chamisa's comes not only from the efforts of those in her present world, but also from those who came before, her "grandmothers [who] went to war long ago"—the blue horses of her past, those "Naabeeho women with blue horses" (27). The conversation of life continues across generations, even beyond temporality, into the domain of myth, where real historical grandmothers rode mythical blue horses through the journeys of their long lives.

Gertrude Walters notes in her short poem, "Shimásání (Grandmother)": "Shimásání, you have traveled a long way—. . . Giving / Love / Protection / Understanding" (110). These long travels, carried by the blue horses of myth, faith, and lived history, are those that serve to guide and protect the younger and future generations. "Shimásání, . . . / Here I sit / Watching you / . . . / Trying hard to taste your life / Shimásání . . ." Walters's poem joins the continuing intergenerational conversation of Navajo women explicitly framed in the form of a granddaughter's direct address to her grandmother. Although the conversive structures of American Indian, and in this case Navajo, poetry need not take the overt forms of a second-person direct address, in "Shimásání" this is the case. Walter's listener-reader hears a granddaughter's words (or thoughts) directed to her grandmother and to herself, but which are also shared with the reader as listener, much as a private and personal conversation might be shared with a friend, relative, or trusted acquaintance who happens to be present. Walters thereby invites her reader to identify with her and the granddaughter of the poem in their love of, respect for, and gratefulness to *bimásání* (their grandmother).

The poem begins and ends with the same line, "Shimásání, you have traveled a long way—." The dashes that end each of these lines provide a longer pause, much as the storyteller pauses on occasion to allow time for the listeners' responses (vocalized and silent). In an analysis of the interactive aspects of the storytelling process, Susan Pierce Lamb writes, "The interaction between teller and listener is simultaneous, thus reliant on right brain processing" (15). Through the openness and inclusivity of Walters's conversive style, the reader joins the granddaughter in "Trying hard to taste" the long life of "Shimásání." Of course, if the reader happens to be an old woman, then the poem is, as well, conversively directed to her as recipient of the younger woman's descriptive and actual respect and gratitude.

Esther G. Belin and Luci Tapahonso

Two other poems focusing on childbirth, the first by Esther G. Belin and the second by Tapahonso, join in the conversation of these earlier poems, developing and deepening the thoughts, words, and experiences of all of the poems. Unlike a discursive or dialogic structure in which each poem or individual asserts its or her own subjectivity and primacy at the expense of others, within a conversive style (both literary and critical), the poems and writers comment upon each other, developing conversations within and beyond the written bounds of each poem. Navajo writers such as Tapahonso, Francisco, Walters, and Belin write from and of their own lived experiences, which are informed by their cultural heritages and which, in turn, assume a very real connection with the sacred. For these writers, this connection is manifested in a conversive writing style that points beyond the boundaries of the writers' lived experiences in this world. The worlds of their poems conversively conjoin the worlds of their lives, the worlds of their people (the tribal reality of the Diné) today, historically, and into the future, and within the timeless world of the sacred. In contrast to the Navajo perception of the interdependency of these worlds, a Western orientation posits sharply delineated distinctions between these worlds, often seen in a competitively fearful framework that opposes individual and group against each other, the temporal material world against a transcendent spiritual world, and a chronological delimitation that either focuses on the present without the recognition of the present's integral interrelationship with both past and future, or, in a recognition of such an interrelationship, the present is privileged as the strong vanquisher of a weaker past. Conversely, these poems speak and depict worlds that interact and overlap, not in competition, but in an open engagement unthreatened by the diversity inherent within conversive relations (be those between and among individuals, poems, or worlds). This intermingling of worlds can be seen in Belin's "Bringing Hannah Home."

In the poem, Belin shares with her reader the very private and cultural experience of the burial of a child's placenta. Navajos believe and know that a child will always return to this place that contains the initial source of the child's lifeblood. Belin begins her poem in a very personal conversive style, as if she is sharing the poem and story with a close friend: "we brought hannah home today" (18). Instead of referring to the baby in the objective tone more familiar within Western discourse (e.g., "We brought the baby home today"), Belin personalizes and subjectifies the baby in naming her. In this naming and in the first-person plural pronoun "we," Belin brings the reader into the personal world of the poem. The reader is expected to know to whom the "we" refers and to know who Hannah is. Even if the reader, by chance and in all likelihood, is not familiar with Hannah nor with those who have brought her home, Belin does not leave the reader in the dark as outsider. After a short first stanza, the very next stanza begins with the needed clarification, "two women with a child and a shovel and a frozen placenta . . . hannah was brought into this world / some say fourth others say fifth / five days before. / before we brought her home" (19). Within Belin's conversive style, reader, speaker, and subjects of the poem are interwoven in a conversation that traverses diverse worlds, times, realities (literary and lived), and persons.

As the two women dig into the ground, the speaker of the poem shares her thoughts and prayers with the reader. In the digging, this woman (aunt, friend, other relative?) remembers another and more difficult digging— that of her father's grave dug into and from the frozen ground of a reservation winter. Within the poem, Belin interweaves the two changes of worlds, Hannah's entry into and a father's departure from this world:

i thought good thoughts for hannah and her mother
and prayed for us all
remembering those who have passed on and those to be born
and i thought of my children to be born
and i thought of my father who has passed on.

(18)

Even in the immediacy of the burial of Hannah's placenta and her return home (from a hospital or other place of birth), the speaker's prayers (prayers offered by Belin, Hannah's relatives and friends, the poem's persona, and the reader) for Hannah and her mother are also for us all, here now, here before, and here to come. Prayers rooted in the concrete here and now also transcend the limitations of time and space and conversively bespeak an inclusivity inherent within the worldview of the poem. Even in Belin's lack of capitalization, especially in the lowercase "i", we see the conversive focus and privileging of the other rather than of oneself.

We converse with, not to, some other person or persons, and within the bounds of a conversation, we speak with the expectation and hope of the "other's" assertion of her or his subjectivity as manifested in a response, which in turn points beyond the individual speaking self and to the importance and reality of the listener. This is categorically different from the dialectic, discursive, or dialogic structures that privilege the subjectivity of a speaker with the passive objectivity of the listener who only gains subjectivity through his or her own speech. For the Navajo, activity is acknowledged both within speech and within thought. Within a Navajo conversive style, as evidenced in these poems, writers and speakers write and speak in a manner that serves to privilege themselves and their words through the primacy given to their readers and listeners. However, such a conversive style involves the responsibility of the reader or listener to respond in turn and in kind. This is not a reader-response critical approach in which the reader completes the poem (and thereby gains a position of privilege), but a conversive response in which listener-reader continues a conversation that began generations and ages before the actual writing and that will continue into the future—as in the case of the thoughts and prayers "for us all / remembering those who have passed on and those to be born." As Rodney Frey points out, "When a story is being told it is being relived, participated in by those assembled. History unfolds anew" (129). Through the conversive structures present in Belin's poem, her readers actually enter the world and the story of Hannah's homecoming.

Belin ends the poem with Hannah's mother taking "the frozen mass of tissue and blood and life" out of its plastic bag and aluminum foil and placing it in the hole. The poem concludes, "and i felt her heat of tissue and blood and life / squatting with bloodied hands and cold earth / bringing hannah home" (19). The pronoun "her," whose syntactical antecedent is "hannah's mother" but whose "heat of tissue" as well refers to Hannah and to the female speaker's physical response to the ceremony, presents a conversive ambiguity that in one word, *her,* brings the three females together in a homecoming profoundly significant for each: Hannah's arrival in this world and homecoming from the hospital, a mother's new life with her baby daughter ceremonially brought home, the speaker's homecoming with Hannah, Hannah's mother, and her deceased father. This intergenerational and interpersonal homecoming demonstrates the dynamism, fluidity, and inclusivity possible within conversively structured poems.

Tapahonso's "It Has Always Been This Way" (*Sáanii* 17–18) contributes to this conversation, adding her Navajo perspective on the importance of new life. "Being born is not the beginning. / Life begins months before the time of birth" (17)—not only during the baby's life in the mother's womb, but also in the lives and generations that precede the baby's life and that inform the lives of both baby and mother. This is explained in the Beck and Walters volume, *The Sacred,* in the chapter by Nia Francisco: "In the days before pick-ups, cars and hospitals, the whole process of having a baby was a ritual—with the help of a Hataali (singer or medicine man) and a midwife—there were songs sung, spreading of fresh soil, sprinkling of corn pollen, stretching of the sash belt, and untying of tied knots, and letting hair down. Long ago, childbirth was considered a beautiful real life struggle and it was a ritual with the sacred beings watching on" (272). Still, in the worlds of these poems, the sacredness of new life is respected even within the domain of contemporary hospital rooms. The importance given to new life also signifies particular responsibilities given to the mother before and after the actual birth. But these responsibilities for the Navajo are neither privatized nor individualistic but involve the participation of extended family and even the larger tribal community, both of which are expected to insure that the mother is enabled to fulfill her responsibilities, which might mean other individuals taking on some of her other chores or jobs.

Tapahonso also explains the burial of the placenta: "It is buried near the house so the child / will always return home and help the mother. / It has been this way for centuries among us" (17). In this burial, we see the significant conjunction of the personal and private with the communal and public, the specific and material with the sacred and the symbolic, and one baby's spatial connection with her mother's home and the love and care of parents and other relatives for a new child. Even the beginnings of life define the circular domain of the conversive for this particular Navajo baby. "Much care is taken . . . to talk and sing to the baby softly in the right way" (17). The importance of vocalization is emphasized from a child's earliest sounds. The first laugh of the child is conversively responded to by the family members and their celebratory "give-away."

> The baby laughs aloud and it is celebrated with rock salt,
> lots of food, and relatives laughing.
> Everyone passes the baby around.
> This is so the child will always be generous,
>   will always be surrounded by happiness,
> and will always be surrounded by lots of relatives.
> It has been this way for centuries among us.
>
> (17)

The child's happy vocalized laugh is framed within a conversive engagement with the emphasis being not on the subjective vocalizing or laughing individual as an objective end, but rather as a gift from the child offered to those whose response is, in turn, one of giving rock salt and food as gifts to others. With the circularity of a conversive structure, one can only return to one's own point on the circle by going via the other points.

The subjective and self-referential privileging possible within linear oppositions (in which an objective world is defined and understood solely in terms of a subjective and privileged point of orientation) is in sharp contrast to a conversive circularity in which each point is privileged always but never at the expense of any other point. From a Navajo perspective, the devaluation, marginalization, absence, or silence of any person or point on the circle would indicate an incomplete circle and an unfinished and partial conversation. As Robin Melting Tallow (Métis) points out, "the circle has neither beginning nor ending. It has always been. The circle represents the journey of human existence. It connects us to our past and to our future. . . .

We are writing the circle." Analogously, a criticism that is not conversively informed by the reality of the text it approaches is, as well, incomplete and partial—a writing that bespeaks more the structure of a monologue than of a multiply voiced conversive critical engagement between story and scholar. Dennis and Barbara Tedlock have stressed the importance of "learning directly from the Indian" (xiii). Although their focus is ostensibly on the scholarship of anthropologists, their concerns are well-taken with respect to literary criticism as well. As they write, "It is true that anthropologists sometimes describe themselves as students of the Indian; they may indeed appear to be his students while they are in the field, but by the time they publish their 'results,' it is usually clear that the Indian is primarily an *object* of study" (xiii). A conversive strategy places literary scholars within a conversation that includes scholars, writers, literary works, and the larger context in which the literatures exist—without the individualized privileging of discursive or dialogic approaches. This involves a very direct relational engagement between scholar and story that in no wise privileges the assumed priority of the scholar.

Wittgenstein taught us that a 'language game' is a "form of life" (*PI* 11e). Allen (Laguna Pueblo) echoes Wittgenstein's point when she writes, "Literature is one facet of a culture. The significance of a literature can be best understood in terms of the culture from which it springs" (*Sacred Hoop* 54). Tapahonso makes this explicitly clear as she begins the final stanza of her poem, "It is all this: the care, the prayers, songs, / and our own lives as Navajos we carry with us all the time" (*Sáanii* 18). The sacred, the communal, the tribal, the personal, the lived, and the living. Blue horses for Navajo women. As Tapahonso ends her poem: "It has been this way for centuries among us" (18), for centuries, and even beyond into the atemporal and nonlinear domain of the timeless and the sacred.

If our aims are to read these poems and to accept the gracious invitations into their words and worlds, which are offered to us by these women poets, then we need to recognize that different words, languages, and worlds require different responses. Allen pointed out, "The study of non-Western literature poses a problem for Western readers, who naturally tend to see alien literature in terms that are familiar to them, however irrelevant those terms may be to the literature under consideration" (*Sacred Hoop* 54). Specifically in relation to Navajo poetry, the importance Navajos give to the use of language exhorts the literary scholar to approach the poems and her or his scholarship with an analogous degree of respect and graciousness. As

Gary Witherspoon points out, "It is through language that the world of the Navajo was created, and it is through language that the Navajos control, classify, and beautify their world" (7).

For the Navajo, language represents and affects the world—a fact that invites scholars to conversively approach the writing of Navajo poets through an intersubjective relationality in which the poems are understood as speaking and, thereby, creative and living stories. Krupat argues for the importance of "an 'indigenous' criticism for Indian literatures" (*Ethnocriticism* 44). One step in that direction is a conversive strategy in which American Indian literatures are enabled to speak their own stories in conversation with the stories (scholarship) of the literary scholars. The poems of Della Frank, Nia Francisco, Luci Tapahonso, Gertrude Walters, and Esther G. Belin suggest the value of such an alternative conversive approach that enables scholars and other listener-readers toward consciously relational and intersubjective engagements with the poems—thereby allowing the poems their own voices within the scholarly retellings. Barney Blackhorse Mitchell (Navajo) says, "The greatest sacred thing is knowing the order and the structure of things" (qtd. in Beck and Walters 11, 95, 107). This "order and structure" involve the ways in which various elements of creation are interrelated and interwoven. Through a conversive approach to the poetry of these Navajo women writers, in which their poems are allowed to converse together, new insights and meaning are gleaned from the work that can only be seen through the particular conjunctive storytelling relationships. An analogous conversive coming together of other poems would shed even more new light. Such a conversive approach offers an infinitude of connections and combinations and relationships, both literary and lived, which will deepen our understandings of the poems and their story worlds.[3] Rather than literary works made text, this is literary scholarship made story. This story continues in the next chapter, which focuses explicitly on these sorts of connections, noting that relationality is at the heart of all storytelling and also at the heart of American Indian literatures.

RELATIONALITY IN DEPICTIONS OF THE SACRED AND PERSONHOOD IN THE WORK OF ANNA LEE WALTERS, LESLIE MARMON SILKO, AND LUCI TAPAHONSO

Relationality may well be the most crucial element of conversive communications. Conversivity reflects the very real connections that exist within worlds (written, told, and lived), and by its transformative nature it weaves new, mends damaged, and reweaves anew connections previously nonexistent, torn, or completely destroyed. As Barney Blackhorse Mitchell (Navajo) explains in his statement that concluded the previous chapter, "the greatest sacred thing is knowing the order and the structure of things" (qtd. in Beck and Walters 11). This order and structure are not means by which the world is divided, but rather means by which the interconnections and interrelationships throughout all of creation are understood and maintained. Gloria Bird (Spokane) explains, "*Everything* depends upon something else. Our ability as readers to enter as participants of the story ultimately relies upon our ability to make those connections, to forego on an intuitive level the constricting notions we have of language and its use" ("Towards" 4). Whereas discursive literary structures and critical strategies emphasize the capacity to delimit the world and texts through the discernment of distinctions, discordant elements, hierarchized orderings, differences, separations, ruptures, and aporias (whether or not these differences are thereafter reconciled through a range of modern critical methods, or thereafter irreconciled and deconstructed through a range of poststructural critical theories), a conversive approach to the world begins with its primary emphasis on the interrelationality and interconnectedness of all elements of the universe. As Trinh T. Minh-ha writes, "Life is not a (Western) drama of four or five acts" (143)—nor for that matter are the stories, histories, and literatures which, over two thousand years of Western critical analysis, have compartmentalized and crystallized into the diverse samenesses and similar differences, respectively, of the modern and postmodern agendas.

Although critical differentiations can assist close analyses of parts of texts (written and lived), when those sharp delineations are at the expense of the interconnections between the parts, then, from a conversive orientation, everything is lost—both the interrelated whole and the range of meaning between the interrelated parts. This is the oft-quoted, yet significant, dilemma of not seeing the forest for the trees. Salish elder Ellen White notes that her grandfather taught her about this problem. Her grandfather advised her accordingly, "You talk *real good, clear, not too many words,* when you talk about something—use too many words, you lost. Think . . . if you talk about trees, you talk too much about limbs and the cone and the ground, the kids will *think* about that—the tree is gone. They didn't see the tree" (Archibald and White 153). For White and her grandfather, it is much more important to recognize the interconnectedness between the diverse elements of the world rather than to focus on those elements in and of themselves. Jane H. Hill and Ofelia Zepeda (Tohono O'odham) note, " 'individuality' in its stereotyped form is rare in vernacular conversational narrative" (222). As this chapter will show, the sort of individuality noted by Hill and Zepeda is absent in those conversive communications whose inherent structuring is relational and intersubjective. Insofar as language use is concerned, we would need to turn to textually discursive forms of communication to find individuals presented as distinct and separate from each other.

Meaning within a conversive framework comes from the relationships among those elements, not from any analysis of those elements in isolation. Simon Ortiz (Acoma) clarifies this in terms of language use when he explains that much more is lost than gained when breaking down a word, a song, or a story into parts. In *Song,* he writes that he once asked his father about the linguistic parts of a word he had used. "What does that word break down to?" Ortiz asked (2). He then relates his father's response: "[He] looked at me with [an] exasperated—slightly pained—expression on his face, wondering what I mean. And he tells me, 'It doesn't break down into anything'" (2). In Ortiz's telling, his father's response bespeaks volumes about the divergent worldviews and systems of significance and meaning that differentiate between discursively textual and conversively experienced words and worlds. Ortiz continues, "The word is there, complete in its entity of meaning and usage. . . . Language, when it is regarded not only as expression but is realized as experience as well, works in and *is* of that manner" (2–3). The conversive power of language manifests itself within the living reality of interpersonal relationships co-created through story and lives: "A song is made substantial by its context—that is its reality, both that which is there and what is brought about by the song" (6). Ruppert makes the same point about the transformative quality of language in a discussion of Maurice Kenny's (Mohawk) writing: "Through his song and poetry, Spirit—the motivating force behind Native American oral tradition—is expressed and confirmed; it re-animates the world" ("Uses" 90).

Native peoples have traditionally understood that nothing in the universe is isolate. Everything is interconnected, and accordingly, knowing comes from learning and understanding those interrelationships. This chapter investigates the ways by which diverse concepts and persons interrelate to re-in*form* themselves and their worlds. The interrelationships that define the interconnectedness of inclusion are manifest in the living diversity of all of creation—what Gloria Bird refers to as "the major trope of Native American literature, that is, the interconnectedness of all things—of people to land, of stories to people, of people to people" ("Towards" 4). This chapter specifically focuses on two areas that demonstrate such conversive interrelationality: the sacred and personhood. In the discussions of the sacred, I look at the conceptual and actual interrelationships (and clashes) between Christianity and tribal beliefs in the sacred, showing how conversive relationality is manifested both in practice and on conceptual levels. In relationship to notions of identity and personhood, I turn to the conversive interrelationships between human persons and nonhuman persons (animals, plants, other elements of the universe) to demonstrate the intersubjective relationality between diverse persons in the world. The range of possible interrelationships between concepts and realities demonstrates the extent to which those connections (and *dys*connections) serve to form, de-form, and reform our words, worlds, and lives. After a discussion of the role of relationality within conversive storytelling worlds, the chapter turns specifically to how such relationality is reflected in American Indian literary depictions of the sacred and of personhood.

Within dialectical, discursive, and dialogical models of language and the world, differences are affirmed through oppositional distinctions; in contrast, similarities are defined in terms of categorical elements that emphasize sameness within a category by means of a differentiation from those other categories against which the similar elements are understood. This can be seen in Wittgenstein's example of color-blind people, discussed in Chapter 2. As I quoted in that chapter, he writes, "There are people who behave like you and me, and not like that man over there, the blind one" (*RC* 334). Within such oppositional frameworks, both difference and sameness are defined through the construction of boundaries that wall off what is similar from that which is dissimilar. "But when one draws a boundary it may be for various kinds of reasons" (*PI* 499e). Here Wittgenstein makes it very clear that the recognition of differences need not always be understood oppositionally. As Robin Fast points out in her essay "Borderland Voices in Contemporary Native American Poetry," "For different peoples and individuals, these variously realized borders may have quite different origins, appearances, and implications" (508).

Wittgenstein explains that language, the world, and, more specifically, the delineation of boundaries are much more complex than we have previously understood. In regards to boundaries, he continues: "If I surround an area with a fence or a line or otherwise, the purpose may be to prevent someone from getting in or out; but it may also be part of a game and the players be supposed, say, to jump over the boundary; or it may show where the property of one man ends and that of another begins; and so on. So if I draw a boundary line that is not yet to say what I am drawing it for" (*PI* 499e). Within oppositional interpretive frameworks, sameness and difference are understood oppositionally. The notion of oppositional difference is self-evident. Oppositional sameness is somewhat less obvious, but nonetheless divisive. Within an oppositional framework, sameness is necessarily defined against that which it is not. For example, Eurocentric delineations of race defined other races in terms of their differences from the white or Caucasian race. However, more recent discussions of race recognize that the differences and similarities across and within groups of peoples cannot be so simply defined and differentiated and that, although we can note differences between individual persons and among groups of peoples, these differences do not signify essential oppositions but rather those constructed hegemonic concepts of racial difference that reflect little beyond peoples' incapacities to recognize the living diversity of the one human race—humankind.[1]

This concept of unity with diversity is categorically different from both the melting pot image of differences melting down and being lost into sameness and the more recent postmodern salad bowl image in which difference is affirmed but without the accordant affirmation of similarities and overlap between dissimilars. Such oppositional frameworks posit the choice of unity, sameness, and coherence against the diametric alternative of separation, difference, and complexity. From the perspective of coherent unity, complex diversity is perceived as incoherent noise, and from the latter perspective, the former appears as dull monotony. The irony here is that both perspectives evaluate the other in terms of their own position, neither taking the conversive leap toward interrelational engagement. In the previous chapter, I suggested an alternative metaphor to the melting pot or salad bowl images: namely, a garden in which differences are preserved and valued, not in and of themselves, but more importantly through their interrelationships, which reflect the living diversity that defines the garden and, more broadly, the entire world (also see Brill, *Wittgenstein* 8).

An oppositional interpretive framework that stresses difference through division and separation is merely one way of perceiving, describing, interpreting, and evaluating the world and texts. Differences can also be understood through those connections that interweave and interrelate those diverse elements present within and throughout our lived and read worlds. Through these interweavings and interrelationships, difference is affirmed and valued as that which significantly informs the complexity that is the world, our lives, and our stories (or 'language games', in Wittgensteinian parlance). Granted, the differences that make life in the world meaningful can be denied and sacrificed toward those narrow interpretive ends, which insist on reducing a living diversity into a textualized fixity and sameness. As Sarris (Coast Miwok/Pomo) notes about his Pomo relative and informant, Mabel McKay, she adamantly refused to have "any aspect of her world," her stories, or herself "seen as or reduced to anything other than what it is, in all its complexity and difference" (*Keeping* 41). Even seemingly reasonable, if somewhat naive, questions about the symbolism within her stories are, to McKay, a problematic limiting of the stories into particular interpretive frameworks. As McKay would tell Sarris on multiple occasions, "There is more to the story" (28).

There is more to the story in that stories, like lives, are continually developing and expanding with each individual teller, with each new listener, and with each occasioned telling. There is, as well, more to the story than can be fit into any interpretation that is definitionally bounded by its own conceptual limits. Conversive methods of literary scholarship, rather than bounding a text by preconceived interpretive theories, take on a descriptive role analogous to Wittgenstein's philosophical methods of understanding the world. As Wittgenstein transformed what he perceived as the dead rubble of philosophy into the interactive process of philosophical investigations, which self-consciously emphasizes the relationship between the philosopher and the world she investigates, conversive scholarship moves away from the range of critical assumptions about texts, readers, and writers (granted, all concepts whose definitional boundaries have taken on a shifting and amoeboid shape of late) and, instead, emphasizes the interrelational processes of literary scholarship and storytelling, both in its oral and written forms. By focusing on the process of literary scholarship as storytelling rather than on specific critical theories, the scholar is free to engage with and discover aspects of texts otherwise obscured by various theoretical constraints. These theories and criticisms do bring specific aspects of texts into focus, but they can only illuminate that which their method specifically analyzes.

Western criticism and theory have followed the Platonic and Aristotelian methods of analysis that privilege definition, delineation, difference, dissection, and discrimination. A conversive approach presents a descriptive rather than an explanatory or analytic method,[2] emphasizing the value of discerning 'family resemblances' and connections between apparent similars *and* between dissimilars. In no way is difference lost or ignored. In fact, difference is affirmed through the diverse interrelationships that inform the realities of human lives and literary texts. The conversive emphasis on interrelationality can be seen in the ways by which diverse concepts and belief systems are conjoined without a concomitant loss of their original differences, far from the melting pot images of differences melting down into sameness. With the emphasis being placed on the interrelatedness of different elements (or belief systems) rather than on the specific points of contention, it is possible to maintain the diversity of those elements (and beliefs) within a larger interpretive framework that incorporates their differences. As Reed Way Dasenbrock notes in relation to Silko's writing, "Precisely the opposite of the Western tradition of closure and boundedness obtains: stories are valued for their overlap, for the way they lead to new stories in turn" (313).

Bird points out, "We must also be willing to attempt to 'see the world differently'" ("Towards" 4). J. Barre Toelken notes in relation to a story told by the Navajo elder, Little Wagon, "by seeing the story in terms of any categories I had been taught to recognize, I had missed the point" ("Pretty Language" 213). In contrast to discursive structures that reflect critical divisions, deconstructions, and reconstructions, conversive relations manifest the intricately diverse ways by which the various elements of the world and of texts are interwoven within an organically diverse and changing world. Our knowledge of these relationships and structures is directly in proportion to our own contact with those aspects and elements of the world we desire to understand. A. LaVonne Brown Ruoff points out, "Consequently, each literature must be studied within the contexts both of the cultural group that produced it and of the influences on that group resulting from its interactions with other tribes and with non-Indians" ("Survival" 274).

Ruppert explains that this necessitates a critical perspective that explicitly addresses the interconnections evidenced in Native American fiction. "Mediation has a way of utilizing the two perspectives so that neither is subsumed, but rather they exist in a dynamic confluence that can encourage deeper questions in differing audiences" ("Mediation and Multiple Narrative" 211). The complexities involved in the dynamically evolving interrelationships of stories and lives, what Michael M. J. Fischer refers to as "the inter-references, the interweaving of cultural threads from different arenas" (230), call for scholarly strategies capable of comparable dynamism and responsiveness. This is why James Clifford advocates the "new interest in revaluing subjective (more accurately, intersubjective) aspects of research" for work in cultural studies ("Ethnographic Allegory" 107). A conversively based approach is crucial for responding to and with conversively informed literatures. Only through a connective means can scholars begin to really become a part of the interconnective stories that are Indian literatures. Literary scholarship is a retelling of those stories, and such retelling requires that the new teller know the story—and within a conversively informed framework, such knowing involves being a part of the story, being transformed by the story, and being able to serve as the instrument enabling others' participation in the story, too.

Interconnectedness, relationality, inclusivity are the hallmarks of conversive scholarship and of conversive stories. Frey notes in "Storytelling among the Apśaalooke (Crow Indians)," "The human, natural, and spiritual worlds are intimately linked, interdependent each with the other" (131). Peggy Beck and Anna Lee Walters (Pawnee/Otoe-Missouria) emphasize that this interdependence encompasses everything: "One of the important concepts Native American tribal people share with respect to the sacred is that all things in the universe are dependent on each other" (102). And Silko (Laguna Pueblo) emphasizes the importance of such interrelationality—especially within stories: "There is always, *always* this dynamic of bringing things together, of interrelating things" ("Language" 64).

This interrelatedness is what Wittgenstein describes as 'family resemblance'. In a discussion of the differences and similarities between diverse 'language games', Wittgenstein explains that although we cannot reduce all of language to a specific set of elements or propositions, we can note the ways in which all of language is related in a complex set of interrelationships. He writes, "Instead of producing something common to all that we call language, I am saying that these phenomena [e.g., different 'language games' in use] have no one thing in common which makes us use the same word for all but that they are *related* to one another in many different ways. . . . [W]e see a complicated network of similarities overlapping and criss-crossing: sometimes overall similarities, sometimes similarities of detail" (*PI* 65e, 66e). Wittgenstein repeatedly uses the example of weaving to describe his recognition of the interrelatedness of language use. Through this analogy, he explains that even those very diverse elements that combine to make up one thread are connected through the "continuous overlapping of those fibres," which knits all into one thread (*PI* 67e). What Wittgenstein describes in terms of language use are the multiplicitous connections Beck and Walters describe as inherent throughout the universe. Within Wittgenstein's notion of 'family resemblance', differences are in no wise denied, annulled, or ignored, but are, in fact, affirmed through the recognition of those connections and similarities that unite difference in the world. One area in which this inclusiveness and overlap can be seen is in those stories that communicate people's relationships to the sacred.

Diverse Manifestations of the Sacred

In their volume *The Sacred,* Beck and Walters emphasize the "viability or adaptability" of tribal spiritual beliefs, noting that this adaptability manifested the people's spirituality, not in abstract dogma and religious explanation, but rather in "*practical* systems of knowledge. . . . Classic tribal sacred ways do not try to explain or control all *phenomena* in the universe" (4). The juxtaposition of Eurocentric Christian teachings against tribal beliefs resulted in severely discursive and oppositional divisions between people and their diverse belief systems. However, those Indian peoples who responded in a conversive manner to the different religious traditions found meaningful connections, 'family resemblances', and relationships among the diverse traditions which, within the discursive framework of colonization, could only be understood oppositionally. We can see this clearly in the various ways in which some Indian peoples have been able to accept Christianity as true and important to them without that acceptance being a rejection of their own tribal beliefs and traditions. This contrasts with the predominant incapacity of those who brought Christianity to Indian peoples to see and accept the spiritual 'family resemblances' between Christian and tribal sacred traditions. Ortiz explains that his ancestors perceived and accepted the sacredness of both traditions, transforming Catholic ritual through the framework of Acoma culture and belief: "Many Christian religious rituals brought to the Southwest (which in the 16th century was the northern frontier of the Spanish New World) are no longer Spanish. They are now Indian because of the creative development that the native people applied to them" ("Towards a National Indian Literature" 8).

For many Indian peoples, such acceptance and transformation of seemingly divergent religious traditions were seen as affirmation of the range of beliefs and traditions that center themselves within the domain of the sacred. This is what Kimberly Blaeser (Anishinabe) refers to as "the shifting grounds of religious and spiritual understandings, requiring us to reconsider, reevaluate, reimagine what these terms mean or have come to mean to Indian people as well as what they might come to mean to all people" ("Pagans" 13). In her short story, "The Devil and Sister Lena," Anna Lee Walters depicts diverse interpretive responses to the reality of the sacred. Walters provides the contrasting examples of Lena, an older Indian woman for whom the domain of the sacred is a profound part of her everyday life, and various Christian preachers for whom sectarian theologies and church affiliations seem more important than any meaningful connection with the sacred. Here Walters echoes Mabel McKay's concern about the extent to which the world and "all its complexity and difference" are reduced through narrowing interpretive frameworks—regardless of whether those frameworks take on a literary critical or theologically sectarian focus.

For the preachers depicted in Walters's story, there is only one reality of the sacred which, by their definitions, is necessarily circumscribed by the boundaries of their own sectarian interpretations. What is outside those bounds is defined as wrong, unholy, pagan. This one example demonstrates the reality that Blaeser notes: "The various representations of religion and spirituality in twentieth century Native American literature frequently depict or take for granted knowledge of the historical and philosophical conflict between Christianity and tribal religious practices" ("Pagans" 13). Although such oppositional relations do describe the horrific effects of "the socio-political colonizing force" of the Christian churches (Ortiz, "Towards" 8), a conversive approach is needed to read the unifying and relational story of the sacred that is never oppressive nor divisive, but always inclusive and accepting. For Walters's Lena, the sacred is one reality, even though it may be manifested in diverse forms.

Lena, like many of the other members of her tribe, has accepted the spiritual station of Jesus Christ. Lena accepts that Jesus is a part of the sacred, just as are the traditional spiritual ceremonies of her tribe. Accordingly, Lena occasionally attends church to hear about Jesus: "Lena was a religious woman. She attended church at every opportunity even though an ancient tribal belief had been deeply instilled in her. She did not forsake 'the old way' as she called it, and she taught both ways to the grandchild in her care" (*Sun Is Not Merciful* 63). Lena, again like a number of her fellow tribal members, chooses to attend different churches at different times, I imagine for a range of practical reasons—perhaps one church is on her way to visit a relative, or another church is near the fairgrounds where there are some traditional doings, or perhaps there is a new preacher at a church whom she wants to hear. Lena accepts Jesus fully, but she does not accept the sectarian differences that have interpretively divided up the sacred, which she sees as indivisible. For her, there isn't even any foundational or essential spiritual difference between her faith in Jesus and her faith in her tribe's traditional spiritual beliefs.

To the different preachers frustrated at her inability to understand the finer points which, they believe, prove the truth of their respective churches and the falsity of the others, Lena repeatedly tells them, "It's alla same" (64). However, the ministers, incapable of perceiving and understanding the 'family resemblances' between the diverse manifestations of the sacred, "decided then that the Indian flock were like children who had simple minds and led simple lives. Painstakingly theology was explained to each of these potential converts" (63). Lena looks more deeply at the spiritual essence (what Wittgenstein refers to as the underlying grammatical foundation of any 'language game') within both Christianity and her Indian tribal beliefs, and Lena perceives and understands that what lies at the essential levels of both traditions is the heart of the sacred. The surface differences are less important than the essential reality of the sacred to Lena. Whereas the preachers focus on and emphasize the superficial differences between the "heathen" Indian traditions and Christianity, as well as between the different Christian churches, Lena and her fellow tribal members who accept the two spiritual traditions look more deeply beyond the distinctions of sectarian theology and practice, refusing to narrow the reality of the sacred into any particular interpretive framework.

Blaeser discusses this conflict in her article, "Pagans Rewriting the Bible." She suggests, "Perhaps the true conflict is between religion, which involves the imposition of the already established, the fixed order or structure, and spirituality, which involves the interactive formation of relationships" (23). Although I understand Blaeser's concern here, as a Bahá'í, I am not prepared to accept such a categoric devaluation of religion per se. I know that in my own life and in the lives of other persons affiliated with diverse religions, religion and religious belief can be vehicles for one's deepening of spirituality and faith, just as they can be impediments to that process as well. But Blaeser is completely correct in her emphasis on the extent to which organized religion all too often becomes the barrier between the individual and her or his spiritual growth. This is clearly the case for the preachers in Walters's story. It is Lena who truly values Christianity as well as her tribal beliefs. For Lena, Christianity adds to her faith; but in the examples of the preachers described in the story, Christianity appears to be the impediment to their spirituality and recognition of the common grounds between all manifestations of the sacred.

I would amend Blaeser's hypothesis to note the conflict as one between religious dogma and religious faith (or spirituality). In fact, Blaeser explicitly targets religious dogma as problematic for the sort of spirituality present in American Indian literatures. She writes, "It is the stasis and monologic quality of orthodox dogma that much contemporary Native American literature opposes, whether manifested in Christian or in tribal religions" ("Pagans" 22). Within the bounds of the various definitions of the sacred lies the essential distinction between religious beliefs and practices that have been reified through the monologic and discursive historicity of textualization and doctrinization and those religious beliefs and practices that have maintained their conversive dynamism and openness. C. Jan Swearingen notes these differences in a discussion of the oral (conversive) religious belief and practice among the ancient Greeks prior to the development of the more fixed textualized traditions of later religious institutions that resulted in the sort of stasis described by Blaeser. Swearingen writes, "Greek religious texts, interestingly, never became canonical, and in several traditions were forbidden to be written for reasons parallel to Plato's objections to writing in general" (150).

Within oral traditions, the sacred is manifested in the relationships between each person and all other parts of creation. As Wiget explains in relation to Ortiz's poetry, "The inference, dawning here but enhanced subsequently, is that persons have meaning by virtue of their relationships, and that networks of relationships are founded upon belief in a governing story which establishes a Center. Clearly, if one loses faith in that Center, the networks of relationships disintegrate and one's sense of self collapses" (*Simon Ortiz* 34). That Center, as Ortiz himself notes, is the "Creator Source, the Great Spirit; it is all one. Native American stories are traditionally spiritual, and these stories are truly powerful, wondrous, awesome, and sacred because of their spiritual nature" (rev. of Reed and Blue Cloud 598). In fact, elsewhere Ortiz asserts, "The spiritual aspect of literature is, I would venture to say, a distinction of Native American literature" (qtd. in Manley and Rea 365). "The act of telling a story within a Native American cultural context is an act of spirituality" (rev. of Reed and Blue Cloud, 598). Duane Niatum (Klallam) clarifies, "I want to stress again the importance of the spirit; it has always been our major mode of expression" (33). Hence the importance for scholars and students of American Indian literatures to conversively address the sacred and its various representations within those literatures directly and openly as done by many American Indian writers themselves.

This situation is presented very clearly in one scene from Walters's story when a young preacher comes to visit Lena to try to persuade her to save her soul and convert to his faith. Throughout their conversation, the preacher takes a discursively oppositional stance, talking *at* Lena who, in turn, listens closely and responds to him calmly, gently, and conversively, while trying to help the preacher understand the reality of the sacred conversively rather than discursively. Yet even after Lena communicates her belief in Jesus and her appreciation for the songs in church, the young preacher looks at the old Indian woman and says, "I hear you people don't have religion. Don't believe in God or Jesus" (67).

> For the first time in their conversation, Lena's mouth clamped shut. Her lips pursed tightly. She looked at him with open distrust and sat down again on the makeshift chair. She looked at the girl [her grand-daughter] and said, "I'll tell you what I can. We don't got Jesus. We got something else. It's ever thing. Hard to sit and talk bout it. Can't say it in so many words. So we sing, we dance. What we have is a mystery. Don't got answers for it and don't understand it. But it's all right. Jest live right in it. Side by side." (67)

Throughout Lena's conversation with the preacher, she responds to him openly and conversively, listening closely to his words to understand what he is really saying and why a preacher would be so unable to recognize the reality of the sacred in its diverse manifestations. In contrast, the preacher approaches Lena and her beliefs oppositionally through the colonizing perspective of religious orthodoxy, institutionalized status and privilege, cultural distinctions, and racial prejudice, all of which play themselves out in his antagonistically combative discourse.

Conversive communications involve the co-creative participation of each person involved. The preacher's discursive approach prevents him from speaking *with* Lena and from really hearing her words. Throughout this scene, it is only Lena's granddaughter who listens conversively to her grandmother and to the preacher as well. Conversive relations are intersubjective and transformative. Lena really seeks to help the young preacher man understand the sacred beyond the limits of his sectarian belief. In their interaction, it is Lena who demonstrates the love inherent in conversive relations. The preacher may say that he is concerned about Lena and her salvation, but discursive communication is essentially divisive, competitive, and oppositional. As long as the preacher does not respond to Lena in a conversive manner, recognizing her equal subjectivity and personhood in the world, his words will never have the transformative effect he desires. In fact, his combative stance serves to push Lena further away. In her assertive defense of her traditional beliefs, Lena steps out of her otherwise open and conversive manner with the preacher and distances herself from him—evident in her pursed lips, her look of distrust, and her moving away from him physically by sitting down in the chair that she had previously risen from in order to speak with him. However, discursivity is not Lena's general manner. As the preacher gets up to leave, Lena impishly promises him, "We see you at church come Sunday, preacher" (67). The preacher leaves scowling "while Lena giggled and the child waved"—both demonstrating the sincere friendliness of conversive relations (67). At this point in the story, Lena returns to the affectionate playfulness that characterized most of her conversation with the preacher.

Even though the preacher is discursively oppositional and downright rude to Lena (as further evidenced in Lena's granddaughter's statement later that evening, "That whiteman was sure mad at us today, huh?" [68]), with the exception of Lena's eventual defense of her people's spirituality after the direct attack by the preacher, Lena is consistently open and conversively playful with the preacher, even though her openness seems to only frustrate him the more. Whereas he seeks to justify his own narrow interpretive boundaries for the world, people, and religious faith, Lena's conversive openness is a threat to the preacher, for if he were to really listen to Lena's position, he might have to question some of his own preconceived notions. After Lena's granddaughter asks, "How come he acted mean with us?" Lena responds thoughtfully and sincerely (and I would add, very generously), "Not his fault, baby. . . . He's jest young. And he thinks he knows ever thing" (69). When her granddaughter further asks why her grandmother didn't help him to understand, Lena explains that that would be ineffectual. "Wouldn't do no good, baby. He don't lissen. Don't hear the wind and the rain, the trees, and the grass. Don't hear it, the voice inside the mystery" (69).

For the preacher, the differences between him and Lena are religious. He sees himself as "saved" by virtue of accepting and living within the particular interpretive boundaries of his denomination; Lena and all others outside those boundaries are damned. The irony, of course, is that it is the preacher who, in Wittgenstein's words, "is merely tracing round the frame through which [he] looks at" the sacred, while Lena is the one who more closely approaches the "nature" and reality of the sacred through her refusal to delimit the sacred within set interpretive boundaries (PI 114e)—in Lena's words to the preacher: "It's ever thing. . . . Can't say it in so many words. . . . What we have is a mystery. Don't got answers for it and don't understand it. But it's all right" (67). Whereas this lack of interpretive limits clearly disturbs the preacher, Lena feels neither compunction nor need to enclose the sacred due to human hubris and desire to understand in words and thoughts that which for Lena is beyond the bounds of such comprehension.

The differences between one Christian church and another, between Christianity and Indian tribal beliefs are, to the preacher, oppositionally irreconcilable; yet for Lena, who more comfortably recognizes resemblances and connections between those elements of the world seemingly dissimilar, a conjoint faith in Jesus and "the old way" is neither awkward nor complex, but rather profoundly simple. For Lena, both religious traditions were simply two different aspects of the very same reality—the domain of the sacred.

Lena's acceptance of the two different traditions reflects the extent to which a conversive approach to the world brings diverse elements together through a harmony otherwise impossible. Through this process, tradition is neither denied nor, thereby, destroyed through a forced choice between the two. Instead, both are fully accepted and respected, although not in the sectarian and monologic way of the preacher's proselytizing. As Silko notes about the religious inclusivity of the Mexican Indians who accepted Christianity along with their own tribal beliefs, "The Europeans completely misread the inclusivity of the Native American worldview, and they were disgusted by what they perceived to be weakness and disloyalty by the Indians to their Indian gods. For Europeans, it was quite unimaginable that Quetzalcoatl might ever share the altar with Jesus" ("Indian" 6). Lena achieves her convergence between Christianity and "the old way" through her emphasis on the essence of the traditions, rather than through a dogmatic emphasis on the more superficial aspects such as ritual, theology, and sectarian belief. In Silko's *Ceremony,* the characters of Ku'oosh, Auntie, and Betonie provide striking examples of the range of approaches Indian peoples have taken in relation to the apparent and real clashes between traditions and worldviews. Silko presents an analogous resolution to Walters's Lena in the mixedblood Navajo medicine man, Betonie, who straddles and brings together the diverse worlds that have literally, metaphorically, and physically informed his own self. Unlike Lena, however, Betonie's convergence of worlds does not ostensively embrace Christianity, which is presented in the novel as one of the many restrictive and conflictual elements hegemonically imposed upon Indian peoples by the European invaders.

The problematic acceptance of Christianity by Indian peoples is portrayed by Tayo's self-righteous and bigoted Christian aunt, who is more concerned about how she and her family appear to the rest of the community than about the Christian virtues of charity, love, and humility. Like the preacher in "The Devil and Sister Lena," Auntie's narrow-mindedness about religion, her family, her world, and her self is depicted through her discursively oppositional stance to virtually everyone and everything—a stance that does not change until the end of the novel when Tayo's healing ceremony/experiences give the family a level of respect in the community that Auntie's self-righteous churchgoing never achieved. Throughout Tayo's life, from his earliest years after Auntie takes him in "to conceal the shame of her younger sister" (*Ceremony* 29) to his adulthood as a World War II veteran sick with "battle fatigue," Auntie defines Tayo as "other," less than the rest of the family. She maintains a strict hierarchy of privilege and exclusion between her own son Rocky and Tayo. "She wanted him close enough to feel excluded, to be aware of the distance between them" (67).

Auntie, her family, and her people suffered at the hands of European and Euroamerican genocide, deicide, and, more broadly, the devaluation and destruction of their culture, traditions, and beliefs: "Christianity separated the people from themselves; it tried to crush the single clan name, encouraging each person to stand alone, because Jesus Christ would save only the individual soul" (*Ceremony* 68). When Auntie's Little Sister began drinking and being sexually promiscuous, the response of the Catholic priest was judgment and rejection, whereas the tribal members felt compassion for the young woman whose loss was also a very real loss to the tribe as a collective and interrelated whole and, thereby, to each individual member. "The Catholic priest shook his finger at the drunkenness and lust, but the people felt something deeper: they were losing her, they were losing part of themselves" (68). The various relationships that had woven the tribal community together for centuries had been violently and consistently riven apart through the various ideological institutions of the state developed in the United States as practical applications of the belief in "manifest destiny."

Silko points out that Indian peoples were taught to be ashamed of themselves, of their beliefs, traditions, and histories. Little Sister, for example, learned from her home economics teacher in school how to dress "exactly like the white girls," and in so doing she learned that if she looked like them, she could also attract the white men and perhaps, thereby, be less Indian. But the human connections dependent upon the superficial attributes of dress, lipstick, and hairdos are not the basis of intersubjective conversive relationships between persons; they are the objectifying interactions that translate the larger cultural hegemonic practices into the very personal experience of individual degradation and abasement. As Paul Rabinow notes about the diverse ways colonial ideologies are impressed on people, "With less than 20,000 troops, the French, after all, ran Indochina in the 1920s with a degree of control that the Americans with 500,000 some fifty years later never approached. Power entails more than arms, although it certainly does not exclude them" (259).

Whereas Little Sister translated the lessons of racial and cultural inferiority into her own internalized and actual destruction on the streets of Gallup, Auntie translated those same lessons of inferiority into her own desperate judgmentalism and feelings of superiority. Within such an oppositional framework, one is either on the top or on the bottom, and Auntie struggles to perceive herself as on the top through her perceptual and behavioral devaluation of those around her. When her own mother, Old Grandma, decides to call the village medicine man to help Tayo, Auntie takes on the discursively oppositional voice of the non-Indian world: "You know what the Army doctor said: 'No Indian medicine.' Old Ku'oosh will bring his bag of weeds and dust. The doctor won't like it" (34).

In Auntie's opposition to her mother's decision, she is not only rejecting the value of "the old way," but also being disrespectful to her own mother, an elder in the tribe. Her discursive oppositionality reflects more than anything else her own powerlessness and insecurity. Discursive power is necessarily contingent upon its respondent validation on the part of the disempowered other. When the "other" refuses to play the discursive 'language game', the abject powerlessness of the discourser becomes manifest, as was profoundly evident in the interaction between Lena and the preacher. In Auntie's conversation with her mother, Old Grandma communicates her firm decision to call the medicine man Ku'oosh to help her grandson, and then she tells her daughter to stop worrying about what others might think. With her final comment, "Old Grandma stood up straight . . . and stared at Auntie with milky cataract eyes" (34). Here we see Grandma speaking directly to [in communicating her decision] and with [in responding to Auntie's concerns] her daughter, speaking with the power and concreteness and love that are always aspects of conversive relations.

Silko describes the utter weakness and solitude of Auntie in contrast to Old Grandma. Old Grandma draws on the strength of her interrelationships with her family, with her tribal community, and with the sacred. Auntie, instead, shuts herself off from these sources of strength, and in turn, can only struggle for the illusion of strength through her imagined superiority to others. After Auntie's seemingly strong comments about Ku'oosh and his "bag of weeds," Silko writes: "But her tone of voice was one of temporary defeat, and she was already thinking ahead to some possible satisfaction later on, when something went wrong and it could be traced back to this decision" (34). One battle lost, Auntie looks forward to the next battle in her desperate desire for any sense of discursive presence in the world, regardless of the fact that her presence discursively necessitates the objectification of those "others" whose subjective presences she denies, and regardless of the further fact that in a world in which we are all inter-related, any devaluation of "others" is a devaluation of oneself. As the Jewish Egyptian poet Edmond Jabès writes, "Absence has woven our bond: which binds Nothing to Nothing" (159).

In contrast to Auntie, who devalues and distances herself from her family, her people, and the tribal ways, "Old Ku'oosh" privileges the old ways through a rigid adherence to the traditional tribal practices. When Ku'oosh comes to help Tayo, he brings the old remedies and ceremonies. But as Silko makes clear throughout the novel, the old ways need to be modified to be applicable and efficacious in new times. Ku'oosh helps Tayo somewhat—enough to enable him to keep down some cooked corn-meal, but even Ku'oosh acknowledges the limitations of the old remedies. " 'There are some things we can't cure like we used to,' he said, 'not since the white people came. The others who had the Scalp Ceremony, some of them are not better either' " (38). Although Silko portrays the value of the old ways, she also makes it very clear that even they need to evolve—not through a discursive opposition against what is "other" (as in Auntie's case, or more seriously in the case of Emo and his witchery), but through a conversive relationship with those new elements of a changing world. Betonie echoes Ku'oosh's concerns: "At one time, the ceremonies as they had been performed were enough for the way the world was then. But after the white people came, elements in this world began to shift; and it became necessary to create new ceremonies. I have made changes in the rituals. The people mistrust this greatly, but only this growth keeps the ceremonies strong" (126). Ku'oosh, Auntie, and the most evil character in the novel, Emo, present different stances in relation to the sacred, with varying degrees of distance and disorientation. Having acknowledged that change is good, Ku'oosh, nevertheless, rigidly keeps the old ways as they have been, choosing not to engage at all with new or different ways—at least insofar as the tribal ceremonies are concerned. Auntie, in contrast to Ku'oosh, discursively privileges the Eurocentric ways of the Church, and she does so with a rigidity and oppositionality that devalues her own people's traditions and history, and, thereby, her own self. Most dangerously (for himself and others), Emo, the one character who is completely cut off from the sacred, positions himself oppositionally through an extremely pathological and egocentric monologism that recognizes no conversive connections and interrelationships at all. Emo cuts himself off from all sources of interrelational power, thereby necessitating a continual, almost vampiric, need on his part to drain others of their strengths through his desires to gain the illusory power (albeit potentially very dangerous for his victims) that such witchery begets.

In Margaret A. Farley's discussion of individual autonomy within an existential perspective, she explains that existential relations are "relations of conflict" by which an individual becomes a person in contrast to some "other" or nonperson and, ironically, by which an individual recognizes his or her own subjectivity only "in experiencing [him or herself] being made into an object" by others (192). Farley continues, "For Sartre, the other is always only the other for me" (193). Per her description of existential autonomy and conflictual relations, the local priest (Father Kenneth, who objectifies and patronizes his Laguna Indian parishioners), Auntie, and most horrifically, Emo, all represent the Sartrean theory of human absurdity in which ultimate individualism (found in those who objectify and devalue "others" through the individuals' own assertions of self) ironically intertwines those "individuals" with those "others" they struggle to deny. This is the oppositional lie behind the seductive witchery of discursive oppositionality and power that Tayo learns to reject. Although the power and freedom gained through such conflict are illusory and always contingent upon the collusion (active or passive, conscious or unconscious, by choice or by force) of the oppressed, the effects are nevertheless real and deadly.

The emptiness that is witchery is described in Tayo's thoughts about "the lie": "the lies devoured white hearts, and for more than two hundred years white people had worked to fill their emptiness; they tried to glut the hollowness with patriotic wars and with great technology and the wealth it bought. And always they had been fooling themselves, and they knew it" (191). The lies have alienated Auntie from her family, her people, and herself; they have kept Ku'oosh and the others from remembering the conversive dynamism that is always at the heart of the sacred; and they have completely infected Emo to the point of witchery. It is Betonie (the mixed-blood Navajo medicine man who conjoins diverse worlds and traditions in his own person, life, and spiritual practice) who provides the necessary model for Tayo (and the others) to learn how to live conversively in a world that demands an ever-increasing discursive divisiveness and competition manifesting itself in the all too often horrific realizations of a social Darwinian and Hobbesian struggle of each and all against all for survival (the extreme forms being most evident in Emo and his witchery).

Within the domain of the sacred, the cooperation of each is crucial for the survival of all. After Ku'oosh visits him, Tayo remembers "something in the old stories. It took only one person to tear away the delicate strands of the web, spilling the rays of sun into the sand, and the fragile world would be injured" (38). Just as the loss of each person is a loss to all, so is the return of each person an important part of the healing within families, within the tribe, and even within the entire world. Michael Castro explains, "The old stories give Tayo (and the reader) power by connecting him to the past; to the animals and insects of this place, who are revealed as involved in the same struggle against witchery; as well as to the present, which is seen as [a] new version of an eternally recurrent tale" (*Interpreting* 171). Toward the end of the novel, Tayo is home and sees much that has changed: his brother Rocky and uncle Josiah are dead, the gray mule is gone, recent rain has brought new growth to the valley, and the terror of his past nightmares is gone. And even with all these changes, much is the same: the cat and goat are there following him around, his room is the same, the ranchers still own and destroy much of the mountain, but the mountain is stronger than the ranchers and will outlive them. "The mountain outdistanced their destruction, just as love had outdistanced death. The mountain could not be lost to them, because it was in their bones; Josiah and Rocky were not far away. They were close; they had always been close" (219).

Tayo heals by learning and living the fact that strength and health come from the intersubjective connections that bring people together, rather than through the anger, hatred, and competitiveness that tear people and the world apart. Tayo "could still feel the love they [Josiah and Rocky] had for him" (220), not just Tayo's love for them, but their love reaching across worlds and from beyond time and space to embrace Tayo still. Tayo learns that love endures even beyond the grave, and that even with the deaths of his brother and uncle, the loss does not reach the essence of their relationships with Tayo. "This feeling was their life, vitality locked deep in blood memory, and the people were strong, and the fifth world endured, and nothing was ever lost as long as the love remained" (220). In his work with the Navajo, Toelken learned the importance of such connectedness: "Health, on its part, is seen as stretching far beyond the individual: it concerns his whole people as well as himself, and it is based in large part on a reciprocal relationship with the world of nature, mediated through ritual" (Toelken and Scott 88). Such conversive relations reflect the love that is at the heart of Betonie's changing and transforming teaching/healing stories that Tayo hears, lives, and tells.

Throughout *Ceremony,* Silko emphasizes that everything in the world is subject to change, even traditions and ceremonies. If the ceremonies are to be effective through the healing powers of the sacred, then those ceremonies need to be constructed in ways that will enable the people to connect intersubjectively and conversively with the sacred, as Tayo does on Mt. Taylor with Tseh Montaño. Betonie teaches Tayo the importance of the ceremonies and the sacred, but he explains that one's relationship to the sacred must be reflected in ever-changing ceremonies that reflect and respond to the changing times and needs. Referring to individuals like Ku'oosh, Betonie says, "They think the ceremonies must be performed exactly as they have always been done" (126). But as Betonie further explains, in fact, "the ceremonies have always been changing" (126). Betonie maintains an openly and unashamedly conversive engagement with the world that surrounds him. His hogan is filled with not only the herbs and roots and hides one might expect in a medicine man's home, but also piles of old newspapers and telephone books, boxes and trunks filled with "the junk and trash an old man saves," and overflowing shopping bags—"the leftover things the whites didn't want" (127). Betonie engages directly with the world around him, and that engagement includes an acceptance (albeit not an approval) of all the elements of a changing and complex world. Accordingly, his ceremonies reflect the conversivity that is at the heart of transformative healing. When Tayo and the people are conversively strong in their interrelationships with themselves and others, then change, no matter how difficult it may be as in the forms of death and war, is neither to be feared nor avoided when necessary.

Tayo's healing comes through his own conversive relationships. "He cried the relief he felt at finally seeing the pattern, the way all the stories fit together—the old stories, the war stories, their stories—to become the story that was still being told" (246). As Silko interweaves diverse stories into the one story that is *Ceremony,* Tayo learns to interweave the different stories of his and others' worlds into the one story that is the story of the sacred. The boundaries, categories, and divisions that pull human beings apart—from themselves, from "others," and from the rest of creation—are the discursive constructions of our own making, which mask the underlying connections and resemblances pervading the whole world. Tayo's relief comes from this very realization and from the fact that "He was not crazy; he had never been crazy. He had only seen and heard the world as it always was: no boundaries, only transitions through all distances and time" (246). Transitions, change, conversive connections, and relationships are affirmed within Tayo's living ceremony; here, set boundaries, fixed definitions, rigid ritual, linear oppositions, and discursive constructions and deconstructions have no place.

Throughout *Ceremony,* those forces that serve to separate and divide up the world are portrayed as destructive, while whatever contributes to the interconnectedness of all elements of creation is conversively healing. As Silko herself points out in relation to her work, "What I write about and what I'm concerned about are relationships" (in Fisher 21). Again, it is important to reemphasize that a conversive recognition of the dynamic interrelatedness of diverse persons, cultures, times, and places in no wise signifies a loss of difference. Conversive relations emphasize the connections between different elements of the world. Difference is not, thereby, lost; on the contrary, difference is affirmed through the intersubjectivity of conversive relations that recognizes the subjective status of oneself *and* of others. Moore writes, "Relationality is thus a web" ("Myth" 393). Through Betonie's new ceremonies, the old ways are not lost, but are, in fact, affirmed. The sand painting story that becomes a part of Tayo's life may have a new *form* different from the traditional healing ceremonies of Betonie's or Tayo's peoples, but the "new" ceremony is *in essence* more a continuation of the old ceremonies than are many of the old practices that have lost their efficacy (and, thereby, their meaning) in a changing world. It is Tayo's healing story that possesses the transformative power of conversive relations. As Tayo conversively relates his healing story to the Laguna elders, Tayo and the old men are transformed: Tayo as he is welcomed back into the fabric of his tribe, and the old men as they see the power of the new ways.

A'moo'ooh, you say you have seen her
Last winter
up north
with Mountain Lion
the hunter

All summer
she was south
near Acu

They started crying
the old men started crying
"A'moo'ooh! A'moo'ooh!"
You have seen her
We will be blessed
again.

(257)

Silko explains that Tayo's telling took a long time. After the fashion of the oral storytelling traditions, teller and listeners interact throughout the telling as they co-create the story. Betonie and Tayo co-create Tayo's healing story, and as Tayo tells his story to the others, it then becomes their (Tayo and the old men, and more broadly, the tribe as a whole) collective healing story. Throughout Tayo's telling, the tribal elders repeatedly stop him with questions about specific aspects of the story, particularly those elements relating to time and place. Even in the process of the telling, Tayo is reconnected within his tribe through the intersubjective quality of the men's interactions. Thereby, they all learn the new/old story together and realize the blessings the tribe will receive from Tayo's healing as connections and resemblances come to take the place of separations and differences. In relation to the Jewish storytelling tradition, Peninnah Schram explains, "Since God is found in the specific, the historical, and the relational, God becomes related to our human experience" (41). This is what Toelken refers to as "the reciprocal relationships between people and the sacred *processes* going on in the world" ("Seeing" 14). Through those relationships, transformative healing occurs. As Louis Owens (Choctaw/ Cherokee) points out, "Through ceremony, Tayo is able to 'live into' the complex coherence of Pueblo reality and escape the metanarrative of the western world with its story of separation and ultimate destruction" (*Other Destinies* 175).

Even Auntie goes through her own conversive healing as she begins to open up to closer relationships with her family (including Tayo) and others. Auntie starts to talk directly to Tayo as a member of her immediate family, and no longer in the protective manner she used with her own husband and mother "all those years, with an edge of accusation about to surface between her words" (259). This, in and of itself, represents a significant amount of progress for a woman who, throughout most of Tayo's life, tried to disappear him out of the family. But through Tayo's healing ceremony (which is the entire novel), he and his family are healed back into the tribe as valued members. As Auntie sees that even the women at church start to give her more respect and compassion, she responds with the same words used by Hummingbird and Fly in the story about the effects of *ck'o'yo'* magic: "It isn't easy" (113, 255, 256, 259). In Auntie's words to the church women, her mother, and Tayo, she drops her old accusatory discursive edge. As she finally begins to really converse with Tayo and the others in her life, Auntie is transformed through Tayo's story and through her own story, which she no longer tells through the judgmental blinders of a prejudice that rejected her culture, her history, her traditions, and her self. To Auntie, Tayo's recovery is the living proof of the value of Indian peoples and ways. Betonie's ceremony was successful where white medicine and the church had been incapable of healing him.

Auntie still goes to mass and to the bingo, no longer out of rejection of the other traditions, but more out of long-standing habit. When the church women ask her how she has endured all her difficulties over the years, her response from the Hummingbird and Fly story conversively brings together her churchgoing and the old ways. Auntie conversively relates these recent conversations she had with the women at church and at the bingo, sharing the story with Tayo and her mother in a comfortable and open family telling: "She remarked to old Grandma, dozing beside her stove with the dial turned all the way to HIGH, and to Tayo who was oiling his hunting boots: 'I tell them, "It isn't easy. It never has been easy," I say'" (259). Even through the conversive tellings of Auntie at the bingo, we see connections being made in new and transformative ways. Auntie's years of defensiveness and judgmentalism masked her own internalized rejection of herself as an Indian woman, a rejection that she can finally let go of as the power of Indian ways is clear and manifest in her nephew's healing. As Old Grandma says, "So old Betonie did some good after all" (215).

When individuals like Walters's Lena or Silko's Betonie and Tayo live in relation to the sacred, their lives are significantly informed by the conversiveness of all of creation. Difference is not seen oppositionally as a threat to oneself. One speaks and engages *with* those other elements of the world through intersubjective relations. Difference is recognized and valued as part of the diverse fabric that makes up the world. Yes, there are aspects of the world that are dangerous and/or evil. Many Indian peoples know this profoundly—and not only by virtue of their past five hundred years of survival in spite of the horrific effects of the European and Euroamerican colonization of Native lands, cultures, and peoples. Tayo learns, however, that one cannot vanquish evil through opposition; fighting back only fuels the witchery. Even evil (real or perceptual) needs to be accepted and, ideally, avoided. Because everything participates in the various cycles of life, eventually evil will return upon itself. Harmony and balance in the world can only be achieved through the recognition of the intricate interrelatedness of all of creation and through the acceptance of all. As Tayo learns from Betonie, "his cure would be found only in something great and inclusive of everything" (126). That inclusiveness even includes the acceptance of white people and white ways and the fact that Auntie's attendance at mass and the bingo are as okay as Tayo's going hunting or meeting with Ku'oosh and the other elders. Betonie explains to Tayo, the witchery wants Indian people to hate white people (132). Such oppositional struggle feeds into the destructive desires of witchery. But the way of the sacred is the way of unity—not of sameness, but of unity with diversity in which all the diverse elements of the world are interwoven to make up the stories that encompass human existence. As Blaeser comments in a discussion of Linda Hogan's (Chickasaw) *Mean Spirit,* Michael Horse "seems to embody the cosmopolitan spirit which both allows difference and recognizes the 'unity-in-difference.' He looks beyond the religious forms which are 'culturally biased' and perceives the 'oneness behind the plurality' " ("Pagans" 24).

The conversive worldviews that have informed how American Indian peoples perceived others emphasize the interrelationality of all of creation along with an acceptance of diversity. This stands in stark contrast to Eurocentrically discursive traditions of individualism, uniformity, and conformity. The effects of Western individualism prove to be more the illusion of difference than an actual acceptance of diversity. For Walters's Lena, the doctrinal differences between the various Christian churches and her traditional tribal ways are unimportant. The essence of her faith in the sacred cuts through those differences: "It's alla same." The preacher's inability to fathom the unifying depths of the sacred prevents him from understanding Lena's explanations of her faith in Jesus and in her tribal ceremonies. But I imagine that he will continue to visit Lena, attracted by her infectious good humor, caring, and openness; and perhaps after a while, that young preacher might begin to respond to her in a conversive manner, perhaps beginning to see her as an adoptive grandmother. Lena's concern for the young man might open him up so that he could finally begin to understand her words and ways. We see this very sort of transformation in the title story of Walters's collection, "The Sun Is Not Merciful," in which a young white officer decides not to ticket two elderly Indian women who are fishing without the necessary licenses. In Silko's story, "The Man to Send Rain Clouds," a priest is asked to sprinkle holy water on the grave of an old pueblo man, even though the grandfather was buried according to his pueblo's tradition and did not receive the Last Rites of the Catholic Church. The priest is confused and frustrated by the Indians' disregard for the specifics of Church doctrine and practice, but he finally assents to the request: "He sprinkled the grave and the water disappeared almost before it touched the dim, cold sand; it reminded him of something—he tried to remember what it was, because he thought if he could remember he might understand this" (*Storyteller* 186). The priest might never really come to understand how the Indian people at the pueblo can interweave such seemingly divergent threads of the sacred together into a harmonious blend, but, unlike the young preacher in Walters's story, the priest has learned to accept, albeit begrudgingly, a way of looking at and understanding the sacred that is beyond the bounds of his conceptual horizon.

Throughout Silko's and Walters's writing and the writing of many other American Indian writers, the relationships between beliefs, practices, and persons serve as reminders of the interconnectedness that permeates all of creation. Lorenzo Baca (Isleta Pueblo/Mescalero Apache) comments on the value of the spiritual conjunction between Christian and Indian traditions for the Pueblo Indian peoples: "These Pueblos celebrate something Catholic, somewhat, but also Pueblo. We mix everything to make it work. I think it happens in all religions, anyway" (15). Silko explains, "Pueblo cultures seek to include rather than exclude. The Pueblo impulse is to accept and incorporate what works" ("Indian" 6). Of course, the very real differences between conversively open and discursively oppositional engagements between religious traditions cannot be ignored. When those engagements take the insecure and combative forms evidenced by the preacher in Walters's "The Devil and Sister Lena" and Auntie in Silko's *Ceremony,* the dividing lines are laid down, and divergences are judged and punished. The horrific legacy of the far too common abuses of missionary zeal, ignorance, and racism have been well-documented. But Silko and Walters (along with many other American Indian writers) demonstrate the ways by which comfortable, valuable, *and* empowering convergences can be made between apparently divergent religious traditions. Blaeser explains, "The many voices intersect because all are engaged in the same spiritual (though not necessarily the same religious) dialogue" ("Pagans" 24).[3] This interconnectedness is especially manifest in understandings of the sacred and in beliefs surrounding the notion of personhood. The second half of this chapter turns to the interrelationships throughout all of creation that include humans, animals, plants, rocks, planets, stars, and whatever else is part of creation.

Diverse Manifestations of Persons

Within a conversively informed worldview, all elements of creation are recognized as fellow persons who function in the world (and in stories) through their relationships to each other. Everything is perceived as possessing its own intentionality and manifesting its own subjectivity and personhood after its own fashion and capacity. Human persons will manifest intentionality in ways quite different from, say, a horse person or a plant person. But within the relational framework of a conversive worldview, everything in creation is understood to have its own responsibilities in and of itself and in relation to the rest of creation. This section turns to this way of looking at personhood, noting that such a perspective is prevalent throughout much of contemporary and traditional American Indian literatures and storytelling. In fact, such an orientation is a part of all conversive ways of looking at and engaging with the world. To tell this story about the personhood of all creatures, I will interweave stories from American Indian literatures, the Jewish Bible and the Old Testament of the Christian Bible, and my own life. These diverse stories whose meaningful 'family resemblances' make them kindred stories are all brought together to tell the specific story about the relational intersubjectivity of persons that is at the heart of all conversive storytelling—being both its inevitable method (in the relationship between the storyteller and storylisteners) and its content. This is especially evident in Luci Tapahonso's poem, "For Lori, This Christmas I Want to Thank You in This Way."

This poem interweaves Navajo and Christian sacred beliefs and stories through the unifying thread of relationality that brings beliefs, stories, and diverse types of persons together within the larger story that is the story of the poem. The poem interweaves the stories of the birth of Tapahonso's daughter and the Christmas story of the birth of Jesus, but the story of Jesus' birth is retold and reframed within a familial and tribal context that transforms the biblical story through a new conversive telling. The magic of one religious birth is intertwined with the magic of the birth of Tapahonso's daughter, and both births communicate the conversive interrelationships that exist across diverse times, places, histories, traditions, and peoples. In Tapahonso's Christmas poem, rather than discursively privileging a Christian event at the expense of her Navajo voice, Tapahonso takes the Christian event and incorporates it within the Navajo oral tradition continued in the voice of her seven-year-old daughter's storytelling:

> "baby jesus—'Awééchí'í born somewhere
> on the other side of the world, far, far away
> some sheep, cows and horses saw him and
> they told other sheep, cows and horses.
> and so they know too.
> all of them and all of us know."
>
> (*Breeze* 19)

Here the orally related story of the Nativity, which has been given to literary and religious history in the gospels of the Christian Bible, is conversively reborn in the new oral telling of a little girl. In her story, both Navajo and Christian traditions are affirmed and strengthened in their interconnections within Tapahonso's family and in their underlying spiritual 'family resemblances', which define both traditions as diverse manifestations of the one reality that is the sacred. In Lori's telling of the Christmas story, she explains that humans learned of the birth of Jesus not on their own, but from the animals that were there in the manger. The little girl further communicates that such knowledge came from the repeated tellings of the story—a tradition which she, in turn, continues in her telling with her younger relatives. In this way, Lori shares the Christmas story through a telling that is decidedly Navajo in the personification of the animals, in the intersubjective relations between the animals and humans, in the importance of storytelling, and in her use of the Navajo term for the little baby Jesus ('Awééchí'í).

In "For Lori, This Christmas," Tapahonso demonstrates how seemingly diverse traditions can be conjoined through a conversive acceptance of diversity that, in turn, transforms both traditions and worldviews through peoples' intersubjective interactions with those new beliefs and practices. Sam D. Gill tells us, "Bridging the gap between the earth people and the Holy People is a crucial element in Navajo ceremonial practices" (157). Although Gill was clearly thinking of traditional Navajo ceremonies (as distinct from Betonie's evolving ceremonies or Tapahonso's fusion of Navajo perspectives on the sacred, Christian belief, and Navajo storytelling), Tayo's relationships on Mt. Taylor with Tseh Montaño and Mountain Lion the hunter and Tapahonso's and Lori's Christmas storytelling all demonstrate the power of storytelling to weave and reweave those connections between and within worlds (material and spiritual).

The ceremonies and stories serve not only to bring human beings and human beliefs and practices together, but also to connect human persons with nonhuman beings, as in Tapahonso's Christmas poem. To be more precise, this interconnectedness needs to be rephrased to convey the intersubjectivity of these relations. For Indian peoples, even human relationships with nonhumans (e.g., animals, plants, earth, rain, sky, and spirit beings) are conversive in that they are intersubjective, transformative, and dynamic, being communicated in a range of ways, including through words. Dennis and Barbara Tedlock explain, "For the American Indian in general, it is a world composed entirely of persons, as opposed to the everyday world of ego and object" (xiv). The conversivity evident throughout North American Indian literatures (written and oral) portrays the crucial, yet delicate, interrelationships between human persons and all other persons throughout all of creation.[4] Descriptive psychologists Peter G. Ossorio and James R. Holmes both discuss the nature of persons and what the status attribution of personhood signifies in human interactions. Ossorio posits that a person is someone whose history manifests deliberate action—that which would constitute subjectivity in the world.[5] And Holmes writes, "Up to the present time, we have recognized as persons only those individuals who have the embodiment of homo sapiens, namely human beings. There is however, nothing about the concept of a person that requires persons to be human beings" (30).

As Holmes points out, personhood is a status attribution, the attribution of subjectivity to individuals. He further suggests that such a status attribution need not be applied only to human beings. Specifically in relation to Anishinabe worldviews, A. Irving Hallowell notes that " 'persons' as a class include entities other than human beings"—thereby necessitating a move away from a scientifically objective approach of study for scholars ("Ojibwa Ontology" 21). Frey explains in relation to the Apsáalooke (Crow people), "natural phenomena are animated with volition [and] addressed with kinship terms. . . . The human, natural, and spiritual worlds are intimately linked, interdependent each with the other" (131). The privileging of the one species that possesses mind and the power of ratiocination such that no one else is considered worthy of personhood or subjective status demonstrates the extent to which whatever is without mind (as defined in human terms) is thereby devalued and relegated to a lower status as nonperson and, thereby, object. Throughout the discursively textual traditions of the West, nonhumans and even human beings have been defined as nonpersons and accordingly treated as objects. Women, members of racial, ethnic, and religious minorities, the poor and working classes, the elderly, and children are all too aware of the effects of such human objectification; and an ever-worsening state of our global environment bespeaks poignant testimony to the destructive objectification of those elements of the world that are nonhuman.

Although the Eurocentric legacy of the West has demonstrated a difficulty in relating to "others" intersubjectively—even to the point of an incapacity in recognizing other human beings (such as American Indian and African peoples) as human—the Native peoples of North America had no such difficulty. The European colonizers were recognized by indigenous peoples as fellow human beings, albeit ill-mannered and barbaric. For those Native North American peoples who lived conversively with the sacred at the center of their lives, there was no delineation and differentiation of others from themselves in a manner that led to a subsequent rejection or oppression of those others based on the extent to which that difference diverged from the people's own definitions of self.

Throughout North American Indian literatures (written and oral), Indian peoples are portrayed manifesting a greater respect and care for their fellow nonhuman beings than those peoples of European ancestry have done with their fellow non-European humans. As noted above, Holmes says that personhood is a status attribution of intentionality or subjectivity. Within North American Indian literatures, examples abound of conversive relationships between diverse human persons and also between humans (human persons) and animals (animal persons). Although such conversivity is not limited to human engagements with animals but also includes other nonhuman persons (e.g., plants, the moon and sun, water, and spirit people), I will focus specifically on the human/animal relationship to clarify in what ways such relationships are intersubjective. One clear example, as noted previously, is that of Tapahonso's Christmas poem, in which the Christmas story of Jesus' birth is transformed into a telling that communicates the reality and importance of the intersubjective relationships between humans and animals. As the little girl tells her younger relatives, we humans all learn about the birth of Jesus because of the animals who were there and who told other animals about the birth (*Breeze* 18–19).

Within this telling of the Christmas story, animals are portrayed conversively in their intersubjective communications among themselves (which includes interspecies communication involving sheep, cows, and horses) and, more importantly, with human beings, who learn of the birth of Jesus thanks to the animals who first told the story. Furthermore, the fact that knowledge of such a crucial event within the Christian tradition is dependent upon the storytelling role of animals underscores the extent to which our relationships with animals (and specifically with sheep, cows, and horses—animals particularly important to the Navajo) are also crucial. Although the animals are not anthropomorphized because they are presented as distinct from humans, nevertheless they are portrayed with intentionality (in understanding the significance of the birth of Jesus—a significance evident in their decisions to communicate that event to others), with subjectivity and agency (in their taking on the conversive role of storytellers), and with personhood (in their depiction as knowing subjects analogous to the knowing humans: "so they know too. / all of them and all of us know" [19]). One imagines that the sheep, cows, and horses know in whatever way such animals might "know" such an event. Even though the animals are granted a conversive personhood in the little girl's story, this in no wise signifies a lack of differentiation between the two respective domains of existence (animal or human). A fundamental distinction between the animal ("all of them") and human ("all of us") listeners and tellers is maintained within the telling, even though that difference is bridged through the interrelational telling of animal persons to human persons and a young human person to other human persons. On this note, I'd like to further point out that in the little girl's telling, Tapahonso also emphasizes the importance of children in knowing and communicating such an important event. In this one short story, animals and little children are granted subjectivity, personhood, and, thereby, importance in the world; this is not an individual subjectivity, but rather a subjectivity whose presence is contingent upon an interrelational conversiveness with other subjects in the world (and in stories). Silko writes, "A rock has being or spirit, although we may not understand it. The spirit may differ from the spirit we know in animals or plants or in ourselves. In the end we all originate from the depths of the earth. Perhaps this is how all beings share in the spirit of the Creator. We do not know" ("Landscape" 84).

In her short story "Talking Indian," Anna Lee Walters discusses the conversive relationships that have existed between Indian peoples and animals. She explains that part of "talking Indian" extends beyond the limited domain of speaking specific Indian languages (for example, Navajo, Zuni, or Lakota languages) and involves a way of perceiving, understanding, and interacting with the world. For Walters, one element of "talking Indian" includes the capacity to communicate and interact in an intersubjective manner with animals. In Walters's story, a hundred-year-old man talks about that relationship and how it changed with the arrival of guns, which distanced humans from animals and facilitated a new way of killing that no longer involved the closer relationship necessary in simpler methods of hunting. In Silko's *Ceremony,* Tayo considers such an analogous shift in the arena of warfare as the old Laguna medicine man, Ku'oosh, laments his incapacity to cure many of the Laguna veterans suffering from wartime-related sicknesses. With the technological advancements in warfare, even human beings are distanced from each other and reduced to mere objects to be destroyed:

> In the old way of warfare, you couldn't kill another human being in battle without knowing it, without seeing the result, because even a wounded deer that got up and ran again left great clots of lung blood or spilled guts on the ground. That way the hunter knew it would die. Human beings were no different. But the old man would not have believed white warfare—killing across great distances without know-

ing who or how many had died. It was all too alien to comprehend,
the mortars and big guns. (36)

As killing becomes easier from both technological and psychological vantage points, animals and humans recede into the distance of objectification,
insignificance, and silence. Humans no longer speak with animals (or at
least only in rare and exceptional instances), and human persons even
converse less and less with their fellow human persons who, tragically so,
are not even recognized as fellow persons possessing and manifesting interrelational presence, but are (mis)understood as objects bereft of presence
and whose relative subjective power and positionality in the world are, in
turn, (mis)understood as oppositional threats and impositions to be displaced, disempowered, and destroyed.

Notably, even in Silko's briefly quoted discussion of the horrific effects of
modern warfare, she demonstrates the crucial importance of, and the ease
in, making the simple conversive shifts that bring diverse persons together.
In this passage, her voice shifts to second person in the first sentence signifying a conversive change in which she/Tayo speaks directly and confidentially to her listener-reader. Silko not only writes about the problems
of objectification and alienation, but also provides an example of the sort of
conversive healing necessary to remedy the discursive oppositions that pull
persons (humans, animals, and others) apart. In this example, as in so many
others within the oral tradition and throughout written Native literatures,
linguistic connectors are provided to bridge the gaps between diverse persons and worlds. As Silko makes clear, it is not impossible to live conversively, even though it may take extra effort in a world of increasing violence, objectification, and subjective anonymity.

Within Western discursive traditions, it seems that animals only have
significance when they have some sort of use value placed on them. Domes-
ticated animals are valued for their price in the marketplace (even if that
value includes horrific lives endured at the hands of large agribusiness firms
more interested in their bottom lines than in the care of their animals) or for
their personal value as pets. Wild animals, as well, are granted significance
only when humans can attribute some value to their existence. Particular
species become significant in terms of scarcity values when they are on the
verge of extinction, but until that point, unless they become meaningful
objects for hunters, scholars, environmentalists, or the marketplace, they
are considered insignificant and unworthy of notable human attention. For

example, tree frogs made the headlines a couple of years ago by virtue of their seriously dwindling numbers. In their absences, they've become more significant than they were in their presences. This recent interest in tree frogs reminded me of a story from my youth that demonstrates the value of interspecies conversive relations and the loss that accrues from the destruction of those relationships.

For four years from the ages of eleven to fourteen, I attended (actually, painfully endured) a two-month-long elite summer camp in Maine for girls. During my first summer there, the tree frogs in the woods became my closest friends and my reality checks against a camp that provided the illusion of "roughing it" within an environment of clean and pressed clothes for each dinner time, weekly theatrical productions of recent Broadway musicals, and standardized uniforms with the occasional special day for choice in clothing, which invariably ended up being a competition between who could outdo whom with her designer summer clothes. More than anything else, I remember the days when I would walk into the Maine woods surrounding the bunk houses and sit down and talk with the tree toads.[6] As an eleven-year-old girl newly displaced into a camp environment in which she definitely did not belong, I felt that those frogs were the only persons out there with whom I could sit down and have meaningful and intelligent conversations. The frogs always seemed to understand my confusion with a camp environment that, to me, seemed unreal. My conversations with those tree toads reminded me that I was not crazy and that there was a reality beyond that of the camp. Unfortunately, by the age of twelve or thirteen, the pressures of fitting in had taken their toll, and I stopped going to talk with those frogs. My remaining three years at that summer camp were horrible. I had lost whatever grasp of reality I had held onto in those woods, and I merely drifted through the two months of scheduled activities, which I generally endured and rarely enjoyed. Now, as I look back over those four summers, my strongest and happiest memories are those times from my first year when I would spend the majority of my free time in the woods with those frogs.[7]

As Simon Ortiz explains about his writing, "As a poet, it is important for me to strive to have my poems reestablish and reaffirm relationships among ourselves as a community of people and that community to know itself in relationship to all other forms of life, especially the land" ("That's the Place" 48). Such a connective relationship occurred for me as my conversive scholarship in this chapter "reestablished" and "reaffirmed" my relationships with the poems and stories discussed herein and with "other forms of life" in those tree frogs I knew. Ideally, an evolving, conversively informed approach to literatures will also "reestablish and reaffirm" similar relationships between scholars and our colleagues, students, and listener-readers.

Specifically in relation to our communications with animals, the old man in Walters's story, "Talking Indian," explains to his visitor that "everything we two-leggeds know about being human, we learned from the four-leggeds, the animals and birds, and everything else in the universe. None of this knowledge is solely our own" (*Talking Indian* 30). Here Walters parallels Tapahonso's Christmas poem, emphasizing the knowledge that humans have learned from animals. We humans can teach animals, but perhaps even more importantly, throughout history animals have served as teachers for humans. The biblical story of Noah, his ark, a flood, and the animals provides a clear example of such animal-to-human learning. When Noah wanted to know if the flood waters had receded, he sent forth a dove who eventually returned, we are told, because she could not find any other place to light. A week later, Noah sent her forth again, and this time she returned to the ark with an olive branch, communicating that the flood waters were receding. The Genesis story, which is a written version of a story from the Jewish oral tradition, notes that the dove returns, but it does not explain *why* she returned the second time, nor why she brought the olive branch. According to the story, the third time Noah sends her off, she does not return. On the second flight, because the waters had receded sufficiently for her to bring back an olive branch, she did not *need* to return to the ark nor to Noah. It *is* explained that she returned the first time out of necessity—there being nowhere else to land. What is clear about her second return is that by returning and bringing back the olive branch, the dove communicated to Noah just what he needed to know.[8]

Although the notion of conversive relationships between humans and animals may strike some as far-fetched, I include the Genesis story as a reminder that such relationships are very present throughout the history of written literatures, and most particularly present in those literatures that are closer to their oral roots. In a discussion of the works of Silko and Ray Young Bear (Mesquakie), Moore points out that "relationality across time and space entirely blurs the boundaries of subject and object, of human and nature, of persons" ("Myth" 380). In Walters's short story, the hundred-year-old Indian man notes the extent to which such relationality between human persons and animal persons has been largely lost, but with any hope not irretrievably so (hence his storytelling message and reminder to his visitor): "But old folks always say that the distance between two-leggeds and four-leggeds nowadays hasn't changed four-leggeds in any way. The distance has only changed us two-leggeds, made us worse off, more pitiful. They say that the four-leggeds still talk the way they always have. It's we who've forgotten how to listen. I guess we lost a lot when we quit talking Indian" (*Talking Indian* 32). In this old man's speech, we see a clear description of the effects of the shift from conversive intersubjectivity to discursive objectification. According to this old man, the change in the patterns of communication between human persons and animal persons came about by virtue of human persons no longer listening to the animals. The animals still speak as they did before; they still manifest their conversive subjectivities in the world. It is humans who no longer listen to the animals.

In the textualization of people's lives and stories, human beings have learned to assert discursive subjectivities in the world through the relative oppositionality that demands objects against which those subjectivities are defined. In that process, animals (and those other humans defined as "other") have accordingly been relegated to the subaltern domain of silent and invisible objectivity. Furthermore, an object is defined such that it only has significance through its dependent relationship to some subject— leading to the absurd and profoundly solipsistic philosophical questions such as whether a tree falling in a forest makes any sound if there is no one (read "human") there to hear it—as if trees are incapable of making sounds on their own, and as if animals are insignificant as hearers of such an event! Animals (and, for that matter, trees and all "others" who are nonhuman) are categorically denied any subjectivity whatsoever and are, thereby, not recognized as other persons in the world. Within a discursive framework, subjects speak *to* or *at* "others"[9] rather than conversively *with* their fellow persons. As discursive subjects in the world, humans can talk at or to animals and assume a linear and one-directional linguistic and behavioral role as their keepers. Although humans did receive the capacity to name the animals, nevertheless the Genesis stories repeatedly reflect the extent to which human beings' superiority to the animals is manifested conversively in a mutual respect, interdependence, and appreciation for each other. Noah did not tie a long string to the dove to force her return. He had his desire, and the dove was given a free rein to assert her own subjectivity as well. She did so by returning and telling Noah what he needed to know. Such intersubjectivity bespeaks the conversive relationality that Walters's hundred-year-old man describes as "talking Indian"—when human persons recognized the personhood of animals and when human persons, instead of merely speaking *to* the animals, also spoke *with* and listened to them.

Frey's discussion of these interspecies relationships as represented in the oral literature of the Apśaalooke people emphasizes that "natural phenomena are animated with volition, addressed with kinship terms, able to 'adopt' human children, and a source of transformative power" (131). Frey clearly describes several ways by which nonhumans are understood by the Apśaalooke people to possess intentionality, personhood, agency, and subjectivity. Here I would emphasize that the transformative power Frey notes is less significantly an aspect of the reality of natural phenomena in and of themselves and more importantly a reflection, in the natural world, of the conversive power that is present in any intersubjective relationship. Doris Paul quotes one Navajo man commenting on the lessons of his grandfather: "Know things in nature are like a person. Talk to tornados; talk to the thunder. They are your friends and will protect you" (110). Lee Maracle (Métis/Cree-Salish) notes the importance of such interspecies transformations for human persons, particularly in relation to her own writing: "I heard Raven's song, that's why I wrote *Ravensong*. When I hear Raven sing, I pay attention to that. But coming out of the house is an essential move we're all making. We're all making our way to the other world. We all need to build it from where we are. We need to stand solidly in our own culture, our milieu, our understanding of how Raven and Raven's song work for us and how they lead us in certain directions of change" (in Kelly 85). Maracle's experience directly parallels Tayo's conversive relations with both Mountain Lion the hunter and Tseh Montaño (the personification of Tsepi'na or Mt. Taylor, one of the four sacred mountains of the Navajo). Tayo interacts intersubjectively with the mountain (even making love to it/her [222]) and with her husband, Mountain Lion (the hunter and the hunter's helper), who saves Tayo's life (195–196, 202). It is through Tayo's conversive interactions with Tseh Montaño and Mountain Lion that Tayo learns and is transformed—a transformation only possible by virtue of his intersubjective relations with the woman, the mountain, the man, and the mountain lion as fellow persons in the world.

As Walters, Tapahonso, Silko, and Maracle make clear, when we objectify animals out of our everyday human intercourse, we lose the understandings, experiences, and transformations by which the world and ourselves interconnect, survive, and grow. Farley explains, "It is generally acknowledged that individuals do not just survive or thrive in relation to others; they cannot exist as human persons without some form of fundamental relatedness to others" (189). Here I would like to extend Farley's discussion of human interrelatedness to include the interrelatedness of all persons—human and nonhuman alike. As Beck and Walters point out, "All beings are related and therefore human beings must be constantly aware of how our actions will affect other beings, whether these are plants, animals, people, or streams. . . . Through this interdependency and awareness of relationships, the universe is balanced" (12, 13). Just such a balance is restored to Tayo through his healing ceremony that interrelates the diversity that is Tayo (his mixed ethnicity, experiences, and beliefs) into a unified *person* in the world. Tayo learns to accept all of whom he is, no longer rejecting, hiding, or fighting parts of himself and his history. As Tayo becomes an interrelated and interconnected whole, he is also reconnected in his relationships to other persons in his life (his family members, his tribal community, and all of creation).

The power of conversive connections can be seen in actual practice in recent transformations currently taking place in some of the schools on the Navajo Reservation. These schools are beginning to implement new curricula based on *diné bo'óhoo'aah bindii'a'* (Navajo philosophy of learning), and at the heart of this learning is the transformation and movement of the students toward *hózhó* (beauty, balance, harmony). Herbert John Benally discusses these beliefs, defining "the desired condition, *hózhó* . . . [as a person's living] in harmony with others in society and in nature" (147). Foundational to this philosophy and other similar philosophies throughout Native North America is the emphasis on the people living well through their conversive relations with those other persons in the world with whom they come in contact (human persons in society and nonhuman persons in nature). Interpersonal conversive relationality is the way of living that is exemplified in Luci Tapahonso's poem "For Lori, This Christmas," explained by Anna Lee Walters's Lena, and learned by Leslie Marmon Silko's Tayo.

In *Ceremony,* Tayo heals; his family becomes a conversively unified whole for the first time in the novel; the rains return to the parched land; and even Auntie's brittle insecurities relax their hold on her as she holds her head up high at church and at the bingo as an Indian woman who can finally take pride in the power and value of Indian ways. Again, as Old Grandma keeps repeating, "So old Betonie did some good after all" (215). Dennis and Barbara Tedlock explain, "It is not that the Indian has an older, simpler view of the world, to which we as Newtonian thinkers have added another dimension, but that he has a comprehensive, double view of the world, while we have lost sight of one whole dimension" (xx). The Tedlocks correctly note the greater breadth of Native worldviews, referring to their inclusive expansiveness as "comprehensive." A conversive approach to the world is much more intricate in its diversely interwoven threads, which are continually telling and retelling the stories of the universe in new and changing ways. Betonie's new ceremonies are a conversive intertwining of the old and new, of the Indian and the non-Indian, of a mixedblood Navajo medicine man's healing, and of a mixedblood Laguna veteran's sickness. In Betonie's/Tayo's ceremony, the magical powers latent within the diverse manifestations of the sacred become manifest, just as they do in the Christmas story told by Tapahonso's daughter and in Lena's faith in the "old ways" and in Jesus. Through their conversive engagements with (and within) their literary worlds, these diverse persons inhabiting the story worlds of Southwest Indian literatures repeatedly remind their readers of the significance underlying Lena's emphasis on the importance of recognizing 'family resemblances' wherever they may be; after all, as Lena tells us, "It's alla same."

Although this chapter specifically looks at the interrelationships between human and nonhuman persons and between diverse belief systems and worldviews of the sacred, these are merely two manifestations of the essential connective and transformative forces within conversive intercourse—what John Attinasi and Paul Friedrich refer to as "life-changing dialogues" and "conversion conversations" (43). Throughout Native literatures (written and oral), the conversive forces that demonstrate the power and health of interrelationality are repeatedly evident. Where the stories present examples of disconnectedness, conversive relations are shown to be the means of healing toward balance and harmony. Distances are bridged and traversed; differences are communicated, and thereby shared, and ideally, understood and accepted. The textual oppositionality inherent within discursively defined differences is circumvented by virtue of the conversive acceptance and appreciation of diversity. Difference is never lost within conversive relations; what are lost are separation and discord. Agnes Grant explains, "Much of the oral literature was never perceived as apart from religion, morality and ethics of the community. It is this relationship between the word, the land, and the ceremony linked with the past that gives strength to truly Native contemporary literature" ("Content" 11). By bringing diverse beliefs and persons together through conversive literary examples, Indian writers like Silko, Tapahonso, and Walters remind us all of the transformative power that is present within all conversive relationships—both literary and lived. As Alanna Kathleen Brown writes, "What the study of Native American literature has helped me to understand is concentric knowing, that it is the relation between things, between others, that is of critical importance" (174).

I'd like to end this chapter with a note on the conversive power that exists even in the connections that lie between the literary and the lived. It was only as I worked on this chapter and explored the intersubjective relationships within Indian literatures between human persons and animal persons that I remembered my visits in the Maine woods with those tree toads. My own conversive engagements with the literary works discussed in this chapter recalled a story from my own life that had long since been forgotten. Until this day, I never did tell anyone about those conversations. I guess I figured as a child that no one I knew would understand the power, the meaning, and the reality of those visits. So I never told anyone, and after a while, I even forgot about them. Now, the memory and the story are remembered and shared. As my father would occasionally, and always magically, say at the dinner table, "That reminds me of a story. . . ."

The next chapter builds on the notion of relationality as presented in this chapter. Whereas this chapter specifically looks at depictions of relationality in terms of the sacred and understandings of personhood, Chapter 5 turns to the relationship between a storyteller and a story's listeners and how this relationship is manifested within the writing of many American Indian writers. The chapter takes a close look at two works by Silko to illuminate the range of conversive literary structures within the writing that work to move the reader into the role of a listener-reader. The storytelling relationship between the storyteller and her or his listeners is transformed within a written medium to become a literary storytelling, with readers invited to participate even more actively as co-creative listener-readers who bring the story to fruition in their own lives—as Tayo does with Betonie's healing story. And while the development of the next chapter certainly builds on the past work of reader-response critics and oral discourse scholars, as the chapter moves us even more fully into the realm of conversive literary storytelling, it becomes even clearer how a conversive approach can take us beyond the bounds of these critical approaches as we approach Silko's stories more deeply as listener-readers, rather than just readers.

CHAPTER 5

STORYTELLERS AND THEIR
LISTENER-READERS IN
SILKO'S "STORYTELLING"
AND "STORYTELLER"

In Leslie Marmon Silko's (Laguna Pueblo) *Ceremony,* she provides the example of Betonie, the mixedblood Navajo medicine man, whose guidance and healing help Tayo in his own healing and restoration. The healing ceremony of the novel begins with the story that *Ts'its'tsi'nako,* Thought-Woman, is thinking, continues with the specifics of Betonie's work and words, and continues further with Tayo's entry into the ceremony as a part of the story and then as a storyteller for the other members of his tribe. Silko, Betonie, and Tayo all serve as healing storytellers, weaving the verbal webs that reinscribe the old words, the old stories, the old ways into retellings that provide new ways of seeing, understanding, and interpreting a world in which the old ways are no longer sufficient. These acts of retelling reflect the crucial interweaving of the stories, their tellers, and their listeners or listener-readers in the case of contemporary literary stories. In contrast to those texts that are more literarily informed, the writings of American Indian writers, informed by their respective oral traditions, invite a more directly interactive participation from their readers—readers who within this context are more accurately termed *listener-readers.*[1] This role moves a reader beyond the inherently oppositional domain of discursive literariness and into the intersubjectively relational world of conversive textuality that combines both senses of conversation and conversion.

This chapter looks at the role of the listener-reader, noting its importance within American Indian literatures, and how this role varies based on the conversive and discursive literary structures within actual literary works. The transformational relationship between a storyteller and her or his listener-readers can be clearly seen in Silko's stories, "Storyteller" and "Storytelling." Krumholz, in relation to the entire *Storyteller* collection in which these stories appear, reads the volume "as a ritual of initiation for the reader into a Laguna Pueblo representation and understanding of the world, a reading that emphasizes the potential for the text to transform consciousness and social structures" (90). Just as Betonie's ceremonial healing story works its transformative power through Tayo's own participation in the story, so, too, do Silko's stories, poems, and novels work their transformative magic upon and through the efforts of their listener-readers whose interactive listening-reading is essential to conversive storytelling.

A range of scholars has investigated the role of orality in literature, and in the field of literary criticism, these investigations have led to the development of reader-response criticism. But in the majority of the research, the approaches are still textually rather than conversively informed, in other words, seeing the literary works as texts rather than as tellings. This discursively textual orientation defines the role of the reader within its interpretive boundaries. After a review of the advances made by reader-response critics who have valuably moved critical discussion to privilege the role of the reader, I turn to the work of scholars of American Indian literatures who move the discussion even further down the path of orality and conversivity—thereby opening up the discussion to investigate the role of the reader in new ways. Following this overview, I offer a conversively informed retelling-reading of Silko's "Storytelling" and "Storyteller" to show how literary works are varyingly conversively informed and discursively constructed in ways that invite their readers to become listener-readers.

Folklorists, ethnographers, linguists, and anthropologists have studied the oral storytelling traditions, initially focusing on the content of the stories and more recently addressing the performative aspects of the storytelling experience. What pervades virtually all of these discussions is the extent to which the actual telling of the stories often seems to supersede the actual content of the stories insofar as access into the stories is concerned. This can be clearly seen in the case of the Jewish storytelling tradition that is part of my own heritage. Even though the actual content (the stories, the events, the characters) is a means of defining and remembering oneself as a Jew, as a person of the Book, as a part of a particular and continuing religious and cultural historicity, the actual storytelling process is given primacy as the necessary vehicle for such self-definition. Schram notes that the oral traditions within Jewish culture emphasize "the human connection between a teacher/storyteller and the student/listener . . . [through which] various styles of telling, different versions of stories" are perpetuated (34).

One example Schram discusses is the Passover seder, in which an oral reading of the Haggadah[2] retells and relives the Jewish people's exodus from Egypt and their development into a nation. From the first of the four central questions of the seder ("Why is this night different from all other nights?"), the ceremonial telling is interactive, involving all of the assembled individuals. As Schram points out, "in a real sense, each person is a simultaneous storyteller" (35). Active participation on the part of those present is not only welcomed, but also expected to insure that all have engaged with and become part of the Passover story. Frey, in a discussion of the Crow people, also emphasizes the importance of "performative creativity and participatory dynamics" (129). He writes, "When a story is being told it is being relived, participated in by those assembled. History unfolds anew, to be rewitnessed or witnessed as if for the first time" (129).

As we shall see in the course of this chapter, both within the contexts of stories told orally and within the written stories of American Indian literatures, listener-readers are far more than passive recipients of the stories. They are actual co-creative participants who share not only in the telling of the stories, not only in the creation of the stories, but also and perhaps even more importantly, in the actual events of the stories. For example, in relation to N. Scott Momaday's *The Way to Rainy Mountain,* Jaskoski points out that the work "reaches beyond its powerfully felt and meticulously observed world and invites the reader to participate in what is ultimately a visionary experience beyond the reach of language" ("Image" 77). Many American Indian writers consciously infuse their written work with performative elements from their respective tribal oral traditions to facilitate their readers' transformations into listener-readers. Accordingly, within American Indian literatures, as well as within the various other traditions of oral storytelling (both performative and literary), listener-readers are participants in the storytelling event *and* in the told stories.

This participation in the story reminds me of the Passover seders I attended as a child and young adult, events in which I felt a part of the story that told my history and my life as a girl/woman of Jewish heritage.[3] As

Schram explains, "everyone enters into the story by reciting and by listening to 'We were slaves to Pharaoh. . .'" (37). Again, Frey echoes this point: "In the act of telling a story the listener participates in that reality. . . . The characters and events of the narrative are experientially encountered" (132). For example, in Silko's *Ceremony,* Betonie tells Tayo's story, and Tayo as listener-participant co-creates his story as we see him live its events on Mt. Taylor. And in the telling of the past historical events through which the Jewish people emerged from bondage in Egypt, the participants in the Passover seder share in those events and see themselves as cosufferers, coendurers, cosurvivors. This identification of Jews today with Jews of the past serves to reinforce their sense of cultural and religious identity. The telling is both a discursive recitation of past events and a conversive performance in which those present join those of the past in a lived and living story of survival. Krumholz explains this transformative power of storytelling: "The assertion of ritual properties in written narrative creates a potent model for change, similar perhaps to narratives aimed at religious conversion, in which the narrative seeks to provide a visionary experience" (96). It is this interactive experience that transforms listener-readers through their participation in the story.

The interrelationship between the domains of the written and the oral is far more complex than traditionally understood by scholars. In Finnegan's response to Walter Ong, she problematizes the very notion of an oral/literate divide. Through her examples from Africa, Polynesia, and ancient Ireland, she notes the extent to which the composition and performance of stories varies from culture to culture, and in some cases even within a culture from one contextual event to another.[4] Richard Bauman strongly concurs on this point: "Just as speaking itself as a cultural system (or as part of cultural systems defined in other terms) will vary from speech community to speech community, so too will the nature and extent of the realm of performance and verbal art" (294). In regard to the analysis of an Arizona Tewa text, Paul V. Kroskrity suggests to his fellow anthropologists the importance of "the relationship of narrative texts to the sociocultural contexts in which they are performed and to the native criteria by which they are evaluated" (197). Such reminders are crucial even for those of us working in the area of American Indian literatures. If our scholarly approaches to particular works present Western literary standards for critical analysis to the extent that Native storytelling conventions are lost in the process, then Kroskrity's advice could serve as a helpful reminder to literary scholars, as well as to his fellow cultural anthropologists.

Deborah Tannen, in *Talking Voices,* Kroskrity, in his work with the Tewa people, and Bauman, in "Verbal Art as Performance," delineate various strategies by which storytellers engage their listener-participants with and into the stories. Tannen refers to these as "involvement strategies" (17–29) and differentiates between the linguistic (e.g., repetition, imagery, dialogue), the paralinguistic (e.g., pitch, tempo, stress), and the kinesic (e.g., gesture, physical mirroring). Bauman describes such strategies as metacommunicative framing devices that define the performance within culturally specific bounds. He says that performance is "situated behavior, situated within and rendered meaningful with reference to relevant contexts" (298). Kroskrity lists several specific framing devices or "involvement strategies" noted by his Tewa informants: storytelling conventions (e.g., formulaic introductions and conclusions), archaic words, facial expression, prosodic and paralinguistic effects, song, and "carrying it hither"—situating the narratives for the present audience (195–96). Kroskrity particularly notes the importance of occasional pauses by the narrator, "On these occasions members of an appreciative and responsive audience may periodically interject -úh ('yes'), either as individuals or as part of a group response" (196). Regarding the Crow, Frey writes, "An overt way in which Apśaalooke listeners participate in a story is by acknowledging their involvement aloud. When a story is being told it is the common practice for listeners to periodically say ée, the Apśaalooke word for yes" (133).

The diverse strategies oral storytellers use to involve their listener-participants in the experience of the event and in the story itself, however, are not limited to the realm of the oral event—a fact that raises serious questions about the polarity that Walter Ong delineates between the realms of orality and literacy. In an article on contemporary professional storytellers, Joseph D. Sobol notes strict distinctions between the oral and the written: "None of these [involvement strategies] are available to the writer, except in a refracted and distanced form. He has to rely instead on a range of 'contextualizing' conventions to fill in what is sacrificed to print" (70). Although it is true that writers have to resort to different conventions in order to convey their stories to generally distanced readers, contemporary American Indian writers transform the domain of the alienated and distanced text into a conversive medium that strives to elicit an interactive relationship between the listener-reader and the storytelling-text. As Silko states, "the storytelling always includes the audience and the listeners, and, in fact, a great deal of the story is believed to be inside the listener, and the storyteller's role is to draw the story out of the listeners" ("Language" 57).

Contemporary reader-response critics correctly emphasize the crucial role of the reader, but in so doing, they privilege the role of the reader at the expense of the writer-teller. Reader-response approaches "refocus criticism on the reader" and move "the focus of attention away from the text and toward the reader" (Tompkins, *Reader* ix, xi). Such critics correctly shift the focus of critical activity away from the strict emphasis that earlier formalist critics placed on the text. But a reader-response orientation nevertheless functions within a textually driven domain where readers are definitionally outside the text either as passive recipients or as active creators. Stanley Fish tells us "that it is the reader who 'makes' literature," that he is "in the business of making texts," and that "interpreters do not decode poems; they make them" (11, 180, 327). Jane P. Tompkins writes that Fish "makes the crucial move in reader-oriented criticism by removing the literary text from the center of critical attention and replacing it with the reader's cognitive activity" (*Reader* xvii). Fish notes, "In the procedures I would urge, the reader's activities are at the center of attention" (158). Reader-response critics provide a needed corrective move away from the extreme focus on the text, but such shifts do not enable us to reconceptualize our fundamental responses to literature as literary *critics*. If literary works are still perceived as "texts" rather than as living and telling stories, and literary scholars as "critics" of those texts, then our entries into the worlds of the storytellings behind the texts are accordingly hindered.

A storyteller-writer drawing the story out of her listener-readers offers an experience categorically different from that of a reader-critic making texts. The essential intersubjective relationality between teller(s) and listener(s) is absent to the degree that the reader-response approach privileges the reader's subjective response to an objectified text. The interrelational reader-response experience is between the reader and a text, and intersubjective relationships are between various readers within interpretive communities. Bleich explains, "An intersubjective reading . . . could include several readings of the same text by the same people—that is, several re-readings, each in slightly new circumstances. It includes reactions of other readers as well as the actual readings of these others" ("Intersubjective"

419). Here intersubjective relations remain within the privileged domain of the reader, who is referred to by Tompkins as the "reader-critic" and "reader-oriented critic" (224). Reader-critics interact with the texts they make and with other reader-critics. Bleich further explains that intersubjective readings "are aimed at enhancing the life of the reading community, perhaps at expanding or enriching this community, but they are decidedly not aimed at 'the world'" ("Intersubjective" 419). Absent here is the intersubjective relationship between the storyteller-writer and listener-reader. Rather than the co-creative act of the oral tradition, within a textually discursive framework, the telling becomes the text, and the participant-listener becomes the outside reader (be s/he a passive receiver or an active maker). Unlike stories that are consciously directed at real human persons in the world, when literary stories are interpreted as texts, those texts and their readers form a closed community that is, as Bleich notes, distinct from the world beyond the reading community.

The reader is a crucial player in the process. From a reader-response orientation, the reader makes the text, but within oral storytelling traditions, the reader *and* teller co-create the story. Many American Indian writers consciously work to transform literary techniques by infusing them anew with their oral traditions, thereby providing hybrid texts that are neither purely oral and conversational nor purely literary and discursive or dialogic. This fusion of storytelling traditions results in texts that interweave the literary and oral structures of discourse, dialogue, and conversation into a conversive whole.

A number of literary critics have noted the importance of the oral storytelling traditions of American Indian tribes, particularly in relationship to their connections to and with contemporary American Indian literatures. For example, James Ruppert has discussed elements of the oral tradition evident in the poetry of writers as diverse as Maurice Kenny (Mohawk), Peter Blue Cloud (Mohawk), Wendy Rose (Hopi), Liz Sohappy Bahe (Yakima), Ray Young Bear (Mesquakie), and Elizabeth Cook-Lynn (Dakota).[5] Jahner notes narrative strategies influenced by the oral traditions in the work of N. Scott Momaday (Kiowa) and James Welch (Blackfeet/Gros Ventre).[6] Krupat, Danielson, Hirsch, Nelson, and Krumholz all note levels of orality and dialogism in Silko's *Storyteller*. Krupat especially emphasizes Silko's "awareness of audience"—an awareness that he explains "is entirely typical for a native storyteller who cannot go forward with a tale without the audience's response" ("Dialogic" 62). Danielson echoes this idea in noting the importance of a "creative community . . . [which] consists of listeners as well as artists or tellers" ("*Storyteller*" 330).

Danielson views the orality of Silko's *Storyteller* as a refreshing alternative to the more narrowly linear narrative models of Western literary forms: "So in effacing her own authorship, crediting the community, mixing once-sacrosanct genres, and abjuring linear structure—in short, by denying the standards and customs of white male-dominated literary criticism—Silko reclaims the making of books from the white male critical establishment" ("*Storyteller*" 330). Silko's *Storyteller* provides the oral storytelling experience for her readers through her transformation of the literary into a written form of the oral. Robert M. Nelson notes that "throughout *Storyteller* the development is concentric rather than linear, associational rather than chronologically determined" (42). Bernard A. Hirsch points out that Silko simulates the oral storytelling experience through her writing style. He notes, for example, her voice shifts that demonstrate the "flexibility and inclusiveness of the oral tradition." Accordingly, he explains that "even writing can be made to serve its [the oral tradition's] ends" (2). Krumholz writes, "The book simulates the oral tradition both in the compilation of many stories that create their own interpretive context (functioning like an oral community) and in the lack of discrimination made between the many kinds of stories" (89).

This is clearly the case in Silko's *Storyteller,* and I would posit that in much of American Indian literatures, we can see variations on the underlying theme of traditional oral storytelling, particularly in the intersubjective involvement of the listener-reader. Hirsch notes that Silko fosters "the kind of intimacy with the reader that the oral storyteller does with the listener" (3). Krumholz explains how the stories in *Storyteller* "change us as subjects, as readers" as the book draws its stories out of us (109). Patricia Jones explains, "The oral storytelling tradition which forms the basic structure of Silko's text involves the reader in such a dynamic process. The reader, in effect, becomes participant in the text, connecting stories, finishing them, rewriting them, and constructing his or her own stories in the 'gaps'" (214–15). Although Jones's emphasis on the text and on the reader's role in response to the text is more discursively reader-response than conversively oral, all of these critics note that *Storyteller* is a work that is more of a telling than a text. Krupat explicitly notes about Silko, "Having called herself a storyteller, she thus places herself in a tradition of tellings" ("Dia-

logic" 60). The writer who is a storyteller-writer writes to her readers in a
very different way than do those writers who produce the sorts of static
texts (e.g., textbooks) that "freeze words in space and time" (Hirsch 1).
What is crucial in conversive writing is the relationship, not between readers, but between the teller and the listener. "That is why," Hirsch explains,
"to tell the story correctly, Silko must bring us into the storytellers' presence, to let us somehow see them, learn something of their histories, and
most of all, to hear them tell their stories" (4). Silko even explicitly refers to
the reader of her books as a "listener-reader"—a term that underscores the
categorically different role for readers of American Indian literatures and
all other literatures varyingly informed by their oral roots (in Coltelli, 141).
Two of Silko's pieces whose emphasis on the storytelling tradition is notably
evidenced in their titles, "Storyteller" and "Storytelling," provide clear examples that demonstrate the reality of the storyteller and concomitantly the
necessary role of the storylisteners.

The first, "Storyteller," which is in prose, emphasizes the storyteller; the
second, "Storytelling," in verse format, emphasizes the process of storytelling. Both focus on the importance of stories and the storytelling tradition.
"Storyteller" is a story that I find especially difficult to read, due both to its
content and its method of relating that content. This prose piece portrays
the horrific results of a world in which the process of storytelling is continually disrupted. Kate Shanley Vangen (Assiniboine) emphasizes the politics involved in a white discursive system that impedes and twists the
storytelling and, thereby, human thoughts and lives ("The Devil's Domain"). Rather than maintaining a focus on the process of storytelling and
its continuity in peoples' lives, in "Storyteller," Leslie Silko shows the effects
of the West's privileging of the individualized self distinct from others.

In contrast to the intersubjectivity of oral storytelling emphasizing relationships and their interconnections, "Storyteller" tells the story of the
storyteller whose attempts to tell her story, whose attempts to live intercon-
nectedly with others, whose attempts to interrelate mythopoeic stories with
her life are continually impeded by those around her whose lives as well
have been compromised by a world horrifically out of balance. An intimate
sexual relationship with one of the Gossucks (white people) is related to
bestiality; the storytelling closeness between the narrator and her grandfather (her grandmother's husband) is disturbingly ruptured through their
incestuous relationship; and the narrator's final successful telling at the
end of the story, a telling finally uninterrupted, is nevertheless called into

question by the storyteller's apparent descent into insanity ("she went on with the story, and she never stopped, not even when the woman got up to close the door behind the village men" [32]). The Western privileging of the individual subject, the storyteller, is a privileging that destroys the storytelling process through a rupture that divorces storyteller, listener-reader, and story into three distinct, albeit overlapping, categories. Silko's "Storyteller" represents the lived and told reality of such definitional fissures that erode the essential significance of the intersubjective relationality at the heart of the telling of stories.

Silko's "Storytelling" provides a strong contrast to "Storyteller." In "Storytelling," Silko relates several intertwined storytellings that are varyingly successful. Throughout "Storytelling," worlds and peoples (mythic, historic, lived) are interrelated by means of a conversive intersubjectivity that interweaves seemingly disparate elements into a telling that includes, rather than excludes. Silko uses a range of strategies to enable the listener-reader's entry into the worlds of the story. Here the impediments are more minor than those in "Storyteller." After a close look at the oral conversivity of Silko's "Storytelling," I will return to "Storyteller" to discuss the difficulties of this story in greater detail.

Leslie Marmon Silko's "Storytelling"

In "Storytelling," Silko tells an updated version of the Yellow Woman stories. In this version, a woman leaves her husband and family, returning ten months later with twin baby boys. Silko employs a range of traditional storytelling strategies in order to involve her readers in the story and in its telling. "Storytelling" is framed by the conventional introduction and conclusion, which speak directly to the listener-readers. The introduction relates and interrelates the events of the story to the life of the listener-readers; thereby, the domains of the written and the lived are interwoven in the telling of the story. And in the events of the story, Silko intertwines the domains of history and myth as actual historical events and the happenings of myth are conjoined in the storytelling process. In a discussion of another story from the volume, Nelson points out that even within one story, we find that different "*kinds* of story are occurring simultaneously" (40). He notes four kinds: "(1) an event that took place prior to the telling of it; (2) a storytelling event that occurred in Silko's childhood; (3) the storytelling event that was occurring as Silko composed the text of 'The Laguna People'; and (4) the storytelling event that occurs when this text is read (or reread)" (40). This conjunction of diverse worlds and events (lived and imagined, past and present, historic and mythic) reflects the relational focus of storytelling, where the connections made between realities and domains are emphasized, and a more textual discursive privileging of separate events and subjectivities is deemphasized, if not altogether absent. As Paula Gunn Allen (Laguna Pueblo) writes about the various elements in stories, "In this structural framework, no single element is foregrounded, leaving the others to supply 'background' " (*Sacred* 241). Silko writes, "You should understand / the way it was / back then, because it is the same / even now" (*Storyteller* 94).

Here at the outset of Silko's piece, she speaks directly to her listener-reader, explaining that the events of the story are relevant regardless of when they took place. The dichotomization between past and present is alien to the storytelling tradition. Events and lives of diverse times and places are interrelated as comfortably as if they occurred together. The dissociation of different times and places reflects artificially constructed conceptual boundaries whose delineations disrupt the process of storytelling—a process whose disruptions are portrayed in their raw realities in "Storyteller." Insofar as "Storytelling" is concerned, the reported events of 1967 and those of "long ago" are meaningful today since these are the same events not only of the written stories, but also of our very own lives. Silko clarifies this as she interweaves mythic and past historical events with the storyteller's current life ("it's always happening to me" [*Storyteller* 97]).

The story begins with the "long ago" mythopoeic events of a woman getting water from the river while her husband has gone hunting deer. In this telling, the wife's intentions as she walks to the river are portrayed as innocent. The listener-reader is told that she goes there "to get water." However, waiting for her at the river is Buffalo Man, whose presence does not seem to surprise the woman, who says to him, "Are you here already?" (95). Clearly, the meeting appears to have been prearranged. This story that happened long ago in the past time of historic myth involves a woman who, we assume, had previously been faithful to her husband (as evidenced by his shocked response to her affair with another man), whose husband is gone for days and possibly weeks to hunt, and who is seduced by Buffalo Man. In reading the story, the listener-reader must remember that the seduction and affair between the woman and Buffalo Man are told within a storytelling framework of intersubjective relations in which all adults are assumed to live as interrelated agents in the world. An individual's lack of agency and lack of responsibility to others are considered aberrant and indicative of the individual's need for healing (as in the case of Tayo in *Ceremony*).[7]

Buffalo Man has subjective primacy in his role in the affair: his early arrival at the river, his vocalization of his intentions, which assert his subjectivity with the woman being the object of his desire ("I came for you"), and his directives to her as she asks, " 'But where shall I put my water jar?' / 'Upside down, right here,' he told her, / 'on the river bank.' " (95). However, in the intersubjective conversivity of storytelling, all adult persons are considered as intersubjective agents. Allen points out, "There are no minor characters, and foreground slips along from one focal point to another until all the pertinent elements in the ritual conversation have had their say" (*Sacred* 241). For example, in Buffalo Man's early arrival and also in his waiting for the woman, we see him responding to her. Even his directive concerning the water jar is in response to her initiating that concern.

The intersubjectivity of the story is further underscored by the interaction between the woman and Buffalo Man. Each one's subjectivity proves to be an affirmation of the other's subjectivity, demonstrating the interrelationality inherent in conversively told stories. First of all, Buffalo Man waits *for* the woman. At this point in the story, Buffalo Man is given primacy and his presence begins the third stanza, and yet his primacy serves, in turn, to emphasize the primacy of the woman for whom he came to the river in the first place. The woman's primacy is then asserted in her vocalization acknowledging Buffalo Man's presence ("Are you here already?"). Her subjective assertion immediately returns subjectivity to Buffalo Man. He responds, and we are told, "He was smiling." In his smile, we see his sense of control and, of course, pleasure. Buffalo Man then explains his presence and, we assume, his smile as he conversively returns subjectivity to the woman in his assertion that his presence is because of her.

Buffalo Man's response, "Because I came for you," conveys both senses of the woman's objective and subjective reality in the world.[8] On the one hand, "Because I came for you" signifies the woman's objectified status as the person/object Buffalo Man comes to take away. On the other hand, the woman's subjective agency is signified in Buffalo Man's words, which also convey the sense that what he is doing is *for* her: his actions are therefore responses to her prior agency. After Buffalo Man's response, the woman shyly looks away and asks him where she should put her water jar. Here, as well, we see a concomitant assertion of both one's own subjectivity and that of the other (as evidenced in Buffalo Man's statement, which asserts both his and the woman's respective subjectivities). In her subsequent question about the water jar, we see the woman's assertion of both her own subjectivity and that of Buffalo Man. The question points to Buffalo Man's agency and subjectivity in his capacity to solve her dilemma, but her question also reflects her control and agency as initiator for what the listener-reader is led to believe will be their sexual relations, which, of course, necessitate that the woman not continue holding her water jar. She does not ask Buffalo Man to put the water jar down for her, nor does he take over that job himself. In their interactions and words, each acknowledges the other's personhood.

As this section of "Storytelling" demonstrates, within a conversive framework, each person's vocalization is necessarily an assertion of not only one's own subjectivity, but also the subjectivity of one's listener. Vocalization and behavior are, by definition, co-created by the speaker-behaver and her or his listener-responder. This close look at the river liaison demonstrates the conversive intersubjectivity between Buffalo Man and the woman. However, there is a discursively informed undercurrent that runs throughout the liaison between Buffalo Man and the woman. Buffalo Man is presented to us independently of any other responsibilities he might have. We could read his affair with the woman as an innocent sexual liaison between the two lovers, but the woman is married and a mother. She has responsibilities to others at home, even though, as Silko points out, her affair with Buffalo Man manifests "her uninhibited sexuality, which old-time Pueblo stories celebrate again and again because fertility was so highly valued" (*Yellow Woman* 70). However, the value of fertility and sexual relations within that context does not condone behaviors that seriously conflict with one's responsibilities as a tribal member. Allen writes, "the Keres [of Laguna and Acoma pueblos] can best be described as a conflict-phobic people, while Euro-American culture is conflict-centered" (*Sacred* 238).

Luci Tapahonso (Navajo) helped me to understand the intersubjective relational responsibilities inherent in tribal worldviews.[9] Her poem, "Last year the piñons were plentiful," tells a similar story of a woman who leaves her husband and family one year for another man. Tapahonso clarified that this was not a Yellow Woman story, but that it was based on a story that was told to her about a woman who had gone off in a similar manner. When Tapahonso recounted the story to me, she emphasized the effect of the woman's leaving on her family, how unhappy and worried everyone was. She pointed out that for the entire year, no one ever gave up hope of finding their daughter, their sister, their mother, and wife. They believed that one day she would be found and would come home. She said that they kept looking for her, especially her husband, all that year.

Although it is clear in the Laguna Yellow Woman stories that the woman does eventually return home to her family and community, most scholars have only addressed the woman's freedom in her leaving. To date, no one has really discussed the importance of her return to her family, to her community and tribe, and to her everyday responsibilities. In an interview with Jim Meadows, Tapahonso explains that stories are told to convey meanings that are important for people to learn, that stories teach people they are not isolated in the world, especially in relation to difficulties and hard times. Stories communicate that others in the past have had similar troubles and have survived those hard times: "Well, I think in Navajo tradition, it is probably different in that stories are used to teach, to instruct, maybe sometimes to discipline, to show the listeners how the experience is similar to or is not as unusual as one may think. And this would be in terms of where a person or situation in which a person might be feeling isolated or a person might be feeling bad about a certain situation, and the story is told to show that this has happened before and to show how someone has managed to get free of whatever situation it is." Tapahonso emphasizes the importance of love within the inherent connections of storytelling, between teller and listener, among the various persons involved in the stories. "It is very much a way, I think, showing stories or being a part of telling stories is very much a way in which affection is shown if a person is included within the circle, then in a way it sort of implies that everyone within the circle thinks highly of each other. And so it's a way to show affection and to be included within either listening to or sharing of stories."

The conversive domain of storytelling is an inclusive world in which each involved has a crucial part to play. Of course, there are those characters/persons who for varying reasons are estranged from other persons in the stories. But even the estranged have their place, both in their distance and in their eventual returns. In these estrangements, as in Yellow Woman's estrangement from her family and tribe, there is meaning. And in her return to her family and in her estrangement from Buffalo Man, there is also meaning. Within oral storytelling, characters are given a life that manifests itself in their mix of virtues and fallibilities. In contrast to more textually informed stories in which characters are represented in more static and simplistic ways due to their being more strictly bounded by the written domain of the text, told stories present persons and events with greater degrees of complexity and sophisticated symbolism. This represents what Hirsch describes as "the dynamic relationship between the oral tradition and the life it expresses" (22). Life is much more complex than textual worlds, and those textual worlds that are more lifelike, and therefore more complex, are those texts that manifest greater degrees of orality within their textual tellings.

In her stories, Silko conveys to her listener-readers the conflicted reality of Yellow Woman, torn between her ties to the real world of Laguna and her world of dreams. Even though Silko writes that Yellow Woman's "power lies in her courage and her uninhibited sexuality" (*Yellow Woman* 70), her tellings open up the stories beyond a narrow privileging of Yellow Woman's sexuality. Hirsch explains, "Silko, by juxtaposing different kinds of narratives and subjects, helps us to see vital, rewarding connections that might otherwise go unnoticed" (22–23). Throughout the stories, we also hear the voices of those whom Yellow Woman leaves behind, analogous to the chorus of classical Greek drama reminding us of other views, other feelings, other perspectives—and especially those voices of the people, the tribe, the family. Krupat writes, "For all the polyvocal openness of Silko's work, there is always the unabashed commitment to Pueblo ways as a reference point"—what he refers to as "the centered voice of the Pueblo" ("Dialogic" 65). Melody Graulich comments that in relation to Silko's Yellow Woman stories, Yellow Woman is presented "with choices and map[s] a final, if ambiguous, resolution," noting that in the traditional Yellow Woman stories, the woman chooses "to return to the pueblo, her settled life there apparently satisfying other needs and desires" (16, 17). Clearly any understanding of these stories must follow Krupat's emphasis and center its reading within the Laguna Pueblo Yellow Woman stories, rather than approaching those stories from without. Even though Silko herself points out the value of Yellow Woman's individualistic and "uninhibited sexuality," her stories nevertheless follow the old-time ones with the concomitant and, I would argue, even greater emphasis on the importance of pueblo values and the woman's return to her family, a return that is privileged in its concluding status in the stories. Nevertheless, Graulich is correct in noting the ambiguous endings. Although the woman's return is emphasized as the correct ending to the stories, the importance of her happiness is also emphasized—hence the underlying conditions that would have led to her leaving in the first place.

Stories are open-ended tellings, open to the range of understandings and interpretations found by each listener-reader. Granted, there are understandings of stories that would be deemed misunderstandings, namely, those not grounded in the traditions from which they are told. Tsinaabaas Yazhi (Little Wagon) told Toelken that a young Navajo boy's response to a story demonstrated that "the boy did not understand stories"—a comment that pointed not only to the boy's questions, but also to Toelken's similar inquiries about the stories ("Pretty Language" 213). Toelken explains, "In short, by seeing the story in terms of any categories I had been taught to recognize, I had missed the point, and so had our young visitor, a fact which Little Wagon at once attributed to the deadly influences of white schooling" (213). The relationship between the storyteller and storylistener is a crucial relationship in the success of the telling. Teller and listener both have responsibilities in relation to the telling. Part of the responsibility of the listener-reader involves sufficient familiarity to be able to approach and enter the worlds of the stories.

In Silko's "Storytelling," a conversive intersubjectivity extends beyond the domain of the told story and includes the intersubjective relationship between the teller of the story and Silko's listener-reader. Throughout, Silko shifts the language and events back and forth between the domain of the mythopoeic and contemporary times. Midway in the poem, we hear the husband's reaction to his wife's eventual return: " 'You better have a damn good story,' her husband said" (95). In the clause, "her husband said," Silko provides a voice shift by which she speaks directly to her listener-reader, telling the intimate details of the woman's return and her husband's response. This section is followed by additional spacing during which the listener-reader might respond with a nod or vocalized reaction to the husband's understandable anger. Throughout "Storytelling," Silko interweaves times and places and persons, thereby leveling different stories into one story that is as much about the process of storytelling as it is about the ostensible story lines of marriage, seduction, and human frailty. Silent pauses are provided throughout by means of additional spacing, which the listener-reader is expected or at least enabled to fill with her or his own responses to the story.

The very next section in "Storytelling" continues with the intimacy of a conversational second-person voice as the woman's mother tells her listener-reader, "No! That gossip isn't true. . . . You know / my daughter / isn't / *that* kind of girl" (95–96). The mother's comment is also followed by additional spacing for the listener-reader's response—perhaps a knowing nod or vocalized response acknowledging the mother's assertion about her daughter, perhaps an ambiguous smile or even a suppressed giggle. Silko thereby invites her listener-readers to engage with the storytelling-reading, offering her listener-readers the opportunity to respond to the husband's anger and the mother's self-righteous denial. Silko then interweaves this story with a parallel story of a kidnapping back in 1967: "Four Laguna women / and three Navajo men . . . and the F.B.I. and / state police . . . / hot on their trail / of wine bottles and / size 42 panties . . ." (96).

Here Silko uses the common storytelling devices of comedy and humor to represent human weakness and imperfection, thereby enabling her listener-reader to respond to such human weaknesses as sexual promiscuity with laughter, rather than the self-righteous response of the mother or the anger of the husband. After the story of the kidnapping of the Laguna women and Navajo men, Silko moves into a trickster role along with one of the Navajo men. She shifts the narrative from the voice of the woman storyteller and into the voice of one of the kidnapped characters. Such a voice shift is a traditional storytelling strategy that deflects the focus away from the teller and onto the storylisteners and the different characters in the story. Here it is the Navajo man who tells his story, " 'We couldn't escape them,' *he* told police later. / 'We tried, but there were four of them and / only three of us' " (96; emphasis added). The listener-reader expects the kidnapping to be *of* the Laguna women *by* the Navajo men. But Silko and one of the Navajo men trick us with their joke that the men didn't really kidnap the women; it was the men who were kidnapped! Of course, Silko does not give us the additional information as to whether the police accepted the Navajo trickster's story; nor, for that matter, are we told the eventual facts about the kidnapping. Oral storytelling, although meaningful, is nevertheless aporetic, leaving the listeners and listener-readers to find the truths and meaning for themselves. As Alanna Kathleen Brown notes about the Navajo trickster's story, "Could it be true? That's also part of the fun" (Comment, n.p.). Yes, and also part of the story's meaningfulness. Neither the story nor reality can be pigeonholed—I imagine much to the chagrin and frustration of the police investigating the "kidnapping."

The conjoint joke of the tricksters (the "kidnapped" Navajo man and Silko) further underscores the conversivity of "Storytelling." Unlike the more distanced oppositional forms of discursive and dialogic writing, tellings (oral and written) involve the necessary intersubjective interaction of the listener-reader. The Navajo man tricks the police, but in his trick, the listener-reader finds herself/himself tricked as well. Here the trickster storyteller (Silko) identifies her listener-reader with the duped police. But in the tradition of storytelling, the listener-reader cannot be left alienated from the story or from a trickster storyteller. Even though Silko has tricked her reader and constructed a discursive opposition between herself and the reader (much like the oppositional relationship between the Navajo man and the police), this step into discursivity is shown to be simply the tool of the trickster storyteller.

In "Storytelling," the reader is never really divorced from the teller nor from the story. Immediately after the joke about the "kidnapping," Silko reestablishes the close connection between the storyteller and listener-reader by returning to the intimate and trusting voice of a confidante: "Seems like / it's always happening to me" (97). At this point in "Storytelling," the mythopoeic events of Buffalo Man and his lover, the past events of a 1967 "kidnapping," and the storyteller's own responses to those seductive "brown-eyed men from Cubero" all merge into one telling intimately shared with the listener-reader. "Storytelling" ends with the woman's husband leaving her and going home to his own mother because of his wife's inadequate explanation for her prolonged absence, infidelity, and two new children. This ending is vocalized by the storyteller stepping into the role of the woman who has returned home with twin baby boys. First she speaks directly to her husband, telling her own story unsuccessfully; then she shifts to her listener-readers, speaking directly and confidentially about her husband's response and her own story.

Her failed story indicates that the Navajo trickster's story and the storyteller's story of "those brown-eyed men," albeit delightfully entertaining, probably failed as well. But then stories have many different aims and results, and even if the Navajo men ended up in jail and even if the woman's husband left her, we as listener-readers of this story (these multiple stories which, in essence, are one) are reminded that sometimes things just happen, which aren't always as we intend. Even when such complications happen in our own lives, "Storytelling" and the very nature of storytelling itself reminds us that such things have happened in the past to others, that such things have happened in those "long ago" mythic times, and that life and the world continues. Insofar as "Storytelling" is concerned, perhaps after a while, the wife will tell her story more completely and convincingly, including her hopes and desires, her loneliness and vulnerability, and maybe after telling her story better, just maybe her husband might return home. As these final ruminations upon Silko's story indicate, "Storytelling" (the story and the process) is not bounded even by the literary (written or oral) limits of the story but extends beyond the ostensive frame of its words.

Stories extend backward across generations all the way into mythic time and forward into the lives of those of us who share in the tellings. No told story is owned by the teller, hearer, or subjects in the story because all are concomitantly tellers and hearers and, thereby, active participants in the story as well. As Trinh T. Minh-ha explains, "The story circulates like a gift; an empty gift which anybody can lay claim to by filling it to taste, yet can never truly possess. A gift built on multiplicity" (2). This multiplicity is the multiplicity of the lived and living voices who together perpetuate the telling and the reality of our world(s)/words. Silko's "Storytelling" is a single written story, yet also one written piece of the larger storytelling tradition, as well as a part of a more specific tradition of Yellow Woman stories. Perhaps even more importantly, "Storytelling" is not just *about* storytelling; it *is* storytelling. Throughout the "Storytelling" process, the range of storytelling strategies that Silko informs her story with serve to pull the listener-reader through the world of the text and into the story, which in turn becomes a new conjunctive story co-created through the interaction between the listener-reader and the teller-text. Danielson explains, "These pieces constantly guide the reader's attention back to the act of storytelling as creation, to the creative in all aspects of human inter-action" ("Storytellers" 21).

Leslie Marmon Silko's "Storyteller"

In contrast to the conversive literary style of "Storytelling," Silko's "Story-teller" presents a discursively informed text that keeps the reader at a distance from the events of the story. Silko shows her readers the situation of a young Eskimo woman who is in jail because a white man who was chasing her fell through the ice in the river and died and because she insists on telling the authorities that she was his murderer because she wanted him to die. She tells her story completely and without any lies to her attorney and the jailer, but they do not believe her story. Thinking that she is crazy, they do not really listen to her story. Her words are spoken but to no listener in particular. Silko's story parallels the woman's story with a distancing literary structure that presents the story in a more abstract and distanced third-person voice that serves to keep the reader outside the short story. Whereas "Storytelling" demonstrates the process of storytelling in which tellers and listeners closely interact, "Storyteller" tells the story of storytellers continually frustrated in their efforts to share their stories with others. This is a story about the impediments that prevent storytellers from telling their stories and, more specifically, about the Eskimo woman's struggle to tell her story: "it will take a long time, but the story must be told" (26).

According to the requirements of the oral storytelling tradition, the woman's telling requires listeners who are willing to co-create and participate in a story whose telling persists "year after year as the old man had done, without lapse or silence" (31–32). Yet it is this continuous telling that is portrayed throughout "Storyteller" as dysfunctional and incomplete, for this is storytelling as monologue without any expectation of interactive listeners. Conversive storytelling necessitates not only tellers and listeners (and listener-readers), but also those periods of silence in which the storyteller provides verbal space for the listener-readers' responses. In "Storyteller," we see storytellers who subjectively and monologically tell their stories "without lapse or silence" and often without even listeners. These are the stories that are told within the oppositional framework established by generations of the Gossucks' (white people's) silencing of Eskimo peoples. The Eskimo people have been silenced not only by the Gossucks (and thereby denied their subjectivity in the world as speaking persons), but also through the process of internalized oppression. Silko depicts Eskimo peoples, filled with their own shame and self-hatred, behaving oppositionally against their fellow Eskimos. The woman who is in jail yells for her jailer who "was an Eskimo, but he would not speak Yupik to her. She had watched people in other cells, when they spoke to him in Yupik he ignored them until they spoke English" (18).

The Eskimo jailer is only one of the many people (Eskimo and Gossuck) in this story who reject and abuse the woman. The old Eskimo man who was called her grandfather molested her as a child and maintained an incestuous relationship with her as his prey—"the old man, whose hands were always hunting, like ravens circling lazily in the sky, ready to touch her" (20). This old man who continued to tell *his* story was the very old man who would regularly lie to/with her—"again she had not believed him because sometimes he lied. He had lied about what he would do with her if she came into his bed" (20). The old Eskimo man (married to her grandmother) refuses to perceive her as a granddaughter and refuses to behave toward her as a grandfather; in jail, the Eskimo jailer refuses to recognize her as Eskimo; and in the village, she and her grandparents are shunned by the village people ("the village children . . . were afraid of the old man, and they ran when her grandmother came" [19]).

Throughout "Storyteller," the story/stories are told by tellers without listeners, by tellers who tell without "lapse or silence" because there is no one to fill in those conversive spaces. The telling that is in "Storyteller" is more discursively monologic and oppositional than the conversively inter-subjective and interrelational process that is the essence of storytelling. The village people do not listen to the stories of the woman, her grandmother, or the old man. Krumholz notes, even though "the characters reaffirm the power and continuity of the stories, . . . the situation of the storytellers is perilous" (97). Shunned by the other members of the village, this family and its stories are ignored by the Gossucks and by the other tribal members. Their stories, then, can only be told discursively "to no one in particular" because there really is no one interested in listening anyway.[10] The grand-mother's response is silence and bodily joints "swollen with anger" (19). Even her granddaughter's questions are met with silence as the futility of words consumes the grandmother (verbally and physically). "Sometimes she did not answer and only stared at the girl. Each year she spoke less and less" (19).

Even the connections between "the old woman" and "the girl" are sev-ered in the grandmother's gaze/stare that sees "the girl" objectively and dis-cursively but does not see her granddaughter interrelationally in a manner that asserts the intersubjectivity of both. Even within the family, those rela-tionships that could have been a source of strength and continuance for the old people and their granddaughter are absented and denied. Each help-lessly turns her or his anger and frustration against the others. Whereas the grandmother's dissociation from her granddaughter is evidenced in her stare, silence, and lack of touch ("the old woman had not hugged or touched her for many years" [20]), the old man's disturbing (dys)connection to the girl is evidenced by his speech, his incestuous touch, and his constant lecher-ous watching. The girl's grandmother becomes more and more silent, a silence that in itself is telling for in most native cultures, the old women are the treasure houses of stories—stories that reflect and maintain the health of their families and communities. Trinh T. Minh-ha writes, "In Africa it is said that every griotte [storyteller] who dies is a whole library that burns down" (121). Insofar as Storyteller is concerned, the silent grandmother represents a library closed to all, even herself. And as she becomes more silent, the old man becomes more vocal ("the old man talked more—all night sometimes, not to anyone but himself" [19]). Yet in his increasing vocality, the actual insignificance of his unheard words is expressed. Throughout "Storyteller," Silko depicts storytellers whose words are either unheard or, at best, misunderstood—words whose significance rarely reaches those others (Gossucks and other tribal members) whose own subjectivities discursively insist on perceiving the storytellers as silent, silenced, voiceless, and, thereby, insignificant.

The grandmother and the old man, shunned by the village people and invisible to the Gossucks, in turn silence their granddaughter—the grandmother by her silence and the old man by his speech "without lapse or silence" (32). At the BIA boarding school, the year her grandmother dies, the girl learns that her own words and reality are forbidden. She is beaten for not speaking English, and she is ignored by the other girls, who whisper to each other in English. Words spoken are either not intended to be heard (as in the old man's monologic story, the boarding school girls' whispers, and the young woman's endless and audienceless storytelling at the end of "Storyteller") or they are expressed toward hearers who don't really listen (as in the granddaughter's questions met by her grandmother's silent stare; a red-haired man's words drowned out by the noise from the generators at a construction site; the storeman's words, which first "she did not hear" and which then were heard "only [as] noises coming from his pale mouth" [29]; and finally the young woman's story about how she intended that the storeman die and her Gossuck attorney's refusal to accept her story, saying that he'll "explain to the judge that her mind is confused" [31]).

This is a story more about death than life. We read about the deaths of the Yupik woman's parents, the deaths of her grandmother and the old man, the death of the storeman, and little about these people's lives. "Storyteller" also tells the story of the attempted murder of storytelling, of stories told but unheard and of stories never fully told. However, "Storyteller" is not about the deaths of the storyteller or stories per se. Throughout the piece, stories are told even in spite of seemingly insurmountable barriers (e.g., deceased alcoholic parents, a silent grandmother, an incestuous stepgrandfather, a BIA boarding school, isolation from fellow tribal members, and the U.S. judicial system). There is a resilience in "Storyteller" that, while not explicitly hopeful, nevertheless shows that the stories that need to be told will be told no matter what—even beyond death, if necessary (as in the young woman's continuing the old man's story after his death).

As "Storyteller" ends, the young woman is continuing the story, and as she speaks (perhaps directly to her listener-reader, perhaps to the woman hired to watch her), she tells us about the hunter who had hunted the bear and who, in fact, turns out to be the one who is vanquished as he becomes the prey. Out of exhaustion and frostbite, the hunter drops his knife, and as he does, "the blue glacier bear turned slowly to face him" (32). The bear, previously hunted prey, is no longer the object of the hunter's power. The young woman is no longer the object of the old man's, the storeman's, or the judicial system's power. Like the bear, her strength and voice become apparent in the unmasking of the illusory power of the hunter, the old man, the storeman, and the educational, judicial, and religious institutions that have all served to oppress the woman and her people.

Their power, temporal and discursive, is doomed to its inevitable end as the times change and as institutionalized discursive structures are faced with the intersubjective conversive realities of peoples asserting their own interrelational subjectivities and presences, in spite of the oppositional/institutional discourse that demands their muted, if not silenced, objectification. The mythic power of the story survives as "Storyteller" ends with a storytelling told directly to listener-readers who just might listen. The final paragraph, spoken directly to Silko's readers, restores the intersubjective relationship necessary for a conversive storytelling. Ironically, the storytelling in "Storyteller" occurs only by virtue of listener-readers who are predominantly non-Native. As in the case of Tayo's marginalization from his tribe largely by virtue of his being mixedblood, the Yupik woman is also largely rejected by her tribe. In light of her peripheral (and subaltern) status among her people, we should not find it surprising that the renewal of her storytelling begins with a non-Native listener (the Gossuck attorney) and continues with the largely non-Native audience of Silko's readers. As Trinh T. Minh-ha points out, "The story circulates like a gift; an empty gift which anybody can lay claim to by filling it to taste, yet can never truly possess" (2).

Silko's "Storytelling" and "Storyteller" demonstrate ways in which stories are made available to their listeners, ways in which stories are silenced or otherwise made inaccessible to others, ways in which stories are told without listeners at all or with listeners who do not understand (e.g., listeners who do not really listen with the conversiveness necessary for storytelling). In "Storytelling," Silko offers her storytelling gift to her listener-readers, who are invited into the world of storytelling throughout the piece, just one part of the larger story told by storytellers throughout time and across cultures. As Trinh T. Minh-ha further explains, "The story never really begins nor ends, even though there is a beginning and an end to every story, just as there is a beginning and an end to every teller" (1). The connections within the story extend outward to include its listener-readers and its future and past tellers as well.

The presence of interactive listeners is crucial to any telling. Keith Basso notes in relation to the Western Apache people, "every historical tale is also 'about' the person at whom it is directed" (108). Polanyi explains that the intersubjectivity of everyday conversation and storytelling necessitates the importance of stories' relevance to their listeners. "The 'message' of the story [must have] sufficient generality so that it can be seen to be applicable to circumstances outside of the story-world" ("Nature" 53). The story must tell a story in which the listeners can find or place themselves. Silko refers to storytelling as the weaving of a spider's web in which the structure gradually emerges as the web/story is spun ("Language" 54). Frey notes that it is through the weaving of this structure that the listener becomes involved in the story: "Concerning oral literature, then, in the act of weaving the fibers of words into a story, the story is brought to life through the imagination of the listener" (133). Frey further emphasizes that the listener is not passive, but an active participant in the process of storytelling.

Rather than the alternating voices of dialogic interactions, the intersubjective conversivity of storytelling involves conjoint interactions between teller and listener from start to finish. Susan Pierce Lamb emphasizes that "the interaction between teller and listener is simultaneous": "While 'unpacking' an image in his own mind, the narrator provides stimuli to generate one in the listener's mind. Simultaneously, the listener is responding to the perceived message which affects the way the teller communicates the image. All of the above goes on simultaneously and constitutes the process. The teller's and listener's interactions or synthesis generate the synergic event" (15, 14). This synergetic aspect of storytelling further underscores the extent to which active listeners are crucial to any conversive storytelling. Jane E. Hindman points out that the importance of present and active listener-readers is a crucial aspect of the rhetorical strategies of American Indian storytelling traditions. "Unlike Western rhetorics that privilege product over process and discourse over silence, that assign to the speaker/ writer responsibility for meaning-making, Native American rhetorics are listener responsible" (6). Although Hindman is ostensibly correct here, in fact, all literatures close to their oral roots are responsible to both their teller-writers and listener-readers because both are equally essential to any telling. If, as Richard Bauman notes, "language is a basic means through which social realities are intersubjectively constituted and communicated" ("Verbal" 304), then we should expect to find varying degrees of intersubjective conversivity in virtually all language (spoken, performative, and written). The next chapter turns to this very issue, exploring the work of several different American Indian writers (Louis Owens [Choctaw/Cherokee], Lee Maracle [Métis/Cree-Salish], and Sherman Alexie [Spokane/Coeur d'Alene]) and noting how their work varies in its degrees of conversivity and discursivity. Although all of these writers interweave both strategies in their work, how they do so takes on different forms to the extent that their work is more or less textually and/or orally informed.

Conversive relations are, by definition, transformative, and thereby potentially subversive and threatening (insofar as process and change are considered dangerous). When literature is read with a detachment that separates the reader from the world of a text, the transformative process of storytelling is hampered, and the reader is prevented from conversively engaging with the story behind the text. American Indian writers, such as Silko, strive to enable their readers to become listener-readers with responsibilities to the stories they read and to their own receptions of those stories. Vangen explains, " 'Storyteller' teaches a new way of listening (reading)" (117). And Hirsch emphasizes that "the reader's responses . . . [are] a part of the larger ongoing story," and through this process, "both the story and the reader are renewed" (3). The effect of the breakdown between the storyteller/listener relationship is severe for not only the storyteller whose telling is impeded, but also for those of us who never hear the stories necessary for our own restorative healings in the world. "Storyteller" presents the psychological historicities (atrocities) behind the attempts to silence and discount the very real transformative power and truth of storytelling. However, even the horrific events of "Storyteller" cannot stop the stories from being told. The young woman may not be able to tell her story to those in her own world, but there are those of us outside the bounds of her village who do want to hear her story. And in a wonderful act of authorial kindness, Silko finally helps the young woman to really tell her story by offering *Storyteller*'s readers as listener-readers to the woman's story. As "Storyteller" ends, she is finally able to tell her story, and the real storytelling finally begins as Silko's own voice and story and those of the Eskimo woman are interwoven: "It was a long time ago. . . . It was a long time before . . ." (32, 33).

THE CONVERSIVE-DISCURSIVE CONTINUUM IN THE WORK OF LOUIS OWENS, LEE MARACLE, AND SHERMAN ALEXIE

The differentiation between conversive and discursive communication ranges along a continuum that extends from the intersubjective relational intimacy of a personal conversation or an oral storytelling to the oppositional combativeness of an argument or debate in which the discursive structure merely masks the underlying monologic positions of the speakers. Literary works that fall along this continuum manifest various aspects of orality and textuality merely by virtue of their nature as *literary* texts, written works that straddle the oral domains of storytelling and poetry within the medium of writing. Whether those works are novels that aspire to the orality of conversation in their dialogic heteroglossia or poems whose ancient oral voices are literarily transformed onto paper, literature conjoins both worlds of the oral and textual by its very nature. This conjunction is evident in American Indian literatures whose writers straddle diverse worlds in their very own lives. In fact, within the body of American Indian literatures, the writing varies in its degrees of conversivity and discursivity, with some writers reflecting their oral traditions directly and powerfully in their writing, and other writers relying more heavily on other literary traditions. This chapter looks at the works of several Native writers, Louis Owens (Choctaw/Cherokee), Lee Maracle (Métis/Cree-Salish), and Sherman Alexie (Spokane/Coeur d'Alene), to show the literary diversity throughout American Indian literatures. All three of these writers straddle diverse tribal and nontribal cultures and ancestries, and, as this chapter demonstrates, their work reflects a great diversity of literary strategies and effects.

Much has been written about mixedblood writers whose works reveal conflicted identities and senses of self, but more important than identity issues for many of these writers is their own decentering of self. The extent to which American Indian writers "talk Indian" (Walters, *Talking Indian* 29) or write in a conversive manner is more a product of the extent to which the sacred is at the center of their personal and literary worldviews. Grant explains, "Much of oral literature was never perceived as apart from religion, morality and ethics of the community. It is this relationship between word, the land, and the ceremony linked with the past that gives strength to truly Native contemporary literature" ("Content" 11). Conversely, the extent to which the sacred is decentered and other realities are tenuously given center stage reflects the degree of discursivity in those writers' works. Among the writings of Owens, Maracle, and Alexie, each demonstrates varying combinations of orality and textuality, conversivity and discursivity, the sacred and the secular. These variations cannot be reduced to discussions of blood quantum or tribal affiliation, although these are certainly defining elements in the writers' works. What is involved in defining the extent to which a writer's work is more or less conversive reflects the whole range of each writer's personal, familial, tribal, and national historicities. Before turning to the work of Owens, Maracle, and Alexie, the chapter begins with a discussion of the differences between conversive and discursive language use. Then a close look at Owens's novel *Bone Game* provides the chapter's first example of a work of American Indian literatures that combines written and oral traditions within one literary text.

The distinctions that can be delineated along the conversive-discursive continuum reflect varying degrees of stasis and dynamism. Conversive communication affects real transformational growth for all participants through the synergy of interactive and co-creative relationships. Discursive communication, however, affects the dissipation of energy through the solitary expression of individual subjectivity and primacy in opposition to the objectivity and secondary status of one's hearer. As Gayatri Spivak points out in her introduction to *Of Grammatology*, "there is no other language but that of 'objectification'" (ix). James Clifford comments on the process of textualization (specifically in relation to the ethnographic enterprise): "The other is lost, in disintegrating time and space, but saved in the text" ("Ethnographic Allegory" 112). The other is saved as textual object; what Spivak does not point out, however, is that while objectification is the necessary effect of discursive language, it is not the necessary effect of conversive language. Tyler writes, "Paradoxically, orality is also the name of the counter discourse that resists the hegemony of the written word by recuperating the past, by reminding us that speech and communication ground all representation, not in the sign's alienation of the world, but in commonsense practices when word and world meet in will and deed" (132). I would amend Tyler's statement to note that although orality is not a "counter discourse" in an oppositional manner, it is an alternative means of communication that is inclusive rather than exclusive. Nevertheless, Tyler's point about the dynamic nature of orality is well-taken and crucial to any understanding of the difference between conversive and discursive structures.

The oppositional nature of discourse necessitates that the power of one's words serve deconstructive and, in their most virulent forms, destructive ends because one's own positionality is codependent upon the displacement of some "other." Within this domain, energy is continually being dissipated through the repetitive process of erasure as names and realities are silenced and disappeared into the traces of what they never really were in the first place anyway, but only appeared to be within the interpretive framework of a discursive hegemony. Deconstruction is nothing new for Native peoples. Simple perusals through the works of the past one hundred years of anthropological ethnography demonstrate the extent to which Indian peoples' realities and words have been constructed, deconstructed, reconstructed, and redeconstructed with each writing. The deconstructive project of Derrida, following on the heels of the anti-essentialism of Nietzsche, has broadened the scope to include the destabilization of all peoples, cultures, realities, lives, and words since everything is text (per Derrida's oft-quoted statement, *"Il n'y a pas de hors-texte"*—there is nothing outside the text). This is an equal-opportunity silencing and writing of all realities, which are understood as nothing other than texts to be objectified and deconstructed. When discourse speaks, the whole world is silenced.

Fortunately, the constructions and deconstructions of the ethnographers and Derrida do not delimit the boundaries of human interpersonal relationship, communication, and knowing. For example, a deconstructive reading of Walter Dyk's Navajo "autobiography," *Son of Old Man Hat,* might note the silence and absence of the son of Old Man Hat in Dyk's ethnographic autobiographical rendering of the Navajo man. Rather than reading the life and times of the Navajo around the turn of the century, Dyk's work would prove to be nothing other than his objectified text that absences the real son of Old Man Hat while giving primacy to Dyk and his interpretive rendering. But such a critical deconstruction of the text denies the very real presence and conversive power of Left Handed, the actual Navajo storyteller who spent weeks telling Walter Dyk some pretty remarkable stories. Within a discursive framework, it is Left Handed's voice that is silenced through Dyk's ethnographic and editorial mediation; however, within a conversive framework, Left Handed's trickster voice comes through clearly and powerfully, circumventing Dyk's mediation and undercutting Dyk's discursive primacy.[1] From the earliest days of ethnographic recording and translation, Indian peoples' voices have been misread and misinterpreted through the interpretive scopes of Western discourse that silence, dismiss, and vanish those others whose speech does not fit the oppositional modes of phallogocentric monologue and dialogue. Within this framework, the voices of indigenous peoples' throughout the world have been vanishing through their translations from conversive communication to the imposition of Western discursive structures. But this is merely the illusion of the vanishing Indian. As Yvor Winters noted over fifty years ago in his open letter to the editors of *This Quarter,* "this notion of interpreting the Indian is too much for me. They are in need of no assistance whatsoever" (33).

The voices of American Indian peoples have been speaking powerfully and consistently from the beginning of time. They have never truly been silenced, dismissed, or vanished in fact; they have just not been listened to, not been heard, not been understood in terms of a conversive mode—what Anna Lee Walters (Pawnee/Otoe-Missouria) describes as "talking Indian." The choice not to take discursive space in the world in no wise signifies silence. For many Indian peoples, such discursive space is seen as unimportant and, in fact, meaningless in relation to the more important concerns of living in balance and harmony within the sacred space of an intersubjectively relational world. This juxtaposition between discursive and conversive worlds and words can be seen throughout the history of European and Euroamerican contact/combat with the indigenous peoples of North America. The analyses of many ethnographers, anthropologists, historians, linguists, and literary critics have framed this history within their own discursive oppositions of categorized difference and sameness (more often than not reduced to externally imposed racial categories). American Indian peoples, however, have spoken their own realities and experiences through a conversive manner scarcely heard by scholars incapable of hearing the subjective voice of the presumed objective other—unless the other speaks a language and discourse that sufficiently mimics or adopts the predominant Euroamerican discourses. As Richard Handler comments on the anthropological discourse of the Native other, "we act upon objects, but do not interact with them" (172).[2]

All American Indian writers to different degrees perform balancing acts between tellings and texts as the two, at times, are conversively interwoven within the fabric of a written telling and, at other times, discursively combative in a textual clash that demands oral compromise. Finnegan explains, "oral literature is still a living art and there is constant interplay between oral and written forms" ("Literacy versus Non-literacy" 115). This can be seen in the works of many mixedblood Indian writers whose writings reflect the divergent ways in which discursive and conversive worldviews and strategies of communication intermingle and clash in the development of a hybrid literary style that bespeaks the realities of those writers who are "split at the root."[3] However, the reality of the mixedblood is much more complex than the simple addition of two partial identities. As Ruppert notes, "To overcome isolation and find identity, the half-breed must reject simplistic, internalized dualisms which divide the world and themselves into good and bad, White and Indian, traditional and contemporary" ("Uses" 107). Specifically in relation to mixedblood Indian peoples, Allen (Laguna Pueblo) writes, "a half-breed cannot be wholly white or wholly Indian, but must balance carefully the two in recognition of the good and evil in both, in terms of personal significance" ("Stranger II" 17). "The breed is an Indian who is not an Indian. Breeds are a bit of both worlds, and the consciousness of this makes them seem alien to Indians while making them feel alien among whites" (Allen, "Stranger I" 3).

Michelle M. Motoyoshi explains that mixedblood people manifest elements of both cultural/ethnic backgrounds, but that the extent to which mixedblood people reflect their particular multicultural backgrounds is largely dependent upon their parents' acceptance of their multiethnic and multiracial children (79). Motoyoshi further notes that the realities of mixed-race people serve as the sign of a society's acceptance (or lack thereof) of its demographic and cultural diversity (88–89). Unlike individuals whose backgrounds are less varied, the mixedblood demonstrates an "extra-sensitivity to race issues which is brought about by being privy, in a sense, to each group's attitudes toward the other" (Motoyoshi 78)—hence the likelihood of the feelings of alienation that Allen notes. The mixed-blood is, in varying ways, a part of each group and, as well, is distanced from each group, thereby resulting in a profound sense of being racially and culturally other. But the genetic diversity of the mixedblood, in and of itself, is insufficient to demonstrate the complex diversity to be found in the litera-tures by different American Indian and Canadian First Nations writers. Perhaps even more importantly lies the interstice of the mixedblood that serves as a sign of the divergent ways by which Indian writers' works straddle worlds and words.

Jodi Lundgren discusses the reality of straddling Native Canadian and Eurocanadian worlds in the works of three Métis women writers.[4] Lund-gren notes that in the works of Maria Campbell, Beatrice Culleton, and Lee Maracle, the Métis are characterized through their particular cultural and ethnic heritages rather than through an emphasis on race (63). In fact, Lundgren suggests, "Ethnicity, not race, is what may form the basis of a truly multi-cultural society" (76). The multicultural backgrounds of the Métis preclude their identification with one racial group or another, even though, as Reed Way Dasenbrock notes, "The temptations in studying such bicultural writers is to deny their biculturality, to privilege one of their formative cultures in the name of authenticity or the other in the name of universality" (317). But to do so would be to deny their actual historicities in the world. In regards to the novel *Halfbreed,* Lundgren writes, "Campbell delineates the history of the Métis and demonstrates that they are a unique group, distinct from white Canadians, and 'completely different from' their 'Indian relatives'" (65). This condition of difference is what makes the Métis people "extra-sensitive" to the situations of other people of color, resulting in "the expression of solidarity with other people of colour" (66). The Métis's straddling of worlds demonstrates both their identification with divergent backgrounds and histories and their rejection and differ-ence from those realities. But as Blaeser (Anishinabe) points out, the notions of marginality or borders are insufficient to explain the complexities of the mixedblood. "In fact, the existence of the mixedblood resists even that definitiveness. Mixedbloods exist in the place of contact between age-old tribal traditions and contemporary adaptations, as well as in the place of contact between the stereotypical definitions of Indian identity and the reality of Indian existence" (*Gerald Vizenor* 155). This place of contact that

Blaeser notes manifests itself in language as the place of contact between conversive and discursive worlds and words.

The Métis writer manifests her mixed heritage within her written language. Lundgren notes the endemic racist and sexist foundations of the dominant Canadian discourse that even pervade the work of Native writers. For example, Lundgren describes Lee Maracle as a writer who "adheres (slavishly) to its rules (even dialogic discourse must repeat the convention it 're-marks')" (69). Lundgren underscores the extent to which Maracle reacts against Native people's and women's objectification through Maracle's usurpation of the dominant discourse as speaking subject. But such investments in Western discursive structures pose potential hazards for any person struggling to reposition herself out of the subaltern. The dilemma is that any such attempts at repositioning realize the lie of discursive displacement and marginalization through a tragic collusion of the "other" in the discourse that inevitably repeats its monotonous iteration of who's on top and who's not. Schwab explains, "Only when the colonized's own native culture has been relegated to the political unconscious and become internalized as the Other, only then is the process of colonization successfully completed" (130). One sign of the internalization of colonization is the perpetuation of the discursive structures of power, regardless of who is the speaking subject and who is the disempowered other. Any continuation of the 'language game' of discursive power relations lends credence to the concomitant process of objectification.

Whereas Lundgren views Maracle's writing as largely discursive, she describes Campbell's writing as having a "colloquial, conversational tone": "At the same time as she defies [white readers'] expectations [about the Native other], Campbell encourages white readers to enter the text through the door of familiarity rather than to look at the 'Indian' through a 'study window'" (73). Lundgren sees Maracle's writing as strongly discursive and Campbell's as strongly conversative, but, in fact, all Native writers, as this chapter demonstrates, whether they are Métis, mixedblood, or fullblood, raised on or off the reservation, straddle both discursive and conversive worlds to varying extents, writing in diverse styles that reflect a mixed convergence and divergence of orally based and textually informed realities and voices.

The continuum that ranges from the strictly discursive to the openly conversive is evident in the divergence between the varying forms of the written and the oral. Swearingen writes, "The examination of the literacy continuum or spectrum has demonstrated that even within 'oral' cultures there are varying degrees of preserved and spontaneous discourse, formulaic and innovative language used in diverse combinations for a variety of purposes" (149). This diversity of forms is evident within the literatures of all peoples, and especially so in the case of writers whose lives and words straddle diverse worlds—a situation that bespeaks the reality of most, if not all peoples in America. Frank Shuffelton notes in the introduction to *A Mixed Race: Ethnicity in Early America,* "From the moments when John Smith met Powhatan or Hobomok and Squanto stepped out of the forest, the ethnic others who were both saviors and threats to the English immigrants, American culture has come out of a continuing series of confrontations and collaborations between men and women from every place on the surface of this globe" (14). This diversity is reflected in how our stories are told and written. Investigations into the work of Louis Owens, Lee Maracle, and Sherman Alexie will show the varying extents to which their literary structures manifest discursive and/or conversive manners of communication. As Edward Sapir noted seventy years ago, "Human beings do not live in the objective world alone, nor alone in the world of social activity as ordinarily understood, but are very much at the mercy of the particular language which has become the medium of expression for their society" (209). Regardless of the differences between Owens, Maracle, and Alexie, all of whom reflect different tribal, national, generational, and gendered backgrounds, each writes in a hybrid manner conjoining both discursive and conversive literary styles. At times, the conversive discursivity is jarring and profoundly unsettling; at other times, a happy marriage of diverse cultures and languages is achieved, reflecting what Motoyoshi suggests might be "prototypes" for an evolving multicultural world (89).

Louis Owens's Bone Game

Louis Owens's novel *Bone Game* depicts the conversive discursivity common within the works of many mixedblood writers. Owens is of Irish, Choctaw, and Cherokee descent, and his writing depicts the diversity of engagements that occur among persons of different cultural, ethnic, and historical backgrounds. Often, these engagements are discursively oppositional (from the extreme violence of a serial murderer in *Bone Game* to the subtler, yet at times insidious, dialogic competitiveness that seems to pervade much of contemporary discourse). However, at other times, Owens presents the intimacy of conversive relations between characters who, in his writing, more often than not, tend to be Indians, mixedbloods, or women.[5]

Bone Game takes place in and around the University of California at Santa Cruz, where a serial murderer has been abducting and sadistically murdering young women. Owens frames the horrific murders and the decadent lifestyles of the University of California students within the historical context of the brutally sadistic treatment perpetrated against California Indian peoples by the colonizing Spaniards, focusing specifically on the life of one particularly sadomasochistic Spanish priest who was found murdered (tortured and hanged) in 1812. Padre Andrés Quintana's life and death at the mission of Santa Cruz serve as the historical sign of a continuing legacy of violence, terror, and the ominously intertwined bedfellows of sexual denial and sexual aggression. Enter Cole McCurtain, a mixedblood Choctaw/Irish professor of English at the university, who finds himself inextricably interwoven within the web of violence and depravity, California's inheritance of generations of physical and sexual abuse, objectification, hatred, fear, and outright genocide. It is only through the combined efforts of Cole's Anglo father Hoey, his mixedblood great-uncle Luther, his mixedblood "grandmother" Onatima, his own daughter Abby, and a crossdressing Navajo colleague that the web of horror surrounding Cole and the university campus is partially unraveled—at least sufficiently for Cole and his family to get out.

Throughout the novel, Owens presents the worlds of Indian, Anglo, and mixedblood Indian peoples in all of their complexities and interwoven historicities (past and present). Although there is evil afoot (in the forms of serial murderers and kidnappers), Owens contextualizes the conditions of his characters such that no one is portrayed stereotypically as either an otherworldly sorcerer terrorizing people through witchery or as an all-wise Indian elder whose sacred (and also otherworldly) medicine is instrumental in overcoming the realized dangers of witchery. The serial murderer who mimics Indian witchery as he terrorizes Cole McCurtain's daughter is an Anglo graduate student who works as Dr. McCurtain's teaching assistant. The elders who come to the rescue are a hodgepodge of McCurtain's Anglo and mixedblood relatives, who are in no wise nostalgized or romanticized beyond their realities as very human, fallible, and humorous people whose greatest strengths seem to come from their love for each other.

McCurtain's world is far removed from the mystical world of Tayo's healing ceremony in Silko's *Ceremony,* even though the two novels overlap as McCurtain's father and great-uncle travel west through the Gallup, New Mexico, region on their way to help Cole. Outside of Gallup, Hoey and Luther see three men abduct a drunk Navajo woman. When they catch up with the men's van at a truckstop, they free the woman and entrap her abductors—one of whom turns out to be Emo from Silko's *Ceremony.* Emo and his Anglo cohorts turn out to have a business abducting women (particularly drunk Indian women) and selling them in California (in light of the novel, one assumes to individuals involved in some sort of extreme sadomasochistic practices).

Owens's depiction of Emo demonstrates the novel's realistic portrayal of evil in the world. Evil is presented as powerless in and of itself and as the product of a history of individual, familial, and cultural oppression and suffering. In *Bone Game,* the witchery of Emo and his partners is presented as the sick business enterprise of three very lost souls who are depicted not as witches, but rather as the warped human beings they are. When Luther asks his nephew, "What you want to do with these witches?" one of the three men says, "We ain't witches" (128–9). Luther suggests burning them, "Onatima said white people used to do that with witches," at which point the other white man says, "We're not witches, for chrisesake" (129). Although the effects of the witchery of these three men is real, in Luther's suggestion of burning, Owens parallels the identification of the men as witches with the suspect, yet analogous, determinations of witchcraft by the white people in Salem, Massachusetts. Through the analogy to European and Euroamerican witch burnings, Emo's and the others' witchery is humanized and concretized as evil human behaviors explicable in terms of particular sociohistorical and psychological factors.

Owens translates the belief in witchcraft out of the domains of superstition and the supernatural and into the very real struggles of individuals imposing their power over others (whom they attempt to disempower). Even the evil of the mythic gambler whose bone game determines whether people live or die is framed within the context of actual oppositional struggles in the world. The choice given in *Bone Game* is either to play the game with the gambler in a sort of Faustian bargain and inevitably lose to the gambler's evil and deadly play, or to try to live out of the reach of the gambler. As Hoey reminds his uncle Luther, "Remember what you always said about evil? . . . How you can't kill it, and it's the white man's way to try? That all we can do is be conscious of it?" (154). Here Owens echoes the wisdom Tayo learns throughout *Ceremony* (126–7, 132, 191, 253). The sadistic evil of Emo, Padre Andrés Quintana, and serial murderers serves as the interwoven sign of the critical oppositionality at the heart of the Western traditions of colonization, enslavement, and genocide. Accordingly, Owens's novel intertwines discursive and conversive literary structures as he presents the divergent worlds of horrific oppositional struggle on the one hand, and on the other hand, conversive interrelationality (most notably manifested in the interactions of McCurtain's relatives with each other and with the world).

Power imbalances in the world take on a discursive form whenever they are communicated in words, and all such imbalances that involve human interactions with others (be those others human, animal, plant, or otherworldly) are as well the domain of discursive intercourse. Cole McCurtain's "grandmother" Onatima (actually the long-time lover of McCurtain's great-uncle Luther) explains that such interactions involve not only those who disempower others, but also those who collusively allow themselves to be disempowered. "It's a matter of power. They would imprison us in their vision and their stories, and we can't let them do that. We have to have our own stories" (140). Onatima makes it very clear that discursive power in the world necessitates the volitional involvement of oppressor and oppressed alike. This is not to deny the extent to which peoples and persons throughout history have been oppressed and enslaved and genocided. However, what Onatima tells McCurtain's daughter Abby is that she has the choice whether to grant evil power that it does not, in fact, actually have. The power that discursive evil wields over her is power that it receives from her own collusive fear and objectified disempowerment.

Discursive evil has no real power in and of itself; discursive power is the illusion of power relatively granted through the other's concomitant disempowerment. Discursive power is fundamentally oppositional. It is always a power *over* some "other" who is necessarily disempowered through an objectification that denies his or her subjective reality as a person in the world. Onatima continues:

Perhaps the man who frightened you today wants to make you see yourself only through his eyes, so that you can only imagine yourself from outside the window looking in. That way, every time you look in a mirror you will see only what the man sees. You will always be outside yourself, and your own reflection will be a trap. When that happens we become like ghosts who can't see our own bodies. Then we have to make others see us so we can know we exist, or we have to use others' lives as our own. That's what they want. It's a matter of power. (140)

As the old woman warns her granddaughter, it is when people perceive themselves as the powerless objects of the other's gaze that they become powerless and, in turn, perpetuate the cycle of oppositional objectification and disempowerment by their own attempts to assert their own power through their subsequent disempowerment of some other. As Onatima says, "Then we have to make others see us so we can know we exist, or we have to use others' lives as our own" (140). This is similar to the process Schwab calls "internalized colonization" (130). As long as people have no sense of their own power as conversively intersubjective persons whose lives and presences in the world are thereby meaningful and substantive, they will continue to live the stories others write and tell about themselves, and they will "become like ghosts who can't see [their] own bodies" (140). Onatima tells Abby, "We have to have our own stories" (140)—stories whose importance serves as the corrective means of what Frey refers to as "re-telling one's own" (134).

In this novel, discursive power and evil cannot be overcome through oppositional struggle because such power feeds on the opposition, the source of its strength. Onatima tries to teach Abby this lesson by conversively sharing her own story with her granddaughter in the hope of transforming Abby through a realization of her own strength and the importance of not engaging in discursive power struggles, of not playing into the hands of mythic or real gamblers. Abby and her father both straddle the worlds and words of conversive and discursive engagements—histories of broken connections, loss, and alienation. Cole McCurtain teaches and lives in California distanced from his relatives and divorced from his wife. His daughter has struggled with the legacy of her parents' divorce and her father's move across the country, a move that has brought Abby to California to be with him. Father and daughter find themselves lost and alone in the discursive reality of a world that defines human subjectivity against others' objectivity. Through the familial reconnection established between the two by Abby's arrival in California, Cole and his daughter begin their processes of transformation away from the discursive disempowerment that surrounds them both and toward the conversive healing that finally protects them from the gambler and brings them home to New Mexico.

Cole McCurtain is haunted by the concretization of the mythic gambler in the person of Venancio Asisara, who comes to him in his dreams. Asisara was one of the Indians who tortured and murdered the Spanish priest Padre Quintana in 1812. From the cruelty of the Spanish priest and the violent retribution perpetrated by some of the Indian people he victimized, to contemporary serial murderers and Cole's alcoholism, Asisara is one link in the chain of a discursively realized evil that continues to perpetuate its sadistic disempowerment of others from generation to generation. The effect of Asisara's presence in Cole's dreams is that Cole retreats into the abyss of his alcoholism, having less contact with others, finding himself progressively more disempowered as he, an English professor at a respected university, becomes afraid of his own words, and thereby, of his own self. No longer writing, Cole's research and creative production fall stagnant. He begins to despise his teaching and his students. At one point, he chooses alcohol over his responsibilities as a professor and tries to get his teaching assistant to lecture in his place. " 'It'll be a good experience for you, and I'm not feeling too well this morning. I think I'm coming down with something.' *Because I shot at a spirit conjured from my dreams. Because of angels and monsters*" (19). McCurtain ends up giving his lecture, but he does so in a discursive manner that oppositionally deconstructs the "ethnostalgic" mystique of Black Elk (43). As McCurtain points out to his graduate assistant, "to an Indian every sentence in English may be a broken treaty" (43).

Cole pulls himself away from the words of his dreams, from the words of his work and world, from the words whose deluge now overwhelms him. He cuts his lecture short, leaving his students feeling cheated and wanting more, wanting their own ethnostalgized mythical reading of Black Elk (Black Elk as constructed as "a one-dimensional holy man, Neihardt's romantic, tragic creation" [42]), and perhaps even more importantly, just wanting more words, a complete lecture from their professor. As McCurtain tells his graduate assistant, "All those f—ing words. . . . You should have done the lecture yourself, Robert. I gave you the opportunity" (43). As McCurtain is haunted by the words of his dreams, those words that surround him on an everyday basis fade into insignificance in a world of broken treaties, ethnostalgic lies, academic arrogance and ignorance, and human loneliness and alienation.

His daughter Abby worries about the extent of her father's silence. As she wanders around his home, she thinks, "There was no sign at all in the house that anyone ever visited. . . . It was as if, except for Alex Yazzie, her father had spoken to no one since he'd loaded the pickup and driven out of the Sandia Mountains of New Mexico" (135). Within a discursive framework, silence signifies a person's subjective absence, and throughout the majority of the novel, Cole's silence and inarticulateness represent his growing incapacity within the discursive world he had defined as his own. The pathological nature of Cole's silences are manifestations of a world in which presence is defined in terms of oppositional struggle. Yet within a conversively relational domain, silence, far from disempowering, is often the manifestation of interpersonal relations and empowerment.[6]

Cole's Navajo colleague Yazzie, like Cole's daughter Abby, is concerned about Cole. He arranges a ritual sweat to try to help Cole, who proves to be a very reluctant participant. Nevertheless, he agrees to the ceremony. In the sweat lodge, the participants offer their prayers for themselves and the world. However, Cole finds himself speechless. "When his turn arrived, Cole opened his mouth and only silence was there. He tried to form the words of a prayer in his mind, but his thoughts remained shapeless, inarticulate. A knot had formed beneath his chest and seemed to be working its way upward into his throat. He closed his burning eyes and in the darkness he saw the painted man" (163). The gambler in his dreams has disempowered McCurtain, even within the safe confines of a sweat lodge. Afterwards, the old man who conducted the ceremony finds Cole and tells him, "Words ain't always important. . . . We just got to empty ourself of the stuff that gets in the way, and sometimes we don't know it worked till a long time later" (164).

Cole's silence is underscored by his complete immersion in a world constructed on discursive lines that insure the proper delineations that separate people from others, fact from fiction, history from myth, and the past from the present. For Cole, it is only in his dreams that the lines and categories of his Anglo-academic world collapse in a necessary implosion that provides the traumatic catalyst for his eventual return. Cole's silence reflects both his incapacity to respond conversively to those around him and his growing disinterest in discursive communication. The discursive paradigm expected of him as a respected university professor is his usual mode of communication, and yet the presence of the gambler (mythical and historical in the person of Venancio Asisara) in his dreams forces him to confront his whole-hearted acceptance of a discourse that has distanced him from his family and his work. Silence serves as the sign of Cole's existential clash between worlds and words, between discursive textual lies and conversive told and lived stories.

Whereas Cole's response to the Californian legacy of the gambler is disempowerment and silence, his daughter's response alternates between a denial of the evil surrounding her (a denial that she manifests in a reckless independence) and a discursive combativeness that, equally foolishly, attempts to fight the evil head on. During a time in which young women in the Santa Cruz area are being abducted and murdered, Abby goes hiking alone in the woods, fishes alone in a stream hidden in the deep recesses of a wooded canyon, and stays home alone in the evening, even though a prayer stick with the flesh from one of the murdered women was left at her father's home. And when face-to-face with the murderers, Abby responds discursively, trying to out-trick them. When Abby goes out one evening with Alex Yazzie (the cross-dressing Navajo), who is dressed as a woman, they end up accepting a ride with a man who turns out to be one of the serial murderers. At gun point, Abby proceeds to try to talk their way out of danger. She begins by lying, "If you let us go now, we'll walk back to the road and say nothing of this" (218). Her lie only gives the murderer more power and alerts him not to trust her: "it's just lying bullshit to try to save your life" (220). Alex and Abby eventually escape, thanks to Alex's martial arts training. Violence is beaten by further, albeit defensive, violence. The legacy of Padre Quintana continues from generation to generation and from one violent act to another. As Venancio Asisara, the gambler of Cole's dreams, tells him, "Eran muy crueles" (7, 241).

Even in Abby's interactions with her father, she demonstrates a discursive distance that reflects the effects of a broken family. Her first words upon her arrival at her father's home are, "Jesus, Dad. What a mess" (58). From her first words of judgment, both Abby and Cole begin their work to move their stilted relationship away from the discursive distance created by the parents' divorce and toward the conversive closeness that strengthens both father and daughter and returns them to their home in the Sandia Mountains outside of Albuquerque. Interestingly, even though Abby moves to California to live with her father, throughout the novel there are very few scenes with them together, either at home or elsewhere. More often than not, each is alone or in the company of Alex Yazzie, who mediates the father and daughter's relationship as Cole's younger colleague and friend and as Abby's lover. With her father, Abby serves as the sign of

Cole's distance from his wife. When Abby tells her father to get cleaned up, he responds, "You're giving orders like your mom" (59). And when Cole rejects Abby's plans to go to school at ucsc, "Her voice thinned toward tears, and he thought of his wife, his former wife. So many of their words had ended that way. In his daughter's face, he saw Mara's" (60).

Just as the horrific legacy of Padre Quintana has passed its traces of violence on from generation to generation in the land of California, so have the effects of the McCurtains' divorce manifested themselves in the ruptured relationship between father and daughter. The arrival of their mixedblood relatives from Mississippi provides the needed familial bond that enables father and daughter to reconnect beyond the lines of a discursively dysfunctional relationship. Both Cole and Abby communicate in conversive manners with their older relatives, thereby transforming themselves and their own relationship through the connective links of their rural mixed-blood Indian heritage. With the support and guidance of Onatima, Uncle Luther, and Hoey, Cole and Abby are able to confront the demons in their lives head on. The entire family returns to New Mexico, and Abby and Alex Yazzie decide to live with her father in the family home in the mountains. Alex undergoes a lengthy healing ceremony back home on the Navajo Reservation to bring him back to harmony from his confused reality in California. And Cole learns the real substance of myth, legend, and dream in his final confrontation with Venancio Asisara in the form of the gambler—a learning that conversively heals him as he re-members himself as a mixedblood professor of English whose roots go well beyond the delimiting domain of discursive academia.

Although ostensibly dialogic, Owens's novel demonstrates the limits of discourse. Whereas Mikhail Bakhtin notes that the novel is an essentially critical and self-critical literary form in which a heteroglossic dialogism places "one point of view opposed to another, one evaluation opposed to another, one accent opposed to another" (314), *Bone Game* presents a world in which the limits of such an oppositional dialogism reach their logical and actual conclusions in a world of horrific violence. The film worlds of director Quentin Tarantino manifest the extreme forms of a Bakhtinian dialogism that can never surmount its inherently oppositional nature. From the sadomasochism of Padre Quintana to that of contemporary serial murders and Tarantino's *Pulp Fiction,* the ultimate limits of discursive epistemologies continue to turn back upon themselves in a never ending spiral of dominance, violence, and submission. Bakhtin is absolutely correct in his assessment of the novel as the literary manifestation of this process. As he notes, "the novel is the sole genre that continues to develop, that is as yet uncompleted" (3).

The world of Bakhtin's discursive heteroglossia is a world that is essentially imbalanced, always striving, not for balance, but for new and different imbalances. This is a process in which those who have been silenced and disempowered struggle to assert their own voices and power over those others who have already achieved positions of subjectivity and privilege. Owens presents the reality of a Bakhtinian dialogism, but in Owens's novel, such a reality is laid bare in all its horrific implications. From the perspective of Native America, what Bakhtin hails as liberatory is seen as not only self-critical but also as self-destructive. Native peoples have traditionally understood the very real conversive power of language. Language can be critical and destructive. But it can also be a creative force that unites diverse peoples and voices into not the unitary voice of a melting pot where diversity is lost, but a multiplicitous one in which diversity is affirmed through interpersonal and intersubjective interaction and conversation. This is what Silko (Laguna Pueblo) refers to as "the boundless capacity of language which, through storytelling, brings us together, despite great distances between cultures, despite great distances in time" ("Language" 72). The world of Onatima, Luther, and Cole is a world that embraces the diversity of peoples, cultures, traditions, and languages.

Cole McCurtain's mixedblood relatives serve as the sign of a conversive reality in which diversity is privileged not through an oppositional discourse but through the lived and spoken connections that bring people together. Onatima demonstrates this conversive acceptance of diversity in her own story, which she shares with Abby. "This is where real power comes from, from all of us—fullbloods and mixedbloods, those who live together and those who live apart. Like me. I'm wearing this dress tonight to remember who I am, because it's easy to forget, and when we forget we expose ourselves to unnecessary dangers" (174). As Frey explains, "The remembering involves a return to and a reuniting" (134). Onatima learned the importance of accepting all of who she is as a mixedblood woman, and this is the lesson that Cole struggles to learn through the course of the novel as the boundaries that circumscribe his discursively constructed world begin to close in on him. The world of *Bone Game* is the discursively objectified world of the novel—the literary legacy of five hundred years of colonization. Bakhtin explains, "Discourse lives, as it were, beyond itself, in a living impulse toward the object; if we detach ourselves completely from this impulse all we have left is the naked corpse of the word, from which we can learn nothing at all about the social situation or the fate of a given word in life" (292). Here life comes from a vampiric attraction "toward the object," the object which is never gained but always sought. Discursive power in its relative reality is never completely fulfilled because such a fulfillment would signify the end of the process of discursive power relations. For Bakhtin, life and novel are necessarily discursively based. Human power is only achievable through the objectification of some "other" whose personhood is reduced to that of the desired object. Within such a framework, human subjectivity is contingent upon a concomitant human objectivity, and analogously, the object receives significance through her/his/its dependence upon the objectifying subject.

Serial murderers are not heroes, but within the discursive structure of the novel (and our world), those who kill serial murderers are perceived as heroes. Robert Malin, who shoots Paul Kantner, and Venancio Asisara, who participated in the murder of Padre Quintana, are hailed as heroes.[7] But within the conversive voice that serves as the grounding and corrective remedy throughout *Bone Game,* the emptiness of such narratological heroics is laid bare. Onatima explains to her granddaughter that when she perceived herself in the discursive manner of a divided world, she was nothing.

> When I was a little girl I wanted to be like my mother, who was French.... My father was an important man among the Choctaw.... I was proud of him, but when we were with white people I saw my father grow small. My mother would take me with her to Vicksburg, where nobody knew us, and we'd pretend that I was just like all the rich white kids there....
>
> And then one day when I was at home playing with my dolls, I looked in a mirror and saw nothing. It was many years before I could see myself again. (139)

Onatima and her parents reflect the clash of discursive and conversive 'language games'. If the predominant 'language game' played is essentially discursive and therefore demands adherence to the rules of an oppositional and objectifying discourse, then those who play the game of discursivity poorly or not at all will inevitably end up losers in the game. Onatima's father, "an important man among the Choctaw," was insignificant within the white world. Onatima and her French mother could gain their largely illusory discursive presence when they would go to Vicksburg and speak French to each other, thereby giving themselves the linguistic appearance of power. Yet within the domain of conversive 'language games', Onatima and her father were accepted and valued, not in terms of appearances (linguistic or otherwise), but on the basis of their realities as members of their tribe and, perhaps even more importantly, as human persons in the world.

The process Onatima undergoes to finally step beyond her desires for discursive presence in a world based on power imbalances is the very same process that Cole begrudgingly embarks upon in his haunted dreams. The narrative structure and world of *Bone Game* are discursively dialogic, but the limits of that 'language game' are repeatedly called into question through their dysfunctional and, at times, horrific effects. Yet, Cole's world is, by definition and birth, the world of the mixedblood—a world whose 'language games' are never purely those of discourse, dialogue, or conversation, but always a combination that straddles worlds and 'language games', at times comfortably, but in the case of *Bone Game,* more often than not awkwardly and even traumatically. Agnes Grant points out, "It is not inevitable, however, that a literary tradition will automatically destroy the oral tradition. The two can exist side by side" ("Content" 6), even within the bounds of one written text. As Owens explains in his critical volume *Other Destinies,* "For the Indian author, writing within consciousness of the contextual background of a nonliterate culture, every word written in English represents a collaboration of sorts as well as a reorientation (conscious or unconscious) from the paradigmatic world of oral tradition to the syntagmatic reality of written language" (6). The 'language games' played by mixedblood writers are 'language games' that necessarily are "split at the root," and their writings are, by definition and birth, discursively conversive. Although each writer and writing is situated differentially along the conversive-discursive continuum, I would argue that the conversive influence is always the most profound and the strongest—even in its apparent absence (as we will see in the case of James Welch's *Winter in the Blood*). The spiritual rootedness and intersubjective relationality of the conversive provides the sort of certain grounds that discursive relations always seek but never achieve due to their relative contingencies of power.

Within the domain of the sacred, power is never a power *over* but rather a power *with*. Whereas discursive power manifests itself in oppositional struggle, conversive power manifests itself in the connections that unite the diverse elements of the world in a harmonious and balanced set of interdependent and intersubjective relationships. The clash of discursive and conversive modes of communication and living has demanded new strategies for people's lives and also for literature. As Allen Quetone (Kiowa) notes about "the Indian way of life in today's world": "There has to be a balancing, a reconciling of ways" (qtd. in Morey 49). Owens and other mixedblood American Indian writers illustrate the range of ways by which such a balancing can be achieved. Regardless of the extent to which discursive worldviews are either denigrated or embraced, it is the conversive that grounds the literatures in the sacred and provides the means toward balance and harmony (individually, familially, tribally, and globally). Luther Standing Bear (Lakota) comments:

> True, the white man brought great change. But the varied fruits of his civilization, though highly colored and inviting, are sickening and deadening. And if it be the part of civilization to maim, rob, and thwart, then what is progress? I am going to venture that the man who sat on the ground in his tepee meditating on life and its meaning, accepting the kinship of all creatures, and acknowledging unity with the universe of things was infusing into his being the true essence of civilization. (249–50)

Whereas the world and words of Owens's novel *Bone Game* represent the world of discursive and realized conflict, it is the balancing presence of conversive relationships that lays bare the limits and dangerous effects of such conflict, otherwise normativized, accepted, and/or condoned. The reality of worlds and words that struggle to achieve a balance between good and evil, between conversive relationships and discursive oppositions, is a part of the writing of all American Indian writers (and, possibly, of all writers). However, each writer develops his or her own interweaving of, and at times clashes between, the diverse voices and worldviews of their stories.

Lee Maracle's Ravensong

In Lee Maracle's novel *Ravensong,* she presents the difficulties that occur due to the conflicting worldviews embodied in discursive and conversive patterns of communication and life.[8] Like *Bone Game,* Maracle's novel takes place over a relatively short time period (although with occasional shifts into mythic, past, or future time) and focuses on the main character's relationship to place. Whereas Owens's novel portrays Cole McCurtain's disorientation within the discursive world of California and his eventual return to the mountains east of Albuquerque, *Ravensong* emphasizes a girl's connection to her Indian village and her eventual departure for college. Stacey's Indian community (on the *other* side of the river from white town) provides her with a stability that is repeatedly called into question through her daily crossings over to attend the white high school. Similar to Owens's novel, *Ravensong* manifests a discursive conversivity that demonstrates the mix of cultures evident within the storied world of *Ravensong.* In contrast, Maracle communicates this world in ways that diverge significantly from Owens's strategies along the discursive-conversive continuum. As Godard points out in relation to her early writing, "Maracle's self-presentation also functions as a critical intervention into the discursive formation: she positions herself as the unspeakable, as paradox confounding discursive norms" ("Politics" 210). Godard continues, noting that the "opposition between orality and writing" is central in Maracle's work (211). Godard is correct in pointing out this conflict that is present in the work of many American Indian writers, but I would posit that the oppositionality between orality and writing in *Ravensong* is merely the discursive appearance of such conflict. In fact, Maracle, like many other First Nations writers, manifests orality within her writing through a conversive literary style. This is what Godard refers to as an "oral text" ("Voicing" 91) and what I would simply refer to as literature.

Owens's novel is largely discursive and dialogic, with several overlapping narrative threads that are resolved by the end of the novel. Even though *Bone Game*'s discursivity is challenged throughout by virtue of the dysfunctionality and danger inherent within the essential disconnectedness of discursive relations, the novel nevertheless is ultimately discursively dialogic in form and substance. The intent of the novel is to move the main characters, Cole and his family, out of the dominant culture's dysfunctional oppositions as manifested in contemporary California lifestyles and back to a more balanced, if not somewhat romanticized, life in New Mexico. In Owens's *Bone Game,* Cole's Indian, mixedblood, and rural white relatives are portrayed as outsiders, as different from the radical differences that are portrayed as the norm in Santa Cruz; however, in Maracle's *Ravensong,* it is the white people who are portrayed as outsiders, as different from the central and centering Indian village of the novel.

The Native orientation of Maracle's novel gives the work a conversive base against which outside discursive forces impinge. Unlike Owens's novel, which discursively struggles against its own discursive boundaries, desperately trying to realize the conversive interrelationality that the novel idyllically achieves in the end, Maracle's novel tells the story of a family and a village desperately trying to maintain the last vestiges of their traditional lives against the imposition of the external boundaries (discursive and real) threatening to crash in upon them. The Indian village is challenged by the peoples' contact with the racism of white Canada and the erosion of traditional tribal spirituality by the combined forces of Christian missionizing, internalized racism, and secular materialism. The form of *Ravensong* is largely conversive; nevertheless, throughout the novel, the conversive connections that bind the people and the world together are threatened by discursive approaches to the world that deny the reality and power of conversivity and demand a continual jockeying back and forth between the construction and deconstruction of power relations and their shifting but ever present imbalances.

The essential conversivity of Maracle's *Ravensong* is evident throughout the work. Even the title represents the crucial interconnectedness of conversive relations. In an interview, Maracle explains that the title and the novel grew out of her own interpersonal and intersubjective relationship to Raven and Raven's song. As Maracle explains, "Raven is the harbinger of social transformation. Raven sings when the world itself is amiss. And some people hear that song. . . . I heard Raven's song, that's why I wrote *Ravensong*. When I hear Raven sing, I pay attention to that" (Kelly 85). In choosing *Ravensong* as the title of the novel, Maracle underscores the crucial importance of human interrelatedness with all of creation. This interrelatedness is specifically manifested in the person of Raven, whose song and message Maracle explains has transformative power, even back to the beginning of time. "Our origin story is that we begin as hidden form, we begin as spirit, mind, and heart, and then Raven calls us into physical being. . . . Raven is the transformer, or the harbinger of transformation, I should say, in our culture" (Kelly 75, 74). Such change is often beneficial, either providing the maintenance of balance, harmony, and personal and social stability, albeit in changing forms and conditions, or serving a remedial purpose in the restoration of balance and health. But change can also be destructive and lead to the disruption of the stability and health of individuals, families, communities, and the entire world. The sadomasochistic behavior of Padre Andrés Quintana in Owens's *Bone Game* has such effects not only on Quintana himself, but also more portentously and lastingly on the tribal community to which he has access. Destructive change can also move an already disrupted and diseased condition into ever increasing degrees of pain and degradation (as in Owens's depiction of the extreme contemporary depravity portrayed in *Bone Game*).

Whereas the destructive change of discursive power relations serves as the underlying 'grammar' of the predominant 'language game' in *Bone Game,* the underlying 'grammar' of *Ravensong* facilitates and emphasizes the articulation of conversive change and interconnectedness, even though that articulation and its concomitant realization are threatened by discursive disconnections. As Maracle says in an interview with Jennifer Kelly, "I don't so much think that it's a connection that we need to find. We have a connection already. It's a human connection. We have an earth connection; that's endangered, though" (74). This connectedness is what permeates *Ravensong,* even though at times those connections are ruptured due to the forced impositions of discursive worldviews and behaviors. From its beginning orientation, with Raven articulating her "deep wind song, melancholy green" (*Ravensong* 9), Maracle firmly grounds her novel within the domain of the mythical and the mystical by means of which the conversivity evident throughout the universe is realized and understood. Maracle expresses that this was a conscious concern of hers: "*Ravensong* tries real hard, without explicitly saying it, to begin with the spiritual and end with it" (Kelly 74).

Just a few pages into the novel, Stacey (the young woman around whom the novel ostensibly revolves) and a number of her relatives head home from a funeral for old Nora, who is described as having had an unhappy life. Stacey ponders the funeral at which few tears were shed and the local priest served his perfunctory purpose, even leaving before the burial was complete. For Stacey, Nora's life and funeral, the lack of tears shed, and the presence of the outside priest all serve as signs of the community's failure to successfully minister to their own internal needs. Stacey's ruminations present her as the young philosopher of the novel. We are explicitly told that she is generally considered to be the one who in her older years would succeed old Dominic in the crucial village role of "the care-taker of the law and philosophy" (95). However, Dominic's premature death due to an influenza epidemic creates a serious fissure in the spiritual and social fabric of the community. As Maracle writes, each death in the village, including that of old Nora, was a "loss [that] was total. An untimely death meant everyone lost a family clown, an herbalist, a spirit healer or a philosopher who seemed to understand conduct, law and the connection of one family member to another. Every single person served the community, each one becoming a wedge of the family circle around which good health and well-being revolved. A missing person became a missing piece of the circle which could not be replaced" (26). After a flu epidemic, the last epidemic the community fights together, "the world floated in, covering us in paralysing silence and over the next decade the village fell apart" (197). In an epilogue, Stacey, as a grown woman, comments on some of the changes that occurred before and after the period covered by the events of the novel. But within the bounds of *Ravensong,* the reader is shown a community whose fabric is conversively intertwined with a strength that still holds the families and the community together, even though that strength is becoming increasingly less solid and more tenuous.

The conversivity of the village relationships enables the community to weather hard times and to adapt to the changing conditions that are increasingly challenging the stability of the village and its members. But each erosion of the community's structure weakens it further. The epidemics caused by the diseases of the white Canadians and worsened by the refusal of many of the white doctors to help the Indian community prematurely robbed the people of too many of their elders too quickly, before replacements had been found. The institutionalized racism of white Canada prevented Stacey's village from having their own school and denied Native peoples the job opportunities available to the white Canadians, further eroding the community as more village members moved away to the larger cities in the hopes of finding work. Even though Stacey is a philosopher, she is too young to take Dominic's place, and her thinking has been problematically disoriented through her years of schooling across the river in white town. Maracle writes, Stacey's "analytic thoughts unfolded in shallow logic" (63–64). She couldn't understand Dominic's "way of talking to animals" (63), and her continual contact with white town left her conflicted about herself, her family, and her village.

Throughout the novel, Stacey's is the voice that straddles worlds and worldviews. Even though she loves her family and community, her approach to the world becomes increasingly discursive as she crosses the river each day. In white town, she sees the whites from the perspective of the Indian outsider whose best school friend never once asks her about her world in the Indian village. For her part, Stacey accepts and perpetuates this distance through her own silence about herself and her world. At times, she becomes overtly rebellious as she asserts her own presence in the world through a discursive rejection of the white power structures that oppress her people. When the principal of her high school orders detentions for her late arrivals, Stacey refuses the punishment:

> Well, I have decided I won't serve any late detentions for a while . . . sir. I was up all night with old Ella, dripping tea into her old bones, trying to save her from dying. I stopped by the river to watch the fish go upstream to spawn. It revived me in a crazy kind of way to think that these little fishes your people claim cannot think could be so passionate about life that they would risk death to procreate, even though at the end of spawning they are all sure to die. At the same time people like Polly choose not to live over a little thing like sex. (66–7)

Polly, a white student, had recently committed suicide after her sexual relationship with a boy in her class became public knowledge. Stacey finds incomprehensible the harsh judgmentalism of the white Christians that would drive a young woman to such an end. Stacey's own confusion, feelings of powerlessness in the white world, and anger at being continually reduced to an objectified subalterity all combine in her eventual eruption of disobedience. Stacey reacts with a discursive attack directed at the high school principal (whom she actually likes—a fact that makes the pathos of her attack that much more poignant). In her rejection of her punishment, "Stacey had just relieved Mr. Johnson of his authority over her. . . . The stripping of Mr. Johnson's authority made Stacey his equal" (67).

Stacey, in her rebellion against Mr. Johnson, who becomes the sign of an oppressive Eurocanadian racism, inadvertently ends up contributing to the very institutionalized discursivity that distances herself from the white community as its oppositional "other." Godard comments on this practice of deconstructive inversion that attempts to subvert the dominant power structures through a rupturing of their foundational claims: "Within this hegemonic order, s/he was constituted as object of the knowledge of subjects. However, through struggle, acquiring some of the strategies and structures of the dominant, the subaltern rises 'into hegemony,' this process constituting a *dis/placement* of the dominant discourse and strategies of hybridization that undermine its monolithic position of power" ("Politics" 193). What Godard does not point out are the very real destructive effects of any contribution to the process of discursive oppositional relations, this notwithstanding the fact that discursive inversions never completely subvert hegemonic power imbalances. Discursivity perpetuates oppositional imbalances even though who's on top and who's on bottom might change.

As Stacey gets caught up within the discursivity of white town, she brings her anger and frustration back home across the river and transfers her feelings of subalterity into a superior judgmentalism directed against her own. Stacey increasingly begins to perceive her own community and family through the oppositional eyes of the dominant white society. On rainy days when she arrived at school drenched from the walk from the village to white town, "she cursed [her parents] for not going to school, she cursed them for continuing to live like her grandparents had, as though this world had not changed. It was 1954, for gawd's sake" (24–25). And on the way home from old Nora's funeral, she criticizes not only the priest, but also her own community and way of life: "Although she doubted the assurances of everyone around her that Nora had lived a full life, Stacey knew why they had to say that to themselves. No one wanted to face the fact that life here at the edge of the world was empty for anyone" (13)—a statement that parallels Benally's attitude toward his Navajo homeland and his people during his harsher moments of criticism and internalized racism ("just the empty land and a lot of old people, going no-place and dying off" [Momaday, *House* 159]). Here Stacey virtually accuses her people of lying to themselves, lying about Nora's life, and lying about their own empty lives. But no matter how discursively and actually powerless Native lives may be within the oppositional structures of an institutionalized racism, as Stacey's urban Indian village community demonstrates, human lives are nevertheless meaningful and important within the rubric of conversively lived relationships.

The extent to which white Canada discursively devalues Native lives in terms of the institutionalized discourses of power in no way makes those lives meaningless in fact, even though that meaningfulness may be misrepresented, devalued, or altogether absented within the fictions of a racist discourse that perceives insignificance where there often is meaningfulness. Maracle writes, "The value of resistance is the reclaiming of the sacred and significant self" ("Oratory" 11). This is not the resistance that attempts to take discursive power through a disempowerment of others. The resistance that Maracle notes here is the resistance that is conversively empowering. But Maracle's voice is the voice of the Métis, straddling conversive and discursive worlds and positions. Even though the strongest emphasis is always laid upon the individual's and the community's rootedness within the domain of the sacred, the seductiveness of discursive battle pulls Stacey and Maracle into the struggles for discursive power. Maracle explains, "I want to know who is going to be there with me, resisting victimization—peacefully or otherwise—and always stubbornly and doggedly struggling to reclaim and hang on to my sacred self" ("Oratory" 11).

The difficulty Maracle finds in her struggle to "reclaim and hang on to [her] sacred self" is the essential conflict between discursive and conversive languages and worldviews. When she steps into the political struggle, the 'language game' is that of discursive oppositionality, and the underlying grammatical rules of that 'language game' or form of life are rules that preclude the conversive presence of the sacred (unless the sacred is narrowed and bounded by a discursive phallogocentric theology that redefines it within an institutionally hierarchized and oppositional framework). But this is not the sacred of conversive openness and the acceptance of difference.

The resistance that Maracle advocates and that Stacey manifests in her altercation with her high school principal parallels what Paulo Freire refers to as the conscientization of the oppressed. Freire emphasizes that the oppressed must learn "to perceive social, political, and economic contradictions, and to take action against the oppressive elements of reality" (19). As Freire explains, individuals need to unlearn their disempowered realities in the world and see the lie of the dominant discourse. This is the lie that Silko so powerfully elucidates in *Ceremony* as Tayo frees himself and the spotted cattle on Mt. Taylor: "He cut into the wire as if cutting away at the lie inside himself. The liars had fooled everyone, white people and Indians alike; as long as people believed the lies, they would never be able to see what had been done to them or what they were doing to each other. . . . [W]hite thievery and injustice boiling up the anger and hatred that would finally destroy the world: the starving against the fat, the colored against the white" (191). Silko and Tayo are both mixedbloods whose worldviews are strongly conversive. In fact, *Ceremony* traces Tayo's change from a discursive anger and self-hatred that is destroying himself and his growth through a conversive healing that centers him within the loving arms (literally in the mythical person of Tseh Montaño) of the sacred. For Silko, one needs to learn the lie, but not in order to fight back, as Freire advocates.

As Silko and Owens remind us, fighting back only feeds the witchery and continues the cycles of discursive and actual violence and oppression. Sarris (Coast Miwok/Pomo) notes the limits and dangers of the sort of dialogically oppositional pedagogy Freire suggests: "But dialogue can become a circumscribed mode of discourse that excludes, often unknowingly, the student's experience" (Sarris, *Keeping* 155). This is particularly the case for those students whose worldviews are largely conversive. Maracle (whose background combines a Métis/Cree-Salish heritage and an urban upbringing) lives and writes a world that bridges both discursive and conversive forms of life. But discursivity and conversivity are not simply two different ways of living and perceiving that can be interwoven into a harmonious fabric of diverse human lives and cultures.

Discursivity is definitionally in opposition to conversive ways of perceiving and living. The essence of discourse is oppositional. Its mode is oppositional. Its manifestations are oppositional. Hence the inevitable struggle involved in re-membering oneself in relation to the sacred. Yet, for Maracle, regardless of the real world oppositional struggles she writes about and lives, what is at the heart is, and must be, the spiritual: "the reclaiming of the sacred and significant self" ("Oratory" 11). Within a discursive framework, individual significance comes from one's own assertions of relative subjectivity through a concomitant disempowering objectification of some other. Within the domain of the conversive, individual meaningfulness comes from one's intersubjective interrelationships with other persons (human and otherwise) in the world. In *Ravensong,* this is part of the message that Raven keeps trying to get Stacey to hear. As Franchot Ballinger explains, such trickster figures serve to "encourage us to see the world through the collective social eye and thus beyond the individual self" (28).

Throughout *Ravensong,* Maracle interweaves the commentary of Raven, who has been watching the changes affecting the people and village community. Raven speaks directly to the people and to her companions, Cedar, Wind, Cloud, and Crow, but few of the people still possess the ability to understand the speech of nonhuman persons. Raven desperately tries to get Stacey to hear her cry, but Stacey is one who has lost the capacity to speak with the animals and other nonhumans. "She knew [old Dominic] had a way of talking to animals" (63), but for Stacey, such abilities were of the dying past. As often as Raven sings her song, Stacey still cannot understand the content of Raven's song, hearing only a raven making noise. One day, after a dialogue with a white boy interested in her, Stacey notices Raven in a tree near the bridge to the village. At first, it seems to her that Raven's cackling was directed at her. "Stacey's attention was drawn to the possibility of Raven having some design on her. She shook her head, convincing herself it was just a crow—a foolish crow" (75).[9]

In this one scene, Stacey's conflicted identity pulls her away from her natural inclinations toward the conversive (in which she responds to Raven's call and a male schoolmate interested in her) and into a discursive stance in oppositional distance to "a foolish crow" and her schoolmate Steve. As Raven cackles at Stacey, she is automatically drawn to Raven's call, noticing that Raven did seem "to be laughing at her" (75). But then Stacey's discursive presence rejects such intersubjective connections with a bird. Stacey does not even perceive Raven as a raven, convincing herself through her Western logic that Raven is just "a foolish crow," thereby denying Raven her ravenhood. By referring to Raven in such a fashion, Stacey also objectifies Raven's subjectivity by denying Raven her proper name as manifested in its capitalized form. No longer a subject with whom Stacey can intersubjectively relate, Raven's personhood and individuality are denied as Stacey reacts to Raven as only another "foolish crow." Stacey's objectification of Raven erases Raven from Stacey's perceived world of significance.[10] Within a discursive framework, only those with subjective status possess a signifying presence over those "others" whose subaltern signified condition is, in turn, contingent upon their passive attachment to some objectifying subject.

Stacey objectifies not only Raven and places her (Raven) under erasure, but also her schoolmate, Steve. As in her conflicted relationship with Raven, Stacey shifts back and forth in her relationship with Steve. When she separates the weeds in the back yard of a white friend in order to bring the medicinal comfrey leaves home, she finds herself opening up with Steve in a conversive manner and sharing with him aspects of her Indian world that she had never shared with any other white person. "For some reason she started telling him what each plant was and what the villagers used them for" (73). For a while, both Steve and Stacey converse comfortably, even to the point of a magical moment when Stacey laughs with him about her white friend's mother throwing valuable plants away as useless weeds. Here Stacey is conversively open with Steve just as she would be with another Indian. But then the discursive racism of white Canada intervenes and the vulnerability of such openness with a white boy presses Stacey back into a discursive mode: "then she got a little nervous. It was the first time she had taken any white boy into her confidence. Steve did not seem . . . to be affected by her taking him into her confidence. She had lurched onto dangerous territory without realizing it" (73). The institutionalized racism of white Canada has taught Stacey the dangers of openly relating in a conversive manner with non-Native peoples. The reserved and thoughtful Stacey openly laughs in a way that is rare for her, even with her own people, but she then catches herself and responds through her own objectification of Steve as the dangerous white "other." By virtue of the racist institutions of power that define their worlds, Steve is not a fellow person in the world with whom Stacey believes she can relate as a coequal subject. She reactively objectifies his humanity out of him as she refers to him as "the green lizard of human disruption we innocently let inside our houses" (74).

Previously, old Dominic had warned Stacey of such dangers, but in Dominic's telling, he was referring to the abusive Indian husband of Madeline, one of the village women. The warning was not about race, but about those human beings who have lost their own personhood and have descended to a level even lower than the animals. As Stacey protectively retreats into a discursive response to Steve, she places him in the same category as "the old snake who abused his wife" (74). But what Dominic told Stacey was the importance of avoiding such oppositional relations altogether. Stacey remembers Dominic's words: " 'Maybe humans want oneness with all humans. . . . Maybe the spirit is our source of affection and it gets trapped inside the layers of poison we are fed in the course of our lives.' Stacey realized now that Dominic had been warning her, not explaining Madeline's attachment to her vicious husband" (74). Dominic had warned Stacey about the "layers of poison" that infect people's spirits such that their open and loving intersubjective engagements with other persons in the world are impaired. Even though Dominic emphasizes the oneness of all human persons (regardless of the distinctions of race, gender, class, ethnicity), Stacey is understandably, even if not justifiably, afraid of Steve (a white male); she has been well taught the lessons of racism. She ends up crossing the bridge to the village without Steve, sending him off with scarcely a word.

The distance Stacey erects between herself and Steve is the distance of the racist and sexist barriers of the dominant white and androcentric history of Canada. Stacey's own objectifying perception of Steve as a conjoint symbol of the white oppression of Indian peoples and the male domination of women leaves Steve hurt and disempowered as she asserts her discursive power over him. "He had the same look on his face that Mr. Johnson [her principal] had. The slave had just given an order to the master, which made him an ex-master. Neither man knew what it was to be an ex-master, so both were confused and hurt" (75). Discursive relations necessarily empower at the expense of some "other's" inevitable disempowerment. When Stacy's white friend Carol (who is described as having no interest in Stacy's life in her Indian village [32]) objectifies Stacey as an Indian girl, she disappears her; and when Stacey objectifies Steve as the white enemy, she disappears him as well. Within the domain of discursivity, persons (human and nonhuman) in the world are objectified out of their own independent conversive realities and into the constructed realm of dyscursively codependent oppositional relations. Stacey's distancing of Steve is certainly understandable within the historical framework of Canadian racial relations, but it is clear that both Stacey and Steve lose out due to the sociohistorical conditions that push them apart.

Throughout *Ravensong,* Steve is the only young person (Indian or white) who really seems to value Stacey and the defining aspects of her personhood. He makes supreme efforts to court Stacey in terms of her cultural and idiosyncratic framework, even though the barriers that impede their knowing each other continually stymie his approaches toward her. Only rarely are the barriers let down such that they can relate in a conversive manner. However, the conversive pulls in their relationship are always presented as Stacey's and Steve's more natural and comfortable inclinations. The discursive stances that push them apart are presented as the constructed relations of three hundred years of a Eurocanadian racism against Canada's First Nations peoples.

Interestingly, the discursive relationship between Stacey and Steve parallels her disconnectedness with her own people and their traditions, with white people and their ways, and more specifically, with Raven. Where Steve serves as the sign for white society, Raven serves as the sign for traditional Indian ways. In both cases, it is Stacey who objectifies Raven and Steve and who rejects any substantive conversive relations with either the young man or the bird. Poignantly, Stacey rejects even the possibility of intersubjective relations with both through her denial of their essential conversive personhood. When Stacey leaves Steve at the bridge, we are told, "She decided to turn the lizard out at the arc of the bridge" (75). Immediately thereafter, Raven critiques Stacey's behavior. Stacey ignores Raven, "convincing herself it was just a crow—a foolish crow" insignificant to Stacey (75). In response to Stacey's disregard, "Raven straightened up, thrust her head forward, letting go an indignant shriek. Stacey flinched, focussed her gaze on the rest of the trek home, and thought no more about Raven" (75). Here and elsewhere throughout the novel, it is Raven who serves as the reminder of the importance of conversive connectivity to all of creation. Raven's shriek attempts to wake Stacey and the village people to the dangerous changes facing them, but in their rejection of Raven, Stacey and her people displace themselves further away from their village world.

The barrage of epidemics leave a genocidal legacy of death and disease that also serves as the sign of the people's increasing dis-ease in a world that pulls them out of their own realities in the world and that permits them no other place than in the interstice between their world of the village (a world that is being eroded ever more quickly) and the domain of a racist and phallogocentric society. Raven's silence through the majority of the second half of the novel ominously signals the continuing erosion of the village world. Is this silence due to Raven's absence or incapacity to speak, or is this a perceived silence on the part of the remaining characters who, unlike old Dominic, are no longer capable of hearing and understanding Raven's song?

The novel begins with Raven singing her mourning song of a dying world. Raven's song is picked up by wind, who continues the song with wind's own input. "Wind changed direction, blowing the song toward cedar. Cedar picked up the tune" (9). Cloud continues the song as Raven weeps. In Maracle's description of the natural chorus singing a mourning song for the village people (and, in fact, for the entire earth and its inhabitants), Maracle exemplifies the conversive reality of different singers whose voices and words speak to and with each other. And each singer's contribution is transformed by the singing of the other singers. Raven sees the coming catastrophe (the eventual destruction of the village), but Raven understands that even catastrophic change is part of the world's cycles of transformation. "Change is serious business. . . . Humans call it catastrophe. Just birth, Raven crowed. Human catastrophe is accompanied by tears and grief, exactly like the earth's, only the earth is less likely to be embittered by grief" (14). Old Dominic tried to get Stacey to understand that the way of the village people was to respond in this conversive manner such that sufferings are grieved over, but not to the extent of becoming embittered by "the layers of poison we are fed in the course of our lives" (74).

As Raven sings her song of change and suffering, rain and cedar weep, but Raven explains that catastrophic change may be necessary to finally get the attention of the human beings (Indian and non-Indian) who have forgotten how to understand Raven's song. *Ravensong* tells the story not only of Raven's warning song, but also of the people's distance from Raven—a distance that incapacitates any sort of sustained conversive response on the part of the people to Raven and to her song. Yet the conversive pulls of community and family are still strong, even if the connections to past tribal traditions are eroding with ever greater rapidity. As Stacey gets ready to leave the village for college, the conversive pulls of the village and her family enfold Stacey when everyone in the village comes to visit and offer her advice. All are involved in her leaving. Even Raven reappears, after a lengthy absence throughout much of the book, although only as an observer. This time, Raven remains silent—a portentous silence that indicates that there is no one left in the village to listen to Raven. Old Dominic talked to the animals, and he was grooming Stacey to eventually become the philosopher and lawgiver of the village in her older years. But Dominic's premature death cut short Stacey's tutelage and stole the last member of the village capable of speaking with the animals in the old ways.

The conversive spirit underlying the reality of all human beings (even though that reality has been severely compromised and silenced through the discursive divisions and oppositions that destroy interpersonal connectivity) survives nonetheless, even in its apparent absence. As Stacey's mother considers her daughter's upcoming departure from the village, she "hope[s] the Raven spirit that snapped behind Stacey's eyes would not be culled out of her by [the] inhumanity" of non-Indian people (193). Raven's presence on the eve of Stacey's leaving serves as the reminder that conversive relations and communication throughout all of creation are still possible. Raven is still there and is still watching over Stacey and her people—perhaps simply waiting for someone to listen. The world for Stacey and her village community has irretrievably changed. Raven's silence signifies this fact. But the change does not signify the impossibility of conversive relations even in light of the eroding and divisive forces of discursive oppositionality in whatever forms they may take (e.g., the forms of racism, sexism, ageism, classism, ethnocentrism, and logocentrism). In light of such divisiveness, the domain of conversivity and the sacred has been decentered from the heart of people's interpersonal relations, but decentering is not necessarily destruction.

Raven may be shut out from the everyday lives of the village people, but Raven is still there. If the conversive call of the sacred and the mythical is unheard, that does not mean that the call is no longer present, nor, for that matter, incapable of being heard. Earth and Raven watch as the village readies Stacey for her departure. Earth weeps for the weakening of the village and for the villagers who do not see the impending dissolution of their community and the underlying fabric that has held it together for generations. But as Raven understands (as did Dominic), the spiritual alienation of the village people is emblematic of the spiritual disconnectedness of all peoples. No longer is human interaction limited within small tribal or village groups; all must learn to live together with the conversiveness that signifies human interrelations informed by the centrifugal force of the sacred, which holds all together within its universe. As Maracle writes,

> Both the earth and Raven knew all the people belonged to them. Raven could never again be understood outside the context of the others. . . . The earth wept for the tragedy that would next befall the villagers. She knew there was no other way for them to understand white town without this next change. Until the villagers began to feel as ugly inside as the others, none could come forward to undo the sickness which rooted the others to their own ugliness. (191)

In a discursively embattled world, no individual or group can live conversively with those whose reality and behaviors are essentially discursive. If the conversive domain of the sacred is to return to the earth, it must include all peoples, not only the people of the village. As Stacey doubts her leaving on her last night in the village, Raven steps forward and brings Stacey's grandmother into her dreams. Gramma tells her, "We will never escape sickness until we learn how it is we are to live with these people. We will always die until the mystery of their being is altered" (192). Here anthropological analysis of the other is inverted in a conversive manner in which the understandings of diverse peoples prove necessary for multicultural and multiracial harmony. In regards to interpersonal interactions and understandings, Hallowell writes, "Consequently, it seems to me, it is of some importance to determine what aspects of culture are relevant to perception, how they become involved in the perceptual experience of individuals, the role they play in the total structuralization of the perceptual field and the consequences of this fact for the actual conduct of the individual" ("Cultural Factors" 170). Such knowledge is significant for any group or individual in relation to any other group or individual. As Stacey's Gramma tells her in a dream, perhaps in this way, balance and harmony will be restored in the world.

Whereas Cole McCurtain in *Bone Game* needs to be extricated from the dangerous web of the discursive and evil power games surrounding him in Santa Cruz (necessitating that he leave California and return home to the Sandia Mountains east of Albuquerque), Stacey (whose Indian identity has been more firmly rooted in her family's and village's traditions) must be sent out into the world beyond her village to learn new/old ways of living and being in the world. For Cole, the issue is his reconnection with the real power of the sacred as manifested in the traditional Indian spiritual ways of his mixedblood relatives, and his disconnection with the disempowering forces of discursive relations. Stacey, on the other hand, has been reared in the interconnected web of her family and village, but the discursively realized racism of the dominant society has infected her as well as others in the village. In order to heal, she first needs to leave the village to learn a new conversive language that is stronger and more inclusive than that of her village. "Ahead lay a land of strangeness—a crew of sharp-voiced people almost unintelligible to the people behind them" (196). Stacey's leaving facilitates her eventual transformation into a new language and way of living in the world that includes whites and other non-Indians along with Indian people.

Conversivity knows no boundaries and excludes no one. In order for Raven's song to return, all need to begin learning to communicate as fellow persons in the world, white and Indian alike. Stacey's hard times lie before her—difficulties that are necessary for her eventual return to the sacred. In *Bone Game,* we see Cole in the grip of the evil of the world, but his sickness and pain are the catalyst for his healing through the conversive love and guidance of his family and Indian friends. Stacey's sufferings are yet to come. In a brief epilogue to the novel, a much older Stacey explains to her son that the sufferings and losses of their people were due to the absence of the sacred, the absence of the transforming power of conversive relations, in three words: "Not enough Raven" (198). She and her sister, mother, and friend tell young Jacob the story of the sufferings of their family and people. In their telling and tears, Stacy's mother digs out an old and long unused hand drum, and the four women sing an old grieving song, perhaps the very song sung by Raven, wind, cedar, and rain at the beginning of the novel. After twenty-five years of difficult times living in the dominant white society, Stacey and her family finally remember Raven—but many years were needed to finally remind them of the importance of Raven and of returning to Raven's conversively transformative song.

Sherman Alexie's First Indian on the Moon

The straddling of words and worlds evident within the writing of mixed-blood writers can also be seen in the works of Indian writers whose writing is much more tribally informed. Swearingen notes, "most discourse is structured by both written and oral conventions. A given speaker or writer is, at any given time, choosing and mixing from a number of such conventions" (149). Accordingly, we should expect to find a diversity of ways in which Indian people reflect the juxtaposition of discursive and conversive literary forms. In the writings of Sherman Alexie, we see many of the same elements noted in Maracle's and Owens's novels. Alexie's poems and stories in *First Indian on the Moon* embrace both discursive and conversive styles in a conjunction that is inevitably disjunctive, disconcerting, and effective in communicating his worlds and words. Alexie, an enrolled member of the Spokane tribe through his mother (his father is Coeur d'Alene), writes in a powerful voice that speaks the realities of worlds that continually push each other to the point of discursive and actual implosion. Whether the results are burning cars, a trailer fire, alcoholism, domestic or racial violence, smallpox blankets, broken treaties, or human alienation and loneliness, for Alexie, the process is always the same: the clash of worlds that rarely gives more than temporary (and in fact illusory) respite from the unfulfilled dreams and lived pain that is the reality on either side of the divide.

Unlike Maracle and Owens, Alexie grew up on an Indian reservation (Spokane). Alexie (also a generation younger than both Maracle and Owens) writes the harsh contrast between the world that he grew up in and the American Dream. The hopes that Maracle and Owens center in the conversive forms of the sacred, be those forms articulated by Raven or Onatima, take on the shape of a crushed aluminum can in Alexie's writing: "Pick up a chair and smash it against the walls, swing it so hard that your arms ache for days afterwards, and when all you have left in your hands are splinters, that's what we call history. Pick up an aluminum can and crush it in your fingers, squeeze it until blood is drawn, and when you cannot crush the can into any other shape, that's what we call myth" (38). The history that is one of broken treaties, smallpox blankets, racial genocide and cultural deicide, unemployment, shoddy HUD homes,[11] urban relocation, commodity food, and trading post shelves lined with Spam, white bread, soda pop, and candy is the history of defeat that Alexie rails against in the image of a smashed chair—the sign of a disempowering frustration and anger turned inward in a self-destructiveness that results in sore arms, splinters in one's hands, and one less piece of furniture in one's home. Within the worlds Alexie lives and portrays in his writing, neither history nor myth have left a legacy of strength and survival, of hope and dream. The traditional strength of myth has eroded to the forces of the church, the state, and manifest destiny, leaving a hollow emptiness that can be destroyed no more effectively than a crushed aluminum can will bring back the beer, stop one's parents from drinking, or destroy the emptiness of a life without hope.

Throughout Alexie's writing, he displays a critically discursive stance against virtually anyone and anything. This is an equal-opportunity anger that perceives the weaknesses and failures of both Indian and white worlds. Like Maracle and Owens, Alexie lives and writes in the interstices between the divergent stories of different worlds, what he refers to as "the in-between / between tipi and HUD house / between magic and loss" (43). In "Reservation Mathematics," the reality of the in-between is expressed in the pain of living a legacy of collusive duplicity.

> Mixed-up and mixed-blood
> I sometimes hate
> the white in me[12]
> when I see their cruelty
> and I sometimes hate
> the Indian in me
> when I see their weakness
>
> (43)

Alexie speaks the cruelty and weakness that are also depicted by Owens and Maracle in *Bone Game* and *Ravensong*. Be it the cruelty of Padre Quintana and the contemporary serial murderers, the weakness that sickens and incapacitates Cole McCurtain, the cruelty of the white doctors who refuse to cross the bridge to the Indian village to save Indian lives, communities, and cultures, the weakness of the Indian lives lost to the epidemics of curable diseases, or the cruelty and weakness that are part of any discursively lived life, all three of these writers portray the desires and fears embedded in the disempowering processes involved in those discursive attempts to gain subjectivity in worlds and words that have relegated Indian people to the domain of objectified silence and displaced absence.

And yet, the interstice is not only a place of pain and anguish, but also a place in which lives are born and lived with joy as well as with pain. When human lives come together in the loves and joys of fancydancers, basketball players, and lovers, then the conversive magic of human interrelationships transforms the interstice into the here and now as meaningful as any here and now anywhere on the planet. The reservation dreams of the fancy-dancers and the basketball players are the same dreams of all human beings trapped within the discursive lies of oppositional relations, relative (in)sig-nificance, subjective power, and objective weakness. Within a discursive framework, all dream "of a life larger than this one" (43)—of lives uncon-strained by the linear walls that define and differentiate inside from out-side, success from failure, subject from object. As Alexie writes, "It doesn't matter if it's a triangle, rectangle, or square. They're all the direct opposite of a circle. I've been dreaming of a life / with a new shape" (43), a life in which Indian people fit, a spherical planet on which circles and lines con-join with the inclusiveness that makes room for all peoples. The fractionat-ing and divisive mathematics of a racist society ("the 3/16 that names me white / and the 13/16 / that names me Indian" [43]) separates people not only from each other, but also from themselves in a personal schizophrenia where struggles to survive inevitably prove self-destructive.

Alexie writes, "An Indian man drowned here on my reservation when he passed out and fell down into a mud puddle. There is no other way to say this" (40). Within the domain of discursivity, one is either subject or object. If the dominant discourse is that of affluent white America, Indian Amer-ica has few other options beyond that of objectified others passing out and drowning in mud puddles. What a generation ago was a joke on the comedic soap opera *Mary Hartman Mary Hartman,* in which one character fell asleep and drowned in his chicken noodle soup, in the real world of reservation America becomes the tragedy of a man's death. From the per-spective of the subaltern, the humor of the dominant discourse becomes hollow as the jokes turn on the "other" in the form of everyday lived trage-dies and sufferings. Yet even in the pain manifested in a desperately egocen-tric lyric that discursively struggles to assert the oppressed self, Alexie transforms that discursive style into a poetic medium that communicates the fear, pain, and anger of a divisive world through its contrast with the life-giving force of conversive interrelationships. The power of such con-nections pervades virtually every piece in *First Indian on the Moon*—in either its presence or its painful absence. In Alexie's brief telling of the mud puddle drowning, he communicates the pathos of that loss, particularly in his emphasis that the reality must be communicated in its facticity and history: "There is no other way to say this" (40). The anonymity of the man signifies his condition in the world as a nonperson, an unnamed object, the loss of which is discursively insignificant. But to Alexie, this man is neither object, nor anonymously distant. He is an *Indian* man who, Alexie tells us, "drowned *here* on *my* reservation" (40; emphasis added). Alexie reaches out and conversively communicates his own loss in this man's loss, one more human erasure for Indian America, one more erased American Indian in the history of manifest destiny, one less [non]person on his reservation. As Alexie's telling makes poignantly clear, this man's loss is neither insignificant nor meaningless and definitely worth the telling.

Whether it is in the example of the three Indian winos of "Freaks," the racist stares in a Perkins restaurant in "Seven Love Songs," the clumsiness of a waiter in "Billy Jack," or the pained patience of children waiting for hours in a car while their parents drink in an Indian bar ("Influences"), Alexie lays bare the discursive lies of centuries of broken treaties and eternities of diseased blankets. Yet even in his anger, the anger of generations of frustration, despair, and hopelessness, the dreams of reservation basketball players comes through consistently and powerfully—even when those dreams are sought in a cheap bottle of wine. The dreams of treaties that won't be broken, the dreams of loves that will mend the torn weavings of broken relationships and families, the dreams of the conversive power of myth, all these survive even beyond the pain of loss. "I would steal horses / for you, if there were any left, / . . . / I would offer my sovereignty, take / every promise as your final lie, . . . / I would wrap us both in old blankets / hold every disease tight against our skin" (55). In a poem directed to a Jewish woman, Alexie relates, "we are both survivors and children / and grandchildren of survivors" (80). Even with the horrific legacies of Sand Creek and Wounded Knee or Auschwitz and Buchenwald, there is a transformative power within the conversive relationships of *First Indian on the Moon* that enables hope, survival, and love. As Alexie emphasizes in his poem "Split Decisions,"

> When the bell rang at the end of the fight
> after Joe Frazier had floored Ali with a left hook
> you must remember that Muhammad Ali was still standing
>
> he stood up.
>
> (91)

In the additional spacing before the final three words, Alexie emphasizes the importance of survival, especially in the face of defeat. In Muhammad Ali's survival and success in his first lost fight, Alexie reaches out beyond the poem, speaking directly to his listener-readers in the conversive second-person voice of the traditional storyteller ("you must remember"). Alexie's conversive voice shift to his readers pulls them into the poem, insisting on their involvement in the world of this poem, in the world of Alexie's conversive experience and reading of the Frazier/Ali fight. As Michael Castro writes in a review of Alexie's *The Lone Ranger and Tonto Fistfight in Heaven,* "It is an atmosphere drenched with alcoholism, hopelessness and despair. But the stories tend to engage rather than depress the reader" ("Indian" 5C). Regardless of the content of Alexie's writing (both in prose and poetry), the connective pathways among writer, writing, and reader are continually delineated and made navigable for his listener-readers.

In Alexie's love poems directed to specific women, there is an analogous openness that is, however, more guarded by the protective walls that cir-cumscribe those relationships. Here the poems open themselves up to their readers whose roles are, nevertheless, defined as outsiders, yet at times, welcome voyeurs. In the voice shifts spoken directly to his readers, Alexie opens himself up most fully and conversively through direct second-person address, often in the form of authorial explanations directed to the reader ("There is no other way to say this" [40, 90]), and most powerfully in the one shift to his tribal language in the final and title poem of the volume in which he expresses his love for his wife.

> I love you
> and I will say it in my own language
> I'll say it in the little piece
> of my own language that I know
> and I'll say it like it's the last thing I'll ever say:
>
> quye han-xm=enc, quye han-xm=enc, quye han-xm=enc.
>
> (116)

Within the intimate domain of a love poem, a conversive style is more the norm than that of discourse (unless it is a poem that focuses on rejection, impediments to the relationship, or other divisive oppositions). But conversivity in a love poem is safe. The poem speaks the closed world of the lovers—a world the reader penetrates, but rarely beyond the outside role as voyeur. Even though the published poem opens itself up to many readers, the poem and its conversive world are nevertheless bounded by their own limits.

Throughout *First Indian on the Moon,* Alexie repeatedly draws the boundaries between Indian and non-Indian worlds, lives, and realities, and yet the 'language games' played out by these boundaries shift throughout the work. In places, the boundaries take on discursively combative forms: for example, where Alexie writes, "Every song remains the same here in America, this country of the Big Sky and Manifest Destiny, this country of John Wayne and broken treaties. . . . Extras, Arthur, we're all extras" (104). The lines are drawn between "America" and the worlds of Indian lives, and it is clear that these lines are the divisive lines of racism, explicitly designed to exclude and erase. In Alexie's voice shift in this final section of a long poem, "My Heroes Have Never Been Cowboys," he underscores the effects of the racist exclusions of America as he turns away from his reader to speak to a fellow Indian ("Extras, Arthur, we're all extras"). As extras in the Great American Western, American Indian peoples are incidental, scarcely significant within the definitional boundaries of the 'language game' of Manifest Destiny. By the end of the poem, Alexie can only speak to a fellow Indian, a fellow extra, because his voice is incidental, insignificant within the boundaries of Manifest Destiny.

Yet, even in the very discursively rooted history that underlies the poem, Alexie continues to shift back and forth between discursive and conversive voices—at times speaking directly and confidentially to the reader, at other times pushing any non-Indian reader away and explicitly speaking to fellow Indian people. When he writes, "Did you know that in 1492 every Indian instantly became an extra in the Great American Western?" (102), Alexie speaks to all of his readers (Indian and non-Indian alike), providing the necessary information for the poem that follows, much as a storyteller who adds the needed information for the listeners to become a part of the story. And when Alexie writes, "We've all killed John Wayne more than once" (103), the "we" includes his readers, but mainly Indian readers. Here the non-Indian reader is positioned outside the poem but welcomed as the outside reader. Ironically, the moments of discursive oppositionality are also some of the moments of greatest openness and vulnerability in Alexie's writing. When Alexie turns away from the reader to speak directly to Arthur, he opens up intimate Indian-only space to non-Indian readers, thereby providing a powerfully conversive entry into his world. As Wittgenstein notes, "Language is a labyrinth of paths. You approach from *one* side and know your way about; you approach the same place from another side and no longer know your way about" (*PI* 203e). Although discursivity and conversivity are mutually exclusive methods of communication in their essential forms, they are often brought together in the works of Indian writers whose lives and stories straddle divergent worlds and words. Owens, Maracle, and Alexie demonstrate that discursive and conversive 'language games' can overlap and interweave in a variety of ways. As Grant emphasizes for readers of Indian literatures, "There must be a recognition of how each writer adapts the Western literary forms and language to the writer's particular vision as a Native writer in society" ("Content" 14).

In Alexie's poem, "My Heroes Have Never Been Cowboys," he demonstrates how ostensibly discursive strategies (e.g, turning away from the reader to speak in a third-person voice to another) can be transformed through the conversive worldviews and methods of the oral tradition and the sacred. Discursive literary structures are thereby reinformed and reconstructed beyond oppositions and into an inclusiveness that welcomes rather than combats. Even in Alexie's anger, there is a graciousness that opens worlds and words to strangers. Even in the final line of the final poem of the volume, "quye han-xm=enc, quye han-xm=enc, quye han-xm=enc" (116), in offering his love in his own language, "in the little piece / of my own language that I know" (116), Alexie opens himself and his world to not only his wife, but also his readers. Within a discursive framework, the language shift serves to push non-Spokane readers away, but within a conversive reading, this shift to the Spokane language offers his readers a powerfully conversive entry into the worlds of *First Indian on the Moon*. This "little piece" of his own language is a precious and powerful gift depending on how it is read and used. As Wittgenstein profoundly reminds us, it is all a question of how we wend our ways through the labyrinthine paths of our words and worlds.

If we expect and demand straight pathways, we never will be able to navigate through and into worlds and words whose realities are much more developed and complex than those of oppositional struggle. It's ironic, but the horrors and complexities of our world are really very simple to understand, the same insecure story played out over and over and over again. Owens, Maracle, and Alexie present this story in its diverse manifestations, particularly in relation to the horrific history of the European, Euroameri-can, and Eurocanadian legacies of racism against American Indian and Canadian First Nations peoples. But it is the story of the sacred, not that of secular struggle,[13] that gives lives their profundity and depth. Blaeser points out the particular power of American Indian literatures and identifies it as rooted in the sacred: "Native American literature, by rejecting orthodoxy and requiring vital engagement in the questions of life, becomes itself a spiritual force" ("Pagans" 30). Maracle emphasizes that for Indian peoples, story and the sacred are inextricably intertwined. "It's all story, memory stored up. And coming to grips with our spiritual subjectivity, coming to grips with it socially and personally" (in Kelly 85). In the works of mixed-blood, Métis, and tribally affiliated Indian writers, the sacred speaks out strongly both in its presence and in its absence. Such presence and absence are manifested in writing to the extent that the writing is conversively informed or discursively constructed. Godard explains, "What character-izes the oral text is its interactive, communal nature, which transgresses the author(ity) in the written text. For the bounded nature of this latter is exploded as the text embraces the shifting relations of author to listener, listener to context and both to extratextual history" ("Voicing" 91). It is the centering force of the sacred that inclusively enables readers to interact interrelationally with the words and worlds of Native North America in truly transformative ways.

Owens, Maracle, and Alexie all demonstrate the necessity of the sacred—be that as a means of surviving the horrific legacy of centuries of sado-masochistic violence, of surviving the erosion of traditional communities through the effects of foreign diseases and their deadly epidemics, or of surviving the more recent ravages of alcoholism, poverty, unemployment, and hopelessness. It is the sacred that is at the heart of any conversive communication, that is at the heart of any coming together, a fact made poignantly clear by each of these writers, albeit in very different ways. In all three works, it is the voice of the sacred interweaving the conversive in its varying forms of prayer, myth, interpersonal love, interspecies relation-ships, dreams, visions, and hope; and it is the voice of conversive faith coming through most powerfully, even in those moments of ostensive dis-cursive struggle. Alexie writes,

Believe me, the Indian men are rising from the alleys and doorways,
rising from self-hatred and self-pity, rising up on horses of their own
making. Believe me, the warriors are coming back

> to take their place beside you
> rising
> beyond the "just surviving"
> singing
> those new songs
> that sound
> exactly
> like the old ones.

(108–9)

Building on Alexie's comments in this poem, I would like to note that
American Indian and Canadian First Nations writers are many of these
new "warriors" who are "singing / those new songs that / sound / exactly /
like the old ones." Although the words may be different, spoken in the
languages of the European colonizers (English, French, and Spanish), and
although those words may take on new forms, written with the tools of the
Western literary tradition, nevertheless, these writers are speaking and
singing their own songs and stories as have their (and our) ancestors since
time immemorial. In so doing, these writers are in the vanguard transforming late-twentieth-century writing back into the storytelling it has been
throughout the ages through a reinfusion of the vital force of the sacred as
manifested in conversive storytelling.

The diversity that exists within the body of American Indian literatures
speaks out strongly against any attempts to reduce those literatures within
the bounds of any set of preconceived critical theories—especially those that
are largely defined within Western literary frameworks. William M. Clements notes, "preconceptions about 'the Indian' and about literature prevent
our understandings of moral orally informed literatures" (1). As is evident in the range of literary strategies and orientations chosen by Owens,
Maracle, and Alexie, each individual writer offers her or his stories in ways
that provide various means of entry into their works. In some cases, the
writing, like that of Owens, is more finely literary, presenting a story that
is largely to be read from without, but with conversively informed vi-
gnettes that serve to bring the reader in more closely as a listener-reader. In
Maracle's novel and Alexie's poetry, their voices are more consistently con-

versive in form, albeit with meaningful shifts to discursive positions that protectively, defensively, and aggressively push their readers away through the expression of generations and centuries of anger and frustration. Of course, how conversive and discursive elements are intertwined in specific stories and texts can vary both within one work and within the range of writing of particular writers, with some work tending more toward a conversive storytelling voice and other writing reflecting a more textually oriented, literary discourse. The conversive-discursive divide is a fluid continuum, and much like the Continental Divide that marks the point of directional and continental flow, different works of literature find their places along that continuum tending more in one direction or the other.

PART THREE

TRANSFORMING LITERARY RELATIONS

... That's the story, words
finding themselves, discovering each other,
always seeking the necessary vision
they must have ... and then back again,
better off this time, ending and beginning.

—Simon Ortiz, *After and Before the Lightning*

EPILOGUE

Conversive Literary Relations and James Welch's
Winter in the Blood

O ur world and our lives are continually changing, and therefore, our
stories need to change and evolve, too. As literary scholars, we tell our
own stories/scholarship to provide helpful pathways into various literatures
for ourselves, our colleagues, and our students. This volume tells the story
of a new role for literary scholars that actually is the resurrection of the age-
old role of storytellers. In *Ceremony* by Silko (Laguna Pueblo), Betonie tells
a new story that is, at the same time, an age-old mythic story and also Tayo's
story; it is Betonie's own personal story, too, all three interwoven into the
new story that heals Tayo and those close to him through their participation
in the story. I see literary scholars in much the same light as Betonie—
guides assisting themselves and others along all of our respective pathways
into and through the stories (told, read, and lived) that we encounter. But
this new-old role means becoming listener-readers who respond, co-create,
and transform the stories and ourselves through conversive interrelationships with/in literature.

The transformative aspect of conversive language use is intertwined
with the spiritual idea of conversion—not in the sense of sectarian conversion, but in the sense of the growth, renewal, and healing that are part of the
sacred. Lee Maracle (Métis/Cree-Salish) explains, "We regard words as
coming from original being—a sacred spiritual being. . . . Words are not
objects to be wasted. They represent the accumulated knowledge, cultural
values, the vision of an entire people or peoples" ("Oratory" 7). And Simon
Ortiz (Acoma) explains, "We begin to regard language too casually, thereby
taking it for granted, and we forget the sacredness of it. Losing this regard, we become quite careless with how we use and perceive with language. We forget that language beyond the mechanics of it is a spiritual

force. Language is more than just a functional mechanism. It is a spiritual energy that is available to all. It includes all of us and is not exclusively in the power of human beings—we are part of that power as human beings"(*Song* 6). Within American Indian stories (oral and/or written), the sacred is manifested in the conversive relations that interweave all parts of the story (including teller and listener) together. This necessitates a scholarship that is conversively relational rather than critically divisive, as well as a scholarship that is accessible to a relatively wide range of readers.

A conversive scholarship significantly diverges from the discursive realm of much of contemporary academic scholarship, in which knowledge is defined in terms of distinctions, differences, and isolable individualities, and in which the scholar manifests a discursive power over her/his objects of study—a power often reflected in a scholarly language inaccessible to anyone besides other scholars. Silko tells us, "I think the work should be accessible, and that's always the challenge and task of the teller—to make accessible perceptions that the people need" ("Stories and Their Tellers" 22). Maracle comments, "Power resides with the theorists so long as they use language no one understands" ("Oratory" 10). Ideally, conversive scholarship moves scholars into this new-old role that includes, not necessarily a simplistic writing style and diction, but certainly work whose accessibility extends beyond the limited domain of the higher ranks of academia. Conversing with and within a written story necessitates a language that does not impede our entry into its story world. Language can facilitate interconnections in the world, and language can also serve as barriers to those connections.

In fact, as I completed the first draft of this book, I listened to my own words and writing and noticed the ways in which my own scholarship and writing evolved throughout the course of this work and developed a more conversive style, tone, and voice. The chapters that were written first were actually less conversive in practice, even though they talked about conversivity in American Indian literatures. These early chapters were more discursive and distancing, in the fashion of the Western literary critical tradition of scholarly objectivity. However, as this book evolved, so did my own writing and scholarship as it became more conversively intimate and relational. The transformational aspect of conversive relations that I was noting within American Indian literatures, and that I was talking *about,* actually transformed my own perspective as a literary scholar and transformed my own scholarship and writing as I began to talk *with* the storytellers, scholars, and character-persons in the stories, all of whom became part of this work. Of course, this necessitated my going back over the earlier chapters and rewriting them to fit more closely within the conversive mode of a storytelling literary scholarship.

Scholars who take such a conversively relational approach to literature enter into an intimacy with stories, thereby involving the scholarship in the larger conversation of life that runs through the literary works and into our own lives. Susie O'Brien suggests, "As readers—as academic readers—we need to continue to look for ways of achieving such an engagement . . . , as Maracle does, with the complexities and contradictions of history" (94–95). Gloria Bird (Spokane) points out, "We must also be willing to attempt to 'see the world differently'" ("Towards" 4). This is especially important in relation to discussions of written stories because, all too often, these writings have been objectified as static texts for critical interpretation. Hirsch notes that writing "is static; it freezes words in space and time. . . . [and] writing removes the story from its immediate context, . . . and thus robs it of much of its meaning" (1). Jack Goody and Ian Watt note "that writing establishes a different kind of relationship between the word and its referent, a relationship that is more general and more abstract" (321). Writing definitely does enable a greater degree of textualization than has been the tradition within oral modes of communication, thereby resulting in the stasis, abstraction, and distancing that Hirsch, Goody, and Watt note. However, pointing out ways by which Silko infuses her writing with the "flexibility and inclusiveness of the oral tradition," Hirsch explains, "Even writing can be made to serve its [the oral tradition's] ends" (2). Wiget notes this conjunction of the oral within the written in Simon Ortiz's work: "The viability of those [tribal] traditions is something Ortiz reinforces in almost every poem or story, by adopting a distinctly 'oral' voice, directly addressing the reader, catching the local pronunciation, casting his work into narrative" (*Simon Ortiz* 49). Ortiz tells us that he began to write largely out of the recognition that "language to me was magic, magic in its purest essence, magic that can create, change, rebuild" ("Always" 57). This transformative power is present in all language that is conversive, co-creative, relational, and intersubjective. And as such transforming language can be manifested in both oral and written forms, just as discursive textuality can be manifested in written or oral forms.

The implications of the orality of American Indian (and other) literatures for literary scholars are manifold, most specifically necessitating substantial shifts in how we perceive, interpret, and evaluate writing whose structures and effects are less textual and discursive and more oral and conversive. Finnegan reminds us, "oral literature is still a living art and there is constant interplay between oral and written forms" ("Literacy" 115). And Greg Sarris (Coast Miwok/Pomo) explains, "Dialogue, self-reflexivity, polyphony, and bifocality characterize many of the newer ethnographic endeavors and textual recreations of oral literature" ("Verbal Art" 109). The conjunctive nature of American Indian literatures (and most literatures) that interweave oral and written traditions together into stories that we refer to as literature demands conversive listening-reading strategies. As Krupat surmises, "a decision in favor of orality or textuality appears to imply correlative choices between performative effectivity or linguistic/referential accuracy, and (so it would seem) between a disciplinary commitment to science or to literature" ("Post-Structuralism" 118). The scholar who chooses to engage American Indian literatures (or, for that matter, any literatures) in a conversive manner brings her or his work and self into the storytelling world of the literatures and essentially tells her or his own new story of that interaction, in much the same manner as Betonie, who demonstrates the importance of new and changing stories and ceremonies for his own life and for those who participate in his stories. Krumholz writes, "In Native American oral traditions, language is neither a lens offering a mimetic representation nor a problematic social structure—language has the power to create and transform reality" (94). This creative and transformative force can also be a part of literary scholarship, but only when it takes on the form and reality of conversive communication, when literary scholarship becomes the storytelling that it always was within more orally based cultures. As many American Indian writers are showing us today, our writing can be infused with the conversive power of orality, both within literary works and within literary scholarship.

Wiget raises the important question of "whether it is possible to write as an Indian apart from the Anglo-authored discourse of Indianness" ("Identity" 261). Clearly, identity politics notwithstanding, American Indian writers demonstrate varying degrees of conversive relations and discursive oppositions within their work (as discussed in Chapter 6). Scholars as listener-readers will need to explore various literary works to ascertain the extent to which orally conversive or textually discursive informed approaches will be more and/or less useful in relation to particular works and writers. In her analysis of a dinner-party conversation that took place in her own home, Polanyi states, "One must understand the culture of the inside speakers in order to 'really understand' the texts which native speakers produce" ("What Stories" 110). Ruoff emphasizes, "My own position is that an understanding of the people, a knowledge of their ethnohistory, and a mastery of literary history and theory are all important to writing good Native American literary criticism. . . . The specialist in Native American literature and criticism has the obligation to become acquainted with Indians as living people, not just as they are represented in texts" ("Recent" 658). The sort of knowledge and understanding that Ruoff calls for necessitates the very sort of interactive relationships involved in a conversive approach to American Indian literatures.

Such a conversive approach involves the recognition of the relationships within and beyond the stories and, perhaps even more importantly, the interrelationships between the scholar and the literatures, as the scholar very consciously becomes a part of those written stories. Our roles as literary scholars are to assist others in their entries into literary worlds, to help others learn to become conversive listener-readers. As Chinweizu writes about African scholarship, "The subservient role of the scholar needs to be emphasized" (15). And as I note elsewhere, in this fashion, we become "signposts guiding readers' ways into literature" (Brill, *Wittgenstein* 54). The work of literary scholars is important, especially now in a world whose textualizing and attenuating influences have robbed us of the depth and complexity that are the warp and woof of oral storytelling traditions. Even so, much of our orality today is mediated through the layers of textuality that precede any telling—hence Wiget's concern about the effects of such mediative discourses. Finnegan warns us, "Thus to take as our yardstick the present circumstances of literature in Western Europe—or rather perhaps those of a generation or so ago—and assume that this is the standard by which we estimate all other literatures is to show a profound lack of historical and comparative perspective" ("Literacy" 143).

Within a conversive framework, the job of literary scholars is, first, to be able to enter and participate in a literary work's story world (a participation that presupposes sufficient knowledge and familiarity to enable one to step behind the text and interact within its storied worlds, including knowledge of the text's originating world, culture, traditions, and language; of the storyteller's person and world; of the storytelling-writing event; and of the range of its conversive and discursive literary structures); and second, to provide literary scholarship that will facilitate the entry of other listener-readers in their interactions with the written story. Chinweizu continues, "in our view, scholarship has to endeavor to illuminate literature, not for the benefit of theory, but for the benefit of the lives of specific people" (13).

Storytelling is a transformative experience. Even as readers, we can transform ourselves into conversive listener-readers and become part of the stories with which we engage. But this means moving beyond the level of textuality, beyond the level of *langue*. Conversive listening-reading involves our moving beyond the superficial level of text and back to the living language, *parole,* of the story. For decades, Louise M. Rosenblatt has been telling us to look at the literature as an event. She writes that readers must interact with the text and that the reader creates a poem out of the text through a transactional process: "The poem is something lived-through, . . . an event in time. It is not an object or an ideal entity. It is an occurrence, a coming-together, a compenetration, of a reader and a text" (126). Rosenblatt definitely points us in the right direction. Helen Jaskoski moves us even closer when she emphasizes the effect once an individual learns a story so well that s/he holds it in memory. "This intimate ownership of a text, and the right to perform it, suggests a different way of looking at literature and its analysis; the memorized text is made a part of the experiencing subject instead of remaining alienated as an object for analysis" ("Teaching" 57). Jaskoski notes the intimacy involved when we interweave a story into our own lives. This is the very personal intersubjective experience of conversive listening-reading. Whereas Rosenblatt's transactional approach creates the literature through the interaction of the reader and the text, the reader is still outside the story interacting with a *text*. It is only through conversive engagements that the storyteller-writer, story-text, and listener-readers are transformed through the direct interrelationships made possible through the power of language.

Wittgenstein makes clear that diverse worlds reflect different foundational 'grammars' and 'language games'. Each 'language game' and world are distinct in their own rights as defined by their grammatical rules or definitional boundaries. However, different worlds and 'language games' overlap to varying degrees and extents—hence Wittgenstein's notion of 'family resemblance'. In fact, some 'language games' and worlds may be sufficiently different from each other such that their languages, cultures, and traditions are virtually untranslatable from one to the other.[1] If not untranslatable, often the 'language games' are divergent in ways such that translation is extraordinarily difficult, as in the difficulties many ethnographers experienced in attempting to translate told stories into textual narratives. In relation to Silko's volume *Storyteller,* Nelson notes that "the development is concentric rather than linear, associational rather than chronologically determined" (42). *Storyteller* demonstrates a conversively informed literary structure; to read this volume through the critically discursive lens of a textually based theory would be to attempt "to sketch a sharply defined picture 'corresponding' to a blurred one"—an endeavor that Wittgenstein refers to as "hopeless": "And this is the position you are in if you look for definitions corresponding to our concepts in aesthetics or ethics" (*PI* 36e).

Within the domain of storytelling (literature), to what extent is the precision of scholarly (scientific) definition really helpful and meaningful? If in the process of such analysis the story is lost, and the transforming connections between listener-reader, teller-writer, and story-text are never made, it seems to me that such scholarship that begins and ends in words is unhelpful in our understandings of the stories within those literatures. Perhaps even more importantly, this results in scholarly work whose words are bereft of the relational power of conversivity—that power that makes all our words transformative, and thereby meaningful. As Simon Ortiz's father responded to his son's inquiries about the parts of words in the Acoma language, "It doesn't break down to anything" (*Song* 2). And as Wittgenstein asks, "Is it even always an advantage to replace an indistinct picture by a sharp one? Isn't the indistinct one often exactly what we need?" (*PI* 34e).

Within the 'language game' of the Western literary tradition, there is the hegemonic assumption that cultures, peoples, and languages are inherently oppositional, with said oppositions described in terms of dialectical, discursive, and/or dialogic assertions of subjective vocality and empowerment, and the concomitant disempowerment of those relegated to the positions of silence, objectivity, invisibility, and subalterity. However, it is far from the case that the literary 'language games' of all peoples have such a hierarchized binary oppositionality as part of their underlying grammar. In fact, many works of American Indian literatures display 'language games' that demonstrate foundational structures that could be more accurately described and understood in terms of conversive rather than discursive relations. Instead of a discursive or dialogic subjectivity that asserts itself at the expense of some silenced or absented other, these conversive literary engagements present subjects whose very vocalization privileges the subjectivity of others. This is an intersubjective relationality that emphasizes the connections between subjects rather than the individualized subjectivities and vocalizations of specific persons or groups—what Silko refers to as "the boundless capacity of language which, through storytelling, brings us together" ("Language" 72). Ortiz explains, "when the totality is considered, language as experience and perception, it doesn't break down so easily and conveniently. And there is no need to break it down and define its parts" (*Song* 3). When all of what is involved in communicative experience is divided up, what is lost is the power of conversive meaning.

Through a conversively informed listening-reading engagement with American Indian literatures, scholars focus on the connections within and beyond texts and the connections co-created by the specific interaction between the reader and the text—an interaction that transforms the reading process into the interrelational acts of storytelling and storylistening. Ruppert touches on this when he writes about American Indian literatures: "Its sources in oral tradition push for a literature in which story becomes reality" (*Mediation* xi). This process realizes and substantiates the text into an experiential process that is real and has substance. Ortiz explains:

> A song is made substantial by its context—that is its reality, both that which is there and what is brought about by the song. The context in which the song is sung or that a prayer song makes possible is what makes a song substantial, gives it that quality of realness. The emotional, cultural, spiritual context in which we thrive—in that, the song is meaningful. The context has to do not only with your being physically present, but it has to do also with the context of the mind, how receptive it is and that usually means familiarity with the culture in which the song is sung. (*Song* 6)

As I have emphasized throughout this book, stories can be realized even in our physical absence from the storyteller, provided we listen-read conversively, establishing our own contexts for the co-creative act as listener-readers. Grant notes, "Oral literature is a special performance; it is unique. It is *one* moment of a tradition. Even when it is written down and becomes 'fixed,' it is still oral" ("Native Literature" 61). And Chinweizu explains, "Literature, as far as we are concerned, is simply a written part of that dialogue which a people conduct among themselves about their history. Their life, not some abstract categories or theories, is the stuff of that history" (13). Conversive readings enable scholars to enter into that conversation.

Readings of American Indian literatures that work largely within the interpretive frameworks of Western and textually informed traditions will overlook the highly developed and intricate tapestries of conversive story-telling worlds. As Chapter 2 emphasizes, meaningfulness within a conver-sive framework is defined relationally in terms of those intersubjective relationships that bring persons (human and nonhuman) together. For those literatures substantially informed by their respective oral traditions, a conversive approach in/to those works will also enable literary scholars to access the meaningfulness within their stories. Paul Zolbrod specifically suggests that an awareness of Navajo poetry will assist our readings of Western texts (92). I'd like to extend Zolbrod's thoughts to include the entire range of conversively informed literatures. Zolbrod writes, "maybe the problems stem from an old way of looking at those texts ['so-called Great Books'], not from the way they were originally conceived. Or maybe non-Western texts can lead us to a new way of conceptualizing them" (92). Non-Western literatures may help us not only to approach Western litera-tures in new ways, but also to describe, understand, interpret, evaluate, and participate in non-Western literatures in ways that Western critical strat-egies cannot. Wittgenstein emphasizes the importance of our stepping be-yond the boundaries of our own worlds as a means of being able to see those limits and their effects more clearly. Fishman echoes this concern when he writes, "The antidote to ethnocentrism . . . is thus comparative cross-ethnic knowledge and experience, transcending the limits of one's own usual exposure to life and values" (306). As Silko points out, conversive language and storytelling manifest the transformative power that brings together the diverse elements and persons in the world.

Investigations in Chapter 4 into the reality of the intersubjective rela-tional worlds depicted in American Indian literatures clarify this crucial aspect of conversivity. When stories are told and written in a manner that directly involves the listener or listener-reader, the result is the very real and concrete transformative power of the word. Dexter Fisher writes, "To study American Indian literature is to study the power of language to shape one's perception of human experience. The word has power because it is the vehicle of the imagination and the means of clarifying relationships be-tween individuals and their landscapes, communities, visions" (5). As Witt-genstein notes, our language in many ways determines the world that we perceive and the world in which we live: "The world is *my* world: this is manifest in the fact that the limits of *language* (of that language which alone I understand) mean the limits of *my* world" (*TLP* 5.62). In other words, each individual has her or his own person-world in which s/he lives. We also live and interact in the broader worlds of family, community, and planet, and each of these worlds are informed by their respective 'language games'. When we interact by means of discursively informed 'language games', our worlds manifest themselves divisively and oppositionally. When we interrelate by means of conversively informed 'language games', our worlds manifest themselves connectively and relationally.

The conversiveness of the oral tradition is evident within most works of American Indian literatures (written or oral), although the extent to which any particular work manifests conversive relations and discursive structures will vary based on the extent to which the world of the text participates in conversively relational and/or discursively oppositional epistemologies. As Chapter 6 demonstrates, mixedblood writers who straddle these domains in their own heritages tend to write in ways that demonstrate a varying range of both conversive and discursive literary structures. Ruppert comments on *Love Medicine* by Louise Erdrich (Anishinabe): "What we have is a novel, a western structure, whose task it is to recreate something of a Native oral tradition. Erdrich uses a Western field of discourse to arrive at a Native perspective" (*Mediation* 134–35). Similarly, *Ceremony* by Silko, *House Made of Dawn* by N. Scott Momaday (Kiowa), and *Cogewea* by Mourning Dove (Okanagan/Colville) interweave discursive structures and conversive relations throughout their textual worlds. More distinctively conversive are the stories from diverse tribal oral traditions and the writings of those poets who have been more traditionally reared (and thereby closer to the conversive orality of their tribes and peoples), such as Luci Tapahonso (Navajo), Simon Ortiz, or Anna Lee Walters (Pawnee/Otoe-Missouria). But as is necessarily the case in the diverse forms of both writing and speech, even the works of these writers demonstrate varying degrees of conversivity.

I would like to end with a brief discussion of *Winter in the Blood,* by James Welch (Blackfeet/Gros Ventre). This novel manifests conversive literary structures, albeit as an undercurrent whose presence is most obvious in its apparent absence. As Anna Lee Walters writes, "We know what is conspicuous by its absence" ("American Indian" 35). Therefore, even those texts that are more obviously discursive can be meaningfully approached and entered through a conversive method. Gerald Vizenor (Anishinabe) notes, "Native American Indian literatures are tribal discourse" ("Postmodern" 4). Even when these literatures are discursive in structure, they nevertheless straddle worlds and words. Vizenor continues, "The oral and written narratives are 'language games', comic discourse rather than mere responses to colonialist demands or social science theories" ("Postmodern" 4).

We can see this in *Winter in the Blood,* in which the fractured relationships between the characters of the novel demonstrate the sort of *dys*cursive[2] communication that presents little beyond the illusion of interpersonal interactions. This absence of conversive relations is depicted in terms of a compromised pathology in which one can only hope to assert one's own subjectivity through the *dys*connections between oneself and others. The unnamed narrator distances and objectifies even his own mother and grandmother by referring to them as "a mother and an old lady who was my grandmother" (2). Concerning the relationship between the narrator and the "girl who was thought to be [his] wife," the most significant connection between them is through his gun and electric razor, which she stole from him the last time she was at his house. The narrator's father and brother, the only two individuals with whom he has had close relationships, are both dead. His grandfather, Yellow Calf, is only known to him as an old man who lives oddly by himself. Years before that, the narrator's grandmother was rejected by her own people. Throughout the novel, Welch presents connections that are defined oppositionally in discursive assertions of subjectivity that declare individual presence necessarily at the expense of those who are objectified as different, other, and thereby insignificant.

When there is the intimation of more substantive connections (such as those between the narrator's mother and her new husband, Lame Bull; between the narrator and his "girl"; or between the narrator and the "other" women with whom he becomes sexually involved), those (dys)connections are compromised through the mediation of land, material possessions, and alcohol. The narrator notes, "Lame Bull had married 360 acres of hay land. . . . And he had married a T-Y brand. . . . And, of course, he had married Teresa, my mother" (13). The narrator's "girl" is repeatedly referred to as "the girl who had stolen my gun and electric razor" (175), these two items being virtually all that differentiates her from other girls. Alcohol is apparently the necessary prerequisite for any of the narrator's sexual interactions with women.

Nevertheless, the dysfunctional universe of *Winter in the Blood* does provide glimmers of the type of conversive connections against which the rest of the novel is juxtaposed. The intersubjective relationships between the narrator and his father, brother, and Yellow Calf (after discovering that

Yellow Calf is his grandfather); the relationships between Yellow Calf and the animals around where he lives; and finally the relationship between the narrator and his horse (Bird) all reflect the conversive sorts of engagements in which one person's speech and presence concomitantly affirms the presence and subjectivity of the other persons. These intersubjective relationships that manifest the transformative power of language and love stand out in Welch's novel, both in their actual power and through their predominant absence. As Beck and Walters explain, "Through this interdependency and awareness of relationships, the universe is balanced" (13). For example, when the narrator visits Yellow Calf, both are transformed and become more than they were before the visits. The narrator gains a grandfather and a history he never knew was his, and Yellow Calf's story gains a new life in being passed down to his grandson. This connection stands out as categorically divergent from the discursively oppositional dysconnections that pervade the novel.

Conversive relations in this novel are rare and largely depicted in terms of the past—of an earlier time scarcely possible today. The discursivity of today's world is presented as inevitable; even with the occasional intersubjective and transformative connections Welch presents, these are the exceptions rather than the rule. The dominant 'language game' is nothing more than the virtual image of that which it reflects but never achieves—namely, those relationships whose connections appear substantive, but never quite achieve actual substantiation. The novel ends with the narrator asserting his own discursive subjectivity as his thoughts wander during his grandmother's funeral, which is attended only by her daughter, grandson, and Lame Bull, who proceeds to jump up and down on one end of her orange coffin to get it to lie straight in the grave. The absence of any other mourners further bespeaks the fractured conversivity of the relationships that pervade the novel. Real connections are absent things of the past. All that one can strive for is discursive subjectivity. As Lame Bull ends his lame eulogy of his wife's mother, the narrator's attention wanders to the girl who stole his gun and razor. "Next time I'd do it right. Buy her a couple of crèmes de menthe, maybe offer to marry her on the spot" (175). Hopefulness, but a lame hopefulness at best.

Throughout Welch's novel, the foundational necessity of conversive relations is manifested most profoundly in their absence, in their past presence, and in the disturbing results that accrue through their absence (e.g., alcoholism, violence, and largely meaningless sexual relationships). The final crèmes de menthe serve as the signs of the meaninglessness and purpose-lessness in much of the narrator's life. However, his ironic thought of offering to marry the girl who stole his razor, thereby placing a marriage proposal within the same context as "a couple of crèmes de menthe," shows his awareness of the ridiculousness of that relationship, and that this time, he'll pursue her with the seriousness that such a relationship deserves. The narrator's greater awareness of his dysconnection to that "girl" is made clear at this point in the novel in the final lines shortly after the narrator's old horse has died: "The red horse down in the corral whinnied. He probably missed old Bird. I threw the [tobacco] pouch into the grave" (176). His pursuit of the girl who stole his razor is juxtaposed in contrast to the conversively meaningful relationship between the red horse and old Bird, and thereby, his own relationship with those two horses as well as his relationship with "the old woman," his grandmother. Even though his relationship with his grandmother was distanced and discordant, it nevertheless had the depth and meaningfulness that is completely absent in his "relationship" with the girl who stole his razor—even though throughout most of the novel, the narrator works hard not to recognize any meaningful connections between himself and any other persons (be they human or animal).

In the end, he throws his grandmother's tobacco pouch into her grave, the pouch that he picks up shortly after she has died and that he returns to her at her burial, as was traditionally done by his people. In fact, when he picks up her pouch from her rocker, he tells us, "I untied it and brought it to the window. It was as soft as old Bird's muzzle. I squeezed it and felt the arrowhead inside. Besides the two pieces of furniture, this pouch and the clothes on her back, I had never seen any of the old lady's possessions, but she must have had other things, things that would have been buried with her in the old days" (132). In his sensitivity to the softness of both the pouch and old Bird's muzzle, he communicates his real relatedness to both his grandmother and old Bird—as much as he tries to ignore and deny such connections in his life throughout most of the novel. Again as the novel ends, the young man thinks of his grandmother in relation to his old horse, and as he thinks how much the surviving horse must miss old Bird, we see him missing both Bird and his grandmother, in his own disconnected and protective fashion. But for him, burying her tobacco pouch with her has the conversive meaningfulness that is absent in his offhand decision to buy the girl who stole his razor "a couple of crèmes de menthe, maybe offer to marry her on the spot" (175). This final offer is most significant in its meaninglessness and absurdity—and in the young man's assertion of his own discursive power as he plans to take the upper hand with that "girl who had stolen my gun and electric razor" (175).

Even in a novel such as *Winter in the Blood,* in which the connections between persons are largely portrayed dysfunctionally and dysconnectedly, conversive connectivity is intertwined with discursive oppositions in this depiction of a world and persons continually at odds with themselves. It is in that depiction of that world and those people continually *at odds* that Welch most powerfully communicates the importance of conversive relations—a reality that is present throughout the novel most notably in its dysfunctional depictions and in its relative absence. Consistent across the tribal peoples of North America is the emphasis on the interrelatedness that is at the heart of a balanced world. As Beck and Walters explain, "All things are related and therefore human beings must be constantly aware of how our actions will affect other beings, whether these are plants, animals, people, or streams" (12). The realization of the significance of one's behaviors on others also includes the effects of one's words because it is through both words and deeds that the relationships throughout the world are created, maintained, strengthened, weakened, or destroyed. This power is evident in not only the prayers, chants, songs, and stories from the oral traditions, but also in the narrator's final thoughts about his two horses—a connection that also points to his grandfather Yellow Calf, who talks with the deer (67–68).

Beck and Walters point out, "Through this interdependency and awareness of relationships, the universe is balanced" (13). When the conversive interdependencies throughout creation are disrupted and made conflictual, the world is defined as dangerous, diseased, partial, imbalanced: as the narrator's grandfather Yellow Calf tells him, "This earth is cockeyed" (68). Those individuals whose lives are analogously discursively oppositional are, in turn, living partial and imbalanced lives—lives that are incomplete, in essence virtual by virtue of being out of touch with that conversivity that is at the heart of harmony and balance. Accordingly, critical methods and theories that are discursively oppositional will be able to shed light most effectively on those texts that are largely discursively informed and which may be literary texts but are not stories. Within a conversively informed storytelling framework, even many of those literary works defined ostensibly as "short stories" are not really stories in the true sense of storytelling. Although some may be largely conversively informed, and like Silko's

"Storytelling," may be actual stories in written form, written works of literature can be more accurately described as virtual stories—namely, literary texts with a number of the superficial aspects of storytelling (e.g., symbolism, heteroglossia and polyvocalism, irony, and humor) but without the essential elements of relationality, listener-reader co-creativity, and the centering force of the sacred. I would also suggest that almost any text (with the exceptions of those whose constructions involve no actual story, perhaps some scientific texts or computer-generated texts) can be approached conversively, provided that the reader makes the effort to become a co-creative listener-reader, reading below the surface level of the text such that the living stories within the texts become accessible in real, tangible, and transformative ways.

American Indian literatures depict the intersubjective relationality that they present as inherent in all of creation, even if that inherence is apparently absent as in Welch's novel. In contrast, discursive positionality offers relationships that are disjunctive, virtual, and largely illusory, with subjects and objects continually jockeying for their own positions of discursive power. Such discursive and dialogic connections represent the ever elusive and receding trace of the actual intersubjective relationships evidenced in conversive stories (lived and told, written and imagined).

From the vantage point of a conversively informed literary scholarship, the Western critical traditions (modern and postmodern) appear to be virtual worlds in which the connections sought are never really achieved due to the interpretive self-referentiality that definitionally privileges subjective positions with the necessary concomitant devaluing of displaced objects. In fact, I would hazard that our contemporary high-tech virtual realities are merely electronic variants of the virtuality that we all live to varying degrees in our poststructural worlds and words. I would further hazard that our high-tech virtual worlds reflect little beyond our desperate attempts to assume (pretend?) a relative concretization of our worlds and lives through their differentiation from the electronic virtual worlds of our own creation, in which signs take on objective status, and objects, ever receding to the convergent point of infinity, take on a distancing that nevertheless gives the illusion of a sought-after closeness and connection. It seems to me that we would do well to heed Wittgenstein's statement, "For our forms of expression prevent us in all sorts of ways from seeing that nothing out of the ordinary is involved, by sending us in pursuit of chimeras" (*PI* 94). Jimmie Durham (Cherokee) explains, "the indigenous people of the Americas are colonized and . . . the colonization is not simply the language of some political rhetoric from past decades" (424–25). Colonization is also evident in the extent to which American Indian (and other) literatures are forced through the mediating sieve of critical discourse and theory. Only when scholars step out of the mode of "speaking for" and instead choose to "listen to" and "speak with" will literary scholarship move more firmly toward conversive relations.

A conversive literary method provides the language and perspective necessary for recognizing and making the connections with, in, and beyond literary works. A conversive practice also transforms the critical reading practice into a storytelling and storylistening event. The scholar listens-reads with and to the story in the prose or poetic work and listens-reads herself or himself into that story world. Through the combination of both conversive and discursive strategies, scholars are able to approach literatures from within as well as from the outside—thereby enabling greater avenues of approach than is possible only through more discursively textual strategies. Crucial to the work of a conversively informed listener-reader are knowledge about the storyteller-writer and her or his world, culture, traditions, history, and language (all of which enable the familiarity that is essential to the co-creative act of conversive communication); knowledge about oral storytelling traditions (historically the academic domain of folklorists, anthropologists, and linguists); and knowledge about the storytelling event (as co-created by the listener-reader's conversive engagement with the literary work and as co-created within its originating context).

Conversive literary strategies are applicable for the vast majority of literary works. Insofar as American Indian literary works are concerned, they can be understood in light of their respective participations along the conversive-discursive continuum. An analogous range of diversity can be found within non-Native literatures. Those more closely connected to their oral roots (such as classical Greek literatures, medieval literatures from the British Isles, African-American literatures, and women's literatures) will tend to demonstrate more obviously a range of conversive literary structures. Even more broadly, those literary works that are largely textually informed may nevertheless manifest elements of their own respective historical oral traditions through occasional or slight vestiges of conversivity. This is certainly the case for *Winter in the Blood*. By means of a conversive approach, we can discern the broad range of storytelling elements that find their ways into works even through the varying layers of textual mediation.

But again this necessitates a shift in critical method to a much greater appreciation of the value and power of orality. As Clifford explains, "Once cultures are no longer prefigured visually—as objects, theaters, texts—it becomes possible to think of a cultural poetics that is an interplay of voices, of positioned utterances" ("Introduction" 12). And it is within this interplay of conversive relations that the remarkable power of storytelling manifests itself in literature and in literary scholarship.

Conversive scholarship is a transformative activity that transforms the words of a text into a story and the reader into its listener. Conversive engagements with literary works move the reader very directly into the transformative world of storytelling. Our readings and interpretations will change, and so might our own lives. Even such apparently small transformations as a memory of conversations in the woods with tree frogs can have a significant effect. But the transformative effects of conversive relations necessitate that readers become listener-readers. In fact, it is we who are in need of relearning, learning to "talk Indian" in the sense of conversive communications, learning to interact and interrelate with stories and lives in conversive ways that bring us together and transform ourselves through the very real and concrete power of those sacred relationships that are at the center of storytelling and life. Conversive relations are nothing new to the world. I have not developed a new method of reading and interpreting literature. What are in this volume are simply the old ways of conversive learning, the old ways of storytelling and storylistening, the old ways that are a part of all of our respective inheritances, however far back we need to go to remember and rediscover the very sophisticated and complex perceptual skills involved in storylistening. Beck and Walters write, "In 'western civilization,' the trend has been to separate knowledge from the sacred" (47). Perhaps it is now time to reverse that trend and to shift to the consciously transformative and intersubjective relations of conversive literary study.

CONVERSIVE LITERARY STRUCTURES

This list includes conversive literary structures that are present in American Indian literatures and that reflect their respective oral storytelling traditions. The list is far from exhaustive, but it provides a helpful grouping of a range of elements that indicate orality and conversivity in literary works. I've also included some references to discussions of these elements by other writers. The references, like the list, are not exhaustive—just an initial listing to direct the reader to some other related discussions.

Conversive literary elements:

1. The literary understood as an extension of the oral—with varying degrees of orality or conversiveness reflected in any work of literature (Silko, *Yellow Woman* 21; Krupat, "Post-Structuralism" 124; Ortiz, "Always" 66; Bataille 17; Simard, "American" 247; Finnegan 24; Chapter 6)

2. Evidenced in more orally informed literary genres (e.g., poetry and drama) than in those that are more literarily or textually informed

3. Circular literary forms rather than linear narrative structures (Simard 245; Chapter 5)

4. Concentric, episodic, associational structure (Nelson 43; Ruppert, *Mediation* 134; Chapters 3 and 5)

5. Interconnectedness, interdependency, relationality (Beck and Walters 11–14; Moore, "Myth"; Blaeser, *Gerald Vizenor* 27; Chapter 4)

6. Holism, "ecosystemic view" (Simard 245; Owens, *Other Destinies* 29)

7. Relationality that is intersubjective (Chapter 4)

8. Importance of the self, but only in relation to other selves; communalism and tribalism (Simard 245; Chapter 4)

9. Sophisticated interweaving of diverse worlds, persons, places, times (Diamond 4; Chapters 3–6)

10. Interweaving of the imaginary and the real, the mythic and the actual, the past and the present (Chapters 3–6)

11. Mythic time and mythic events (Owens, *Other Destinies* 94–95; Chapters 4 and 6)

12. Ritual, prayer, song (Beck and Walters 35–45; Kroskrity 196; Wiget, "Native" 12)

13. Universal themes (Beck and Walters 59)

14. The central focus of the sacred, the mystical, the spiritual (Beck and Walters; Simard 245; Chapter 4)

15. The very real transformative power of conversivity (Attinasi and Friedrich 43, 50; O'Connor 9–10; Bird, "Towards" 7; Chapter 4)

16. Unexpected transitions, voice shifts, juxtapositions (Blaeser, *Gerald Vizenor* 33)

17. Stories and conversations that extend beyond the boundaries of the text (Chapters 3–5)

18. Verbal framing, especially with traditional or formulaic beginnings and endings (Bauman, "Verbal Art" 295; Wiget, "Native" 12)

19. Storytelling conventions or "story words" (Kroskrity 195)

20. Traditional, formulaic, specialized, or archaic words and phrases (Toelken, "Pretty Language" 220–21; Bauman, "Verbal Art" 295; Kroskrity 195; Wiget, "Native" 12)

21. Repeated linking words, sounds, phrases, particles (Wiget, "Native" 12)

22. Repetition—not for memorization, but for learning (Blaeser, *Gerald Vizenor* 33; Wiget, "Native" 12)[1]

23. Figurative language, metaphor, symbolism (Beck and Walters 59–60, 74–75; Bauman, "Verbal Art" 295; Blaeser, *Gerald Vizenor* 33)

24. Varying levels of interpretive complexity (Chapters 1 and 4)

25. Coding (Beck and Walters 59–60; Chapter 4)

26. Ambiguity (Simard 245; Blaeser, *Gerald Vizenor* 33; Chapter 4)

27. Parallelism (Bauman, "Verbal Art" 295)

28. Satire, irony, contradiction (Blaeser, *Gerald Vizenor* 33)

29. Lack of closure (Blaeser, *Gerald Vizenor* 33)

30. Humor (Beck and Walters 31; Blaeser, *Gerald Vizenor* 33)

31. Minimalism; characters, personalities, and emotions evoked rather than fully described (Blaeser, *Gerald Vizenor* 32)

32. Understatement (Blaeser, *Gerald Vizenor* 33)
33. Omission and absence (Kroeber, *Retelling* 19; Blaeser, *Gerald Vizenor* 33)
34. Pauses and silence (line and paragraph breaks, empty spacing on a page) for emphasis and to enable listener-readers to respond to and consider more deeply various aspects of the story (Kroskrity 196; Walters, *Talking Indian* 13–14; Jaskoski, "Image" 69)
35. Polyvocalism, heteroglossia, and pronoun shifts, often with the teller stepping into the voice, role, and person of the individual characters involved (Kroskrity 196; Simard 245; Blaeser, *Gerald Vizenor* 33; Tyler 136)
36. Voice shifts to a second person, direct address enabling the listener-reader's entry into the text, often in the form of a personal intimacy directed to the listener-reader (Blaeser, *Gerald Vizenor* 33; Ruppert, *Mediation* 134; Chapter 5)
37. Conversive intimacy (Ruppert, *Mediation* 133–34; Chapter 3)
38. Narrator's use of first-person plural pronoun of inclusion "we" (Blaeser, *Gerald Vizenor* 29; Chapter 3)
39. A muted authorial presence that does not privilege the author but rather privileges the story and the relationship between teller-writer and listener-reader (Chapter 5)
40. The reader takes on co-creative and interactive role of a listener-reader (Chapter 5)
41. Reader has participating ear rather than objectifying eye of discursive observation (Chapter 5)
42. Situating the story in the listener-reader's world to facilitate the listener-reader's entry into the storyworld (Chapter 5)
43. Emphasis on place identification (Simard 245)
44. Nonhumans (animals, vegetation, rocks, etc.) with subjective status as nonhuman persons and not objectified (Chapter 4)
45. Persons/things/behaviors in the world not understood through a Western semiotic differentiation of signs and objects (Chapter 2)
46. Story characters (human and nonhuman) who *are* living persons; not flattened characters, caricatures, or stereotypes (Chapter 4)

GRAMMATICAL RULES FOR
LITERARY SCHOLARSHIP

*(Encompassing Both Textually and
Orally Informed Traditions)*

As a means of introducing new directions for literary study, I list here a number of underlying grammatical rules that describe in what ways a conversive approach differs from Saussurean or Peircean strains of semiotics. These rules are referred to as 'grammatical' in the Wittgensteinian sense of the underlying grammar upon which 'language games' are based.

Beginning grammatical rules for literary inquiry:

1.   Meaningfulness cannot be determined solely in terms of the presence or absence of signs.

1.1   In some cases, the presence of signs signifies. In other cases, the absence of signs signifies.

2.   The presence of differentiable signs may or may not signify. This signification reflects both objective and subjective relations in the world.

2.1   Within a Western interpretive semiotics, signs signify when distinct and differentiable as such.

2.2   Within a conversively relational system of meaning, signs are meaningful when they are not differentiated from their objective realities.

3.   Meaningful signification is always, by definition, a relational act.

3.1   Within a Western interpretive semiotics, the relationality of signification is primarily focused on the relationship between a sign and object via the vantage point of the interpretant.

3.11 The concept of the interpretant privileges the point of interpretation as necessary to any understanding of the relationship between a sign and object.

3.12 The interpretive relationship between the interpretant and the sign and/or object is deemphasized and thereby devalued.

3.13 The concept of the interpretant (point or angle of interpretation) ignores the interactive objective and signifying effects of the interpretation (Heisenberg's uncertainty principle).

3.2 Interpretation is, by definition, a relational act.

4. Where signs appear insignificant, this insignificance is merely apparent, perceptual, and conceptual and is in no wise essential.

4.1 Within a conversively relational meaning system, objects (or signifying objects/objective signs) only have meaning within conversive relations.

4.2 Within a Western interpretive semiotics, a sign indifferentiable from its object does not signify. This condition is defined as the presymbolic.

4.21 The notion of the presymbolic privileges the "higher" domain of the abstracted sign and accordingly relegates signifying objects/objective signs to a "lower," more "primitive," or less intellectually sophisticated subaltern of signification or the lack thereof.

5. Signs in and of themselves, distinct from objects and interpreting subjects, do not signify, nor do objects or subjects in and of themselves. This independence definitionally denies the significance of signs, the objectivity of objects, and the subjectivity of subjects. (A point is that which has no parts—Euclid.)

5.1 Differentiable signs only signify when in relation to differentiable objects. This relationship is always a constructed one through the interpretive act.

5.2 Differentiable objects only have objective reality when in relation to differentiable signs. This relationship is also a constructed one through the interpretive act.

5.3 A Western semiotic interpretation demands differentiation between signs and objects.

5.4 Differentiable points of interpretation are only significant in relation to the relationships between signs and objects.

6. The subjectivity of objects in the world (as signifying objects/objective signs) bespeaks a circular or spherical semiotic domain in

which the independent points of objectivity, signification, and interpretation are unnecessary for conversive meaning.

6.1   This represents the conversive world of American Indian relational ontologies and epistemologies (as well as those of other peoples whose ontologies and epistemologies are informed by their oral traditions).

6.2   Relational ontologies and epistemologies are conversive.

7.   The absence of differentiable signs in no way signifies or constitutes the absence of signification.

7.1   The presence of differentiable signs within a conversively relational meaning system signifies or constitutes the absence of meaning.

7.2   Within a conversively relational meaning system, the absence of differentiable signs signifies or constitutes the presence of meaning.

8.   Writing and speech are meaningful. So is silence.

8.1   What is an absence within a signifying domain may be a presence within a conversive realm of meaning (and vice versa). Presence can signify absence, but so, too, can absence signify presence.[2]

CIRCULAR AND
SPHERICAL REALITIES

A Brief Geometric Sketch of the
'Language Game' of Conversive Relations

The underlying grammar of the 'language game' of conversive relations is a grammar that posits the following:

1. The reality of objective signs and signifying objects (in other words, persons, both human and nonhuman, in the world).

2. Spherical realities in which meaningful space can be enclosed with two points and two curved lines (relying upon non-Euclidean elliptic geometry and using the sphere as model). This contrasts with the Euclidean dyadic and triadic models that describe signifying regions and relations in semiotics.[3]

3. Circular realities in which meaningful space is enclosed and described by means of only one point and one line that begins and ends with that same point—a point whose meaningfulness is dependent upon the completion of the circle, and whose reality is no more or less important than any other point on the circle. Here again, we rely upon elliptic geometric formulations; our primary model is, obviously, the circle.[4]

Introduction

1. Q.E.D. is the abbreviation for *quad erat demonstrandum* (thus it has been proved), which follows the geometric proofs of Euclid and other geometers.

2. For an extensive discussion of the circumscribed limits of various contemporary critical theories and the theories' ineffectiveness beyond those prescribed boundaries, see Brill, *Wittgenstein*.

3. The recent essay by Attinasi and Friedrich, "Dialogic Breakthrough: Catalysis and Synthesis in Life-Changing Dialogue," comes very close to the actual development of a conversive method of scholarship. Attinasi and Friedrich look at the transformative aspect of conversation, although they do not explicitly discuss the transformative effect on scholarship as well. I highly recommend this article.

4. Here, a hat tip to Helen Jaskoski. By referring to placing the two stories "at the center" of a chapter, I am thinking of Jaskoski's wonderful essay, "Teaching with *Storyteller* at the Center." In fact, the two stories whose development took forms I did not initially intend were from Silko's *Storyteller,* namely the pieces "Storytelling" and "Storyteller" that are discussed at length in Chapter Five.

Chapter 1

1. Clearly, Silko is referring to Wittgenstein's very important work, *Remarks on Colour.* I suspect that Barnes was unfamiliar with Wittgenstein's work and did not have Silko proof the interview notes, in which case the phrase "remarks on color" would have been corrected to identify the volume Silko refers to. In any case, I strongly concur with Silko's recommendation of this volume. It is a solid and readily accessible introduction to Wittgenstein's work. I also recommend the collections *Culture and Value* and *Remarks on Frazer's* Golden Bough as two volumes that would be of direct value and interest specifically to scholars of American Indian literatures and, more broadly, to any scholars with interests in cultural studies.

2. I use the term *in/to* intentionally to convey the tripartite sense of conversive engagement with a work that involves the reader's approach "to" the work, her or his entry "into" the story, and his or her subsequent movement as a participant "in" the story.

3. For a more complete discussion of the notion of critical "fit" regarding appropriate and meaningful applications of various critical theories, see Brill, *Wittgenstein.*

4. Wittgenstein uses the concept of a 'language game' to indicate that any use of language, like a game, is based on foundational rules that are then manifested in their use. The reference to the grammatical rules of a 'language game' refers to those foundational rules and is to be understood metaphorically to indicate whatever is essential to any particular form of communication in language.

5. For a more developed discussion of the role of listener-readers within a written storytelling framework, see Chapter 5.

6. See Wittgenstein's discussion of sign-posts as delineators of rules and customs (*PI* 85, 87, 198). In this example, the individual has the freedom to decide how to respond to the sign-post—by following its direction immediately, another time, not at all, etc.

7. Wittgenstein uses the concept 'family resemblance' to communicate the diverse interconnections throughout the world. For example, the 'family' of chess and logic and mathematics may have certain 'family resemblances' that tell us about those three endeavors, but so too would the 'family resemblances' between the members of the 'family' that includes chess, checkers, hopscotch, and hide-and-seek, and also the 'family resemblances' between chess, European social structures, and the hierarchization within academia. Although the notion of 'family resemblance' can certainly refer to resemblances between human persons within a human family, the concept is much broader and gives the sense of the greater interrelationships throughout the world and the fact that our recognition of those interconnections is important to our understandings of whatever in the world we seek to understand.

Chapter 2

1. For a developed discussion of the role of relationality in oral storytelling and conversively informed literatures, see Chapter 4.

2. Here I need to acknowledge my debt to the Bahá'í Writings (the primary works of Bahá'u'lláh [the Prophet-Founder of the Bahá'í Faith] and 'Abdu'l-Bahá [Bahá'u'lláh's eldest son and the center of the Bahá'í covenant]) for this image of the garden. Both Bahá'u'lláh and 'Abdu'l-Bahá use the image of a garden to reflect the living diversity of humankind. 'Abdu'l-Bahá explains, "If the flowers of a garden were all of one color, the effect would be monotonous to the eye; but if the colors are variegated, it is most pleasing and wonderful. . . . Therefore, although we are of different individualities, different in ideas and of various fragrances, let us strive like flowers of the same divine garden to live together in harmony. Even though each soul has its own individual perfume and color, all are reflecting the same light" (*The Promulgation of Universal Peace: Talks Delivered by 'Abdu'l-Bahá during His*

Visit to the United States and Canada in 1912, comp. Howard MacNutt [Wilmette, IL: Bahá'í Publishing Trust, 1982] 24).

3. It is when Abel is in the hospital in Los Angeles, having been brutally beaten, that Angela comes to visit him. While there, she tells him a story about a bear and a maiden that she tells her own son. Abel's Navajo friend Benally is amazed to hear such a magical story from a white woman, exclaiming, "Ei Yei! A bear! A bear and maiden. And she was a white woman and she thought it up, you know, made it up out of her own mind, and it was like that old grandfather talking to me, telling me about *Esdzá shash nadle,* or *Dzil quigi,* yes, just like that" (170). Ben's response to Angela's story demonstrates its power and interconnective force that are part of conversive (conversative and transformative) storytelling. Angela's story straddles worlds and in some ways serves as a healing medicine for herself, for Abel, and for Ben, who then tells his own Navajo story.

Chapter 3

1. In an interview with Navajo poet Luci Tapahonso, Bruchac discusses the preponderance of mestizo/a Indian writers: "Many of the people in the 'first generation' of American Indian writers in this part of the century who have become well known are people of mixed blood" (*Survival This Way* 278). Both Bruchac and Tapahonso comment on this as a necessary stage for fullblood and more traditionally raised Indians to begin writing and publishing.

2. This shifting role of the critic is discussed at greater length in Brill, *Wittgenstein.*

3. I want to clarify that the reference to the concept of 'structures' does not signify the sort of modernist constructs that poststructuralism rejects. The structures that Navajo elder Barney Blackhorse Mitchell notes are those relational structures that, in fact, exist in the world within and between peoples, other life forms, and things. For Mitchell, there are *real* connections in the world (as opposed to those connections artificially constructed), which can be learned and communicated through life and through stories.

Chapter 4

1. For a comprehensive collection of essays that discuss "scientific" and social constructions of race, I strongly recommend Harding's *The "Racial" Economy of Science.*

2. For a more complete discussion of the differences between descriptively based criticisms and theoretically based criticisms that strive for explanations of texts, see Brill, *Wittgenstein.* This book advocates the practice of a descriptively based critical methodology, arguing that particular theoretical stances should be applied only after a process of descriptive investigations sufficient to determine the value of applying the particular theory. The book specifically emphasizes the im-

this seems obvious

portance of fit—ascertaining which theories and criticisms prove useful to the text and the reader/critic.

3. Although the concept of a dialogue (used by Blaeser) represents exchange and opposition rather than the more conversive interrelational and transformative engagement of a conversation, Blaeser clearly points out the fact that the one reality, which is the sacred, includes that reality's diverse manifestations and representations in the world and in stories.

4. My use of the phrase "throughout all of creation" instead of the more common "in the world" is deliberate. I do so to underscore the fact that for Native peoples, intersubjectivity extends beyond this world to include the clouds and sky, the moon and stars, other celestial bodies, and those realities beyond the limits of time and space (such as Tayo's deceased uncle and brother whose love for him is still as real and conversive as it was when they were in this world). The term *creation* is deliberate as well, conveying the belief in the sacred as an originating creative source.

5. For a complete discussion of this topic, see Ossorio, *Persons*.

6. Although the tree toads are designated as tree *frogs* by naturalists, they are also commonly referred to as *tree toads*.

7. An additional note on my own conversive relations with those tree toads in Maine: interestingly, I do not remember ever running into any other humans (campers or counselors) back in those woods when I went there during that first year.

8. This story can be found in Genesis VIII. Because this story is from the Jewish tradition, I recommend any of the number of translations made directly from the Hebrew by scholars of Judaica. For my reference, I used J. H. Hertz's edition of *The Pentateuch and Haftorahs*.

9. Where I have placed *other* within quotation marks, I have done so to emphasize not only the difference inherent in otherness, but also the hierarchized structuring within discursive oppositions that necessarily defines *otherness* as different *and* therefore less than. *Otherness* thereby signifies subalterity within this framework.

Chapter 5

1. The term *listener-reader* refers to those readers whose roles straddle the written and the oral. The hyphenated term emphasizes the inextricably interwoven and interactive role expected of readers by American Indian literatures. Readers of these texts have analogous roles to those expected of listeners of oral stories.

2. The Haggadah is the written text or script for the Passover seder. The Passover story is told with excerpts included from the Torah. Although basic elements of the Haggadah do not change, there is a substantial degree of flexibility

given in the final texts. There are even revisionist Haggadahs that emphasize the necessary freedom of not only the Jewish peoples but all peoples, and there are Haggadahs that specifically emphasize the importance of women's liberation. But the basic story, that of the Jewish people's freedom from slavery in Egypt and their emergence as a nation, is the foundation for all Haggadahs.

3. Although my religious affiliation is Bahá'í, I grew up in a mixed Jewish/Gentile home, participating in Jewish and Christian traditions and ceremonies and hearng stories from my father's Jewish background and stories from my mother's mixed Anglo-American, Scotch-Irish, and Cherokee history in southwestern Virginia.

4. See Finnegan, *Literacy and Orality.*

5. See Ruppert, "The Uses of Oral Tradition."

6. See Elaine Jahner, "Indian Literature."

7. See the final section of Chapter 4 for a more developed discussion of individual agency and intentionality in relation to concepts of personhood.

8. By referring to the woman's real and lived presence with the mythic Buffalo Man, I do not differentiate between the world of myth and the "real" world of time and place because such distinctions are the constructions of discursive delineations and boundaries. In the domain of conversive relations, mythic and real worlds overlap and merge within the storytelling event. Arnold Krupat explains, "Traditional Native American literary forms were not—and, in their contemporary manifestations usually are not—as concerned about keeping fiction and fact or poetry and prose distinct from one another. It is the distinction between truth and error rather than that between fact and fiction that seems more interesting to native expression" ("Dialogic" 59).

9. The information related in this section was based on a conversation I had with Luci Tapahonso when she was visiting Bradley University to give a reading of her work.

10. The quoted phrase "to no one in particular" comes from the final line of Luci Tapahonso's poem, "The Weekend Is Over." The poem, ostensibly about leaving her family at the end of a weekend visit to drive back [home] to Kansas, nevertheless focuses on the intersubjective and interpersonal closeness of family that is left behind as Tapahonso and her daughters drive to Kansas: "The girls stay awake until we leave our home country—Dinetah. / Then they fall asleep for the next two days of driving. / . . . / 'The land of Kansas,' I say aloud to no one in particular" (*Sáanii* 4).

Chapter 6

1. For a more specific, albeit brief, discussion of the problematic history of ethnographic recordings of Indian peoples' stories, see Brill, review essay of Krupat's *Native American Autobiography.*

2. Holmes provides a powerful analysis of the historical influences in the Euro-centric objectification of persons in the world. He specifically notes the catastrophic effects when metaphors of objectification are translated into real world behaviors.

> If we pretend man is an object or animal, it may, in itself, be a relatively harmless pretense that is useful to biologists or physicists who are interested in certain limited aspects of the embodiment of persons. However, if we come to use the metaphor without awareness that it is a metaphor and treat people as though they "really" or "basically" are objects, animals or organisms, we may lose the ability to distinguish persons from objects, animals or, (in the vernacular of most of psychology) "organisms." . . . Once the awareness of the metaphor is lost, and we no longer are engaged in pretending, metaphors tend to become masks or disguises which hide rather than illuminate. Then, we are duped into believing that the model or metaphor is the way the world is rather than recognizing, as the originators of the metaphors may have done, that the metaphor is simply one way of allocating the facts or one way of describing the world. (23, 22)

3. This refers to Adrienne Rich's essay of the same name, in which she discusses her own writing in terms of her mixed Jewish/Gentile heritage.

4. Métis people are mixedblood Canadians of Indian and European ancestry. The Métis identify themselves through the conjunction of their mixed ancestry, rather than choosing to identify through one heritage and ethnicity or the other. Many of the Métis people live in communities, neighborhoods, and villages that are primarily or even exclusively Métis. A strong similarity in the United States would be the Mexican-American or Chicano/a community whose identity is a mix of Indian and Spanish ancestry, the conjunction of which has evolved into an identi-fiably mestizo/a community—neither purely Indian nor purely white (Spanish), but inextricably an intertwining of both.

5. Although this chapter focuses specifically on the conversive engagements evi-denced by mixedblood and other Indian characters in the works of Louis Owens, Lee Maracle, and Sherman Alexie, it is interesting to note the extent to which women characters regardless of ethnicity also demonstrate the ready conversivity of intersubjective relations. Such a discussion is beyond the bounds of this chapter and book, but investigations into the divergent communications patterns between male-identified and female-identified literary characters/persons along the discursive-conversive spectrum would be a particularly ripe field for future study.

6. For an interesting description of the clash between conversive and discursive interpretive modes, see Anna Lee Walters's *Ghost Singer.* Early on in the novel, there is a scene in which an Anglo historian, his Navajo colleague, and the Navajo man's grandfather learn about one difficult period in Navajo history. As the old man Jonnie Navajo relates a story from that time, showing the younger men where the events occurred, there are periods of silence—silence for processing and digest-

ing the words, silence for understanding. But these periods of silence make the Anglo historian David Drake uncomfortable. "For a few minutes, there was no conversation. The old man was pensive. . . . Willie [the Navajo man's grandson] was quiet, waiting. David was puzzled. . . . 'What's this about?' David asked. 'Sh . . .' Willie quieted him. . . . 'I don't get it,' David said. 'Why is he telling us all this?'" (30). Within the discursively oppositional framework with which David Drake is familiar, silence is space to be filled. But within the conversive domain of oral tellings, silence is space that is already filled, not with new words, but with the old words broadened and deepened through the interpersonal connections strengthened through the shared experience.

7. Tarantino's *Pulp Fiction* is an extreme example. In the film, the demonic and the heroic overlap, such that moral determinations prove meaningless outside the bounds of oppositional struggle, where power is asserted through sexual or physical aggression and human beings are objectified to the point of individual insignificance as little more than pulp or flesh to be assaulted or forced on others.

8. As Wittgenstein repeatedly reminds his readers, a 'language game' is a form of life and cannot be dissociated from the everyday lived realities of our world.

9. The *Audubon Nature Encyclopedia* describes the raven as a very different animal from the crow. In their actual physiology and behavior and in the various stories and myths recounted about these animals, there are categoric differences drawn between the two birds. In light of the following excerpts from the encyclopedia, Stacey's reference to Raven as "just a crow—a foolish crow" takes on a larger significance than the mere misconstrual of an animal. According to the *Audubon Nature Encyclopedia,*

Nearly twice as large as its relative, the crow, the common raven differs from it in possessing a wedge-shaped tail and a thick ruff of feathers on the front of the throat. Its call is more of a croak than a caw. In soaring, the wings are held flat, in eagle fashion, while the crow holds its wings at an angle (1650–51).

There is probably not a bird in history that has figured so directly in legend, superstitions, and folklore as has the raven. The result of this has been its persecution, almost to the verge of extinction in some places throughout its wide range, including much of the eastern part of the United States. A generation ago our northern raven, *Corvus corax principalis,* a subspecies of the common raven, had all but disappeared in the eastern United States. And its local extirpation was largely caused by superstitious ignorance (1651).

An amazing number of people go about under a constant dread of incurring "bad luck" by breaking mirrors, walking under ladders. . . . All these and many other similar puerile superstitions have a stronger hold on people even today, than one might think. . . . Such was the raven's fate (1651–52).

Innumerable legends, stories, and beliefs have been built around the bird from early times, and thousands of people have lived in dread of ravens. . . . Even the sight of the bird was an evil omen, and if one alighted on church or dwelling it was taken as a certain sign of death or disaster. . . . Many of these superstitions of Europe and elsewhere were brought here by early settlers (1652).

The Audubon Nature Encyclopedia (Philadelphia: Curtis Books, 1965)

10. For a more developed discussion of intersubjective relations that cut across human and nonhuman distinction, see Chapter 4.

11. HUD homes refer to the cheap public housing financed by the U.S. Department of Housing and Urban Development.

12. Here Alexie refers to his white ancestry through his Spokane mother, who is part white. Alexie's father is fullblood Coeur d'Alene. Alexie is a registered member of the Spokane tribe.

13. In referring to "secular" struggle, I include sectarian divisiveness, theological debate, and religious war. My understanding of the sacred, as a Bahá'í scholar of American Indian literatures, is that the way of the sacred unites and brings persons and worlds together. Oppositional struggle, in whatever form it may take, is therefore, by definition, a turning away from the sacred, not a manifestation of it.

Epilogue

1. I use the term *translation* more broadly than in the limited linguistic concept of a translation from one language to another. 'Language games' are a part of a particular language (or languages), but what involves a 'language game' includes far more than merely the language. Translation from one 'language game' to another includes such activities as language use, perception, interpretation, evaluation, and behavior. All of these activities are informed by the participants' respective backgrounds and the context for the language use. 'Language game' translation is a far more complex endeavor than the mere translation of words from one language to another.

2. The variant spelling "dyscursive" is used here and elsewhere to convey the conjoint sense of discourse that is inherently dysfunctional.

Appendices

1. Thanks are due to Gloria Bird for making this important point in her talk at the 1995 MLA meeting in Chicago.

2. In her presentation at the 1992 MLA meeting in San Francisco, Joan Retallack noted the presence in absence specifically in relation to John Cage's music and writings. This point was especially helpful for me regarding its related significance in the domain of American Indian cultures and traditions.

3. For a more complete discussion of semiotic geometries (including accompanying diagrams), see Brill, "The Hegemonic Vertex."

4. I describe these geometric models for a conversive semiotics for future developments in this area. One chapter introducing such a schema is insufficient for a complete description of the possible heuristic configurations that could demonstrate the concepts of such an alternative semiotics. But several possible geometric models are suggested herein.

'Abdu'l-Bahá. *The Promulgation of Universal Peace*. Comp. Howard MacNutt. Wilmette, IL: Bahá'í Publishing Trust, 1982.

Alexie, Sherman. *First Indian on the Moon*. New York: Hanging Loose, 1994.

Allen, Paula Gunn. *The Sacred Hoop: Recovering the Feminine in American Indian Traditions*. Boston: Beacon, 1986.

——. "A Stranger in My Own Life: Alienation in Native American Prose and Poetry." ASAIL *Newsletter* 3.1 (1979): 1–10. Pt. 1 of a two-part series; 3.2 (1979): 16–23. Pt. 2.

——, ed. *Studies in American Indian Literature: Critical Essays and Course Designs*. New York: The Modern Language Association of America, 1983.

Archibald, Jo-ann, and Ellen White. "Kwulasulwut S yuth [Ellen White's Teachings]." *Canadian Journal of Native Education* 19.2 (1992): 150–64.

Attinasi, John, and Paul Friedrich. "Dialogic Breakthrough: Catalysis and Synthesis in Life-Changing Dialogue." Tedlock and Mannheim 33–53.

Baca, Lorenzo. "San Lorenzo Day in Laguna." A. L. Walters, *Neon* 15–17.

Bakhtin, M. M. *The Dialogic Imagination*. Trans. Caryl Emerson and Michael Holquist. Ed. Michael Holquist. Austin: U of Texas P, 1981.

Ballinger, Franchot. "Living Sideways: Social Themes and Social Relationships in Native American Trickster Tales." *American Indian Quarterly* 13.1 (1989): 15–30.

Barnes, Kim. "A Leslie Marmon Silko Interview." *The Journal of Ethnic Studies* 13.4 (1986): 83–105.

Basso, Keith H. "'Stalking with Stories': Names, Places, and Moral Narrative Among the Western Apache." *Western Apache Language and Culture: Essays in Linguistic Anthropology*. Tucson: U of Arizona P, 1990. 99–137.

Bataille, Gretchen. "American Indian Literature: Traditions and Translations." *MELUS* 6.4 (winter 1979): 17–26.

Baudrillard, Jean. *Fatal Strategies*. Trans. Philip Beitchman and W. G. J. Niesluchowski. Ed. Jim Fleming. New York: Semiotext(e), 1990.

Bauman, Richard. "Verbal Art as Performance." *American Anthropologist* 77.2 (1975): 290–311.

Beck, Peggy V. and Anna Lee Walters. *The Sacred: Ways of Knowledge, Sources of Life.* Tsaile, AZ: Navajo Community College, 1992.

Belin, Esther G. "Bringing Hannah Home." A. L. Walters, *Neon* 18–19.

Benally, Herbert John. "Diné Bo'óhoo'aah Bindii'a': Navajo Philosophy of Learning." *Diné Be'iina'* 1.1 (1988): 133–48.

Benhabib, Seyla. "The Generalized and the Concrete Other: The Kohlberg-Gilligan Controversy and Feminist Theory." *Feminism as Critique.* Ed. Benhabib and Drucilla Cornell. Minneapolis: U of Minnesota P, 1987. 77–95, 174–81.

Bird, Gloria. "The Exaggeration of Despair in Sherman Alexie's *Reservation Blues.*" *Wicazo Sa Review* 9.2 (fall 1995): 47–52.

——. "Towards a Decolonization of the Mind and Text: Leslie Marmon Silko's *Ceremony.*" *Wicazo Sa Review* 9.2 (Fall 1993): 1–8.

Blaeser, Kimberly M. *Gerald Vizenor: Writing in the Oral Tradition.* Norman: U of Oklahoma P, 1996.

——. "Pagans Rewriting the Bible: Heterodoxy and the Representation of Spirituality in Native American Literature." *A Review of International English Literature* 25.1 (1994): 12–31.

Bleich, David. "Intersubjective Reading." *New Literary History* 27.3 (1986): 401–21.

Bright, William. "Poetic Structure in Oral Narrative." Tannen, *Spoken* 171–84.

Brill, Susan B. "The Hegemonic Vertex: Geometric Consequences for the Semiotic Triangle." *Semiotics 1992.* Ed. John Deely. New York: UP of America, 1993. 237–51.

——. Letter to Naomi Scheman. 2 Mar. 1995.

——. Rev. of *Native American Autobiography: An Anthology,* ed. Arnold Krupat. *Biography: An Interdisciplinary Quarterly* 19.3 (summer 1996): 308–312.

——. "Sherman Alexie." *Dictionary of Literary Biography: Native American Writers.* Ed. Kenneth M. Roemer. Ann Arbor: Gale Pub, 1997. 3–10.

——. *Wittgenstein and Critical Theory: Moving Beyond Postmodern Criticism and Towards Descriptive Investigations.* Athens: Ohio UP, 1995.

Brown, Alanna Kathleen. Comment to the author. Summer 1997.

——. "Pulling Silko's Threads Through Time: An Exploration of Storytelling." *American Indian Quarterly* 19.2 (spring 1995): 171–79.

Bruchac, Joseph. "Contemporary Native American Writing: An Overview." Wiget, *Dictionary* 311–28.

——. *Roots of Survival: Native American Storytelling and the Sacred.* Golden, CO: Fulcrum, 1996.

——, ed. *Survival This Way: Interviews with American Indian Poets.* Tucson: U of Arizona P, 1987.

Castro, Michael. "Indian Consciousness: Poetic Visions Of Tribal Life." Rev. of *The Lone Ranger and Tonto Fistfight in Heaven,* by Sherman Alexie. *St Louis Post Dispatch* 30 Jan. 1994: 5C.

——. *Interpreting the Indian: Twentieth Century Poets and the Native American.* Norman: U of Oklahoma P, 1983.

Chinweizu. "The Responsibilities of Scholars of African Literature." *Research Priorities in African Literatures.* Ed. Beruth Lindfors. New York: Zell, 1984. 13–19.

Clements, William M. *Native American Verbal Art: Texts and Contexts.* Tucson: U of Arizona P, 1996.

Clifford, James. "Introduction: Partial Truths." Clifford and Marcus, *Writing* 1–26.

——. "On Ethnographic Allegory." Clifford and Marcus, *Writing* 98–121.

——, and George E. Marcus, eds. *Writing Cultures: The Poetics and Politics of Ethnography.* Berkeley: U of California P, 1986.

Coltelli, Laura, ed. *Winged Words: American Indian Writers Speak.* Lincoln: U of Nebraska P, 1990.

Cook-Lynn, Elizabeth. "Literary and Political Questions of Transformation: American Indian Fiction Writers." *Wicazo Sa Review* 11.1 (spring 1995): 46–51.

——. *Why I Can't Read Wallace Stegner and Other Essays: A Tribal Voice.* Madison: U of Wisconsin P, 1996.

Crawford, John F., William Balassi, and Anne Esteroy, eds. *This Is About Vision: Interviews with Southwestern Writers.* Albuquerque: U of New Mexico P, 1990.

Danielson, Linda L. "*Storyteller:* Grandmother Spider's Web." *Journal of the Southwest* 30 (1988): 325–55.

——. "The Storytellers in *Storyteller.*" *Studies in American Indian Literatures* 1.2 (fall 1989): 21–31.

Dasenbrock, Reed Way. "Forms of Biculturalism in Southwestern Literature: The Work of Rudolfo Anaya and Leslie Marmon Silko." *Genre* 21 (1988): 307–20.

Deely, John. *Basics of Semiotics.* Ed. Thomas A. Sebeok. Bloomington: Indiana UP, 1990.

Diamond, Stanley. *In Search of the Primitive: A Critique of Civilization.* New Brunswick: Transaction, 1974.

Dorris, Michael. "Native American Literature in an Ethnohistorical Context." *College English* 41 (1979): 147–62.

Durham, Jimmie. "Cowboys and . . . Notes on Art, Literature, and American Indians in the Modern American Mind." *The State of Native America: Genocide, Colonization, and Resistance.* Ed. M. Annette Jaimes. Boston: South End, 1992. 423–38.

Dwyer, Kevin. "The Dialogic of Ethnology." *Dialectical Anthropology* 4.3 (1979): 205–24.

Dyk, Walter. *Son of Old Man Hat: A Navaho Autobiography.* Lincoln: U of Nebraska P, 1967.

Erdrich, Louise. *The Beet Queen.* New York: Holt, 1986.

Farley, Margaret A. "A Feminist Version of Respect for Persons." *Journal of Feminist Studies in Religion* 9.1–2 (1993): 183–98.

Fast, Robin Riley. "Borderland Voices in Contemporary Native American Poetry." *Contemporary Literature* 36.3 (1995): 508–36.

Finnegan, Ruth. *Literacy and Orality.* Oxford: Blackwell, 1988.

——. "Literacy versus Non-Literacy: The Great Divide?: Some Comments on the Significance of 'Literature' in Non-literate Cultures." *Modes of Thought: Essays on Thinking in Western and Non-Western Societies.* Ed. Robin Horton and Ruth Finnegan. London: Faber, 1973. 112–44.

Fischer, Michael M. J. "Ethnicity and the Post-Modern Arts of Memory." Clifford and Marcus 194–233.

Fish, Stanley. *Is There a Text in This Class?: The Authority of Interpretive Classrooms.* Cambridge: Harvard UP, 1980.

Fisher, Dexter, ed. *The Third Woman: Minority Writers of the United States.* Boston: Houghton, 1980.

Fishman, Joshua A. "Language, Ethnicity, and Racism." Saville-Troike 297–309.

Foley, John Miles. "Word-Power, Performance, and Tradition." *Journal of American Folklore* 105.417 (1992): 275–301.

Francisco, Nia. *Blue Horses for Navajo Women.* Greenfield Center: Greenfield Review P, 1988.

——. "Navajo Traditional Knowledge." Beck and Walters 267–89.

Frank, Della. "T'aa Diné Nishli." A. L. Walters, *Neon* 1–2.

Frazer, Sir James George. *The New Golden Bough.* New York: Criterion, 1959.

Freire, Paulo. *Pedagogy of the Oppressed.* New York: Seabury, 1970.

Frey, Rodney. "Re-telling One's Own: Storytelling Among the Apśaalooke (Crow Indians)." *Plains Anthropologist* 28.100 (1983): 129–35.

Gardner, Ethel B. "Ka-im's Gift: A St:lo Legend." *Canadian Journal of Native Education* 15.3 (1988): 101–08.

Gill, Sam D. "Prayer as Person: The Performative Force in Navajo Prayer Acts." *History of Religions* 17.1 (1977): 143–57.

Godard, Barbara. "The Politics of Representation: Some Native Canadian Women Writers." *Canadian Literature* 124–25 (1990): 183–225.

——. "Voicing Difference: The Literary Production of Native Women." *Amazing Space: Writing Canadian Women Writing.* Ed. Shirley Newman and Smaro Kamboureli. Edmonton: Longspoon/NeWest, 1986. 87–107.

Goody, Jack, and Ian Watt. "The Consequences of Literacy." *Comparative Studies in Society and History* 5 (1963): 304–45.

Grant, Agnes. "Content in Native Literature Programs." Mokkakit Conference of the Indian Education Research Association. Winnipeg, 18 Oct. 1986. 1–16.

——. "Native Literature in the Curriculum." *Selected Papers from the 1986 Mokkakit Conference.* Vancouver: Mokkakit Indian Education Research Assn., 1988.

——. "Reclaiming the Lineage House: Canadian Native Women Writers." *Studies in American Indian Literatures* 6.1 (1994): 43–62.

——. *"The Way to Rainy Mountain* in a Community-Based Oral Narratives Course for Cree and Ojibway Students." Roemer, *Approaches* 138–44.

Graulich, Melody, ed. *"Yellow Woman" / Leslie Marmon Silko.* New Brunswick: Rutgers UP, 1993.

Green, Rayna, ed. *That's What She Said: Contemporary Poetry and Fiction by Native American Women.* Bloomington: Indiana UP, 1984.

Gumperz, John J. "Sociocultural Knowledge in Conversational Inference." Saville-Troike 191–211.

Hallowell, A. Irving. "Cultural Factors in the Structuralization of Perception." *Social Psychology at the Crossroads.* Ed. John H. Rohver and Muzafer Sherif. New York: Harper, 1951.

——. "Ojibwa Ontology, Behavior, and World View." *Culture in History: Essays in Honor of Paul Radin.* Ed. Stanley Diamond. New York: Columbia UP, 1960. 19–52.

Handler, Richard. "On Dialogue and Destructive Analysis: Problems in Narrating Nationalism and Ethnicity." *Journal of Anthropological Research* 41.2 (1985): 171–82.

Harding, Sandra, ed. *The "Racial" Economy of Science: Toward a Democratic Future.* Bloomington: Indiana UP, 1993.

Hegeman, Susan. "Native American 'Text' and the Problem of Authenticity." *American Quarterly* 41.2 (1989): 265–83.

Hertz, J. H. *The Pentateuch and Haftorahs: Hebrew Text, English Translation and Commentary.* 2nd ed. London: Soncino, 5732 (1971 c.e.).

Hill, Jane H., and Judith T. Irvine, eds. *Responsibility and Evidence in Oral Discourse (Studies in the Social and Cultural Foundations of Language).* Cambridge: Cambridge UP, 1992.

Hill, Jane H., and Ofelia Zepeda. "Mrs. Patricio's Trouble: The Distribution of Responsibility in an Account of Personal Experience." Hill and Irvine 197–225.

Hindman, Jane E. "'I Think of That Mountain as My Maternal Grandmother': Constructing Self and Other through Landscape." MLA Convention. Toronto, 27–30 Dec. 1993.

Hirsch, Bernard A. "'The Telling Which Continues': Oral Tradition and the Written Word in Leslie Marmon Silko's *Storyteller." American Indian Quarterly* 12 (1988): 1–26.

Hogan, Linda. "Who Puts Together." Allen, *Studies* 169–177.

Holmes, James R. "The Status of Persons or Who Was That Masked Metaphor?" *Advances in Descriptive Psychology* 6 (1991): 15–35.

Hunter, Carol. "American Indian Literature." *MELUS* 8.2 (1981): 82–85.

Hymes, Dell. "Introduction: Toward Ethnographies of Communication." *American Anthropologist* 66.6 (1964): 1–34.

——. *"In vain I tried to tell you."* Philadelphia: U of Pennsylvania P, 1981.

Irwin, Lee. "No Privileged Observers: A Reply to Geertz." *Religion* 24 (1994): 14–15.

Jabès, Edmond. *The Book of Margins.* Trans. Rosemarie Waldrop. Chicago: U of Chicago P, 1993.

Jahner, Elaine. "A Critical Approach to American Indian Literature." Allen, *Studies* 211–24.

——. "Indian Literature and Critical Responsibility." *Studies in American Indian Literatures* 1.1 (1977): 3–7. Rpt. in *Studies in American Indian Literatures* 5.2 (1993): 7–12.

——. "Intermediate Forms between Oral and Written Literature." Allen, *Studies* 66–74.

Jaskoski, Helen. "Image and Silence." Roemer, *Approaches* 69–77.

——. "Teaching with *Storyteller* at the Center." *Studies in American Indian Literatures* 5.1 (1993): 51–61.

Jones, Patricia. "The Web of Meaning: Naming the Absent Mother in *Storyteller.*" Graulich 214–15.

Kelly, Jennifer. "Coming out of the House: A Conversation with Lee Maracle." *A Review of International English Literature* 25.1 (1994): 73–88.

Kroeber, Karl. "Oral Narrative in an Age of Mechanical Reproduction." *Studies in American Indian Literatures* 11.2 (1987): 61–93. Rpt. in *Studies in American Indian Literatures* 5.2 (1993): 72–88.

——. *Retelling/Rereading: The Fate of Storytelling in Modern Times.* New Brunswick: Rutgers UP, 1992.

Kroskrity, Paul V. "Growing With Stories: Line, Verse, and Genre in an Arizona Tewa Text." *Journal of Anthropological Research* 41.2 (1985): 183–99.

Krumholz, Linda J. "'To understand this world differently': Reading and Subversion in Leslie Marmon Silko's 'Storyteller.'" *Ariel* 25.1 (1994): 89–113.

Krupat, Arnold. "The Dialogic of Silko's *Storyteller.*" Vizenor, *Narrative* 55–68.

——. *Ethnocriticism: Ethnography, History, Literature.* Berkeley: U of California P, 1992.

——. "Identity and Difference in the Criticism of Native American Literature." *diacritics* 13.2 (1983): 2–13.

——, ed. *Native American Autobiography: An Anthology.* Madison: U of Wisconsin P, 1994.

——, ed. *New Voices in Native American Literary Criticism.* Washington: Smithsonian Inst., 1993.

——, and Brian Swann. "Post-Structuralism and Oral Literature." *Recovering the Word: Essays on Native American Literature.* Berkeley: U of California P, 1987. 113–28.

Lamb, Susan Pierce. "Shifting Paradigms and Modes of Consciousness: An Integrated View of the Storytelling Process." *Folklore and Mythology Studies* 5 (1981): 5–19.

Larson, Sidner. "Native American Aesthetics: An Attitude of Relationship." *MELUS* 17.3 (1991–92): 53–67.

Lincoln, Kenneth. "Tai-me to Rainy Mountain: The Makings of American Indian Literature." *American Indian Quarterly* 10.2 (spring 1986): 101–17.

Lord, Albert B. *The Singer of Tales.* Cambridge: Harvard UP, 1960.

Lorde, Audre. "The Master's Tools Will Never Dismantle the Master's House." *This Bridge Called My Back: Writings by Radical Women of Color.* Ed. Cherríe Moraga and Gloria Anzaldúa. New York: Kitchen Table, 1983. 98–101.

Lotman, Yuri M. *Universe of the Mind: A Semiotic Theory of Culture.* Trans. Ann Shukman. Bloomington: Indiana UP, 1990.

Ludlow, Jeannie. "Working (In) the In-Between: Poetry, Criticism, Interrogation, and Interruption." *Studies in American Indian Literatures* 6.1 (1994): 24–42.

Lungren, Jodi. " 'Being a Half-breed': Discourses of Race and Cultural Syncreticity in the Works of Three Métis Women Writers." *Canadian Literature* 144 (1995): 62–77.

Manley, Kathleen, and Paul W. Rea. "An Interview with Simon Ortiz." *Journal of the Southwest* 31.3 (1989): 362–77.

Maracle, Lee. "Oratory: Coming to Theory." *Essays on Canadian Writing* 54 (1994): 7–11.

——. *Ravensong: A Novel.* Vancouver: Press Gang Publishers, 1993.

Maranhão, Tullio. "Recollections of Fieldwork Conversations, or Authorial Duties in Anthropological Writing." Hill and Irvine 260–88.

Meadows, Jim. Interview with Luci Tapahonso. WCBU-FM, Peoria, IL. 24 Apr. 1996.

Melting Tallow, Robin. Afterword. *Writing the Circle: Native Women of Western Canada.* Comp. and ed. Jeanne Perreault and Sylvia Vance. Edmonton: NeWest Publishers, 1993. 288.

Momaday, N. Scott. *House Made of Dawn.* New York: Harper, Perennial Library, 1977.

——. "The Man Made of Words." *Symposium of the Whole: A Range of Discourse Toward an Ethnopoetics.* Ed. Jerome Rothenberg and Diane Rothenberg. Berkeley: U of California P, 1983. 414–16.

Moore, David L. "Decolonializing Criticism: Reading Dialectics and Dialogics in Native American Literatures." *Studies in American Indian Literatures* 6.4 (1994): 7–35.

——. "Myth, History, and Identity in Silko and Young Bear." Krupat, *New Voices* 370–95.

Morey, Sylvester M. *Can the Red Man Help the White Man?* New York: Myrin Inst., 1970.

Morrison, Kenneth M. "They Act as Though They Have No Relatives: A Reply to Geertz." *Religion* 24 (1994): 11–12.

Motoyoshi, Michelle M. "The Experience of Mixed-Race People: Some Thoughts and Theories." *The Journal of Ethnic Studies* 18.2 (1990): 77–94.

Murphy, Francis. *Yvor Winters: Uncollected Essays and Reviews.* Chicago: Swallow, 1973.

Murray, David. *Forked Tongues: Speech, Writing and Representation in North American Indian Texts.* Bloomington: Indiana UP, 1991.

Nelson, Robert M. "He Said / She Said: Writing Oral Tradition in John Gunn's 'Ko-pot Ka-nat' and Leslie Silko's *Storyteller.*" *Studies in American Indian Literatures* 5.1 (1993): 31–50.

Niatum, Duane. "History in the Colors of Song: A Few Words on Contemporary Native American Poetry." Scholer 25–34.

Noddings, Nel. *Caring: A Feminine Approach to Ethics and Moral Education.* Berkeley: U of California P, 1984.

O'Brien, Susie. "'Please Eunice, Don't Be Ignorant': The White Trickster in Lee Maracle's Fiction." *Canadian Literature* 144 (1995): 82–96.

O'Connor, June. "On Studying and Being the Other: An Open Letter to Armin Geertz." *Religion* 24 (1994): 8–11.

Olson, David R. "From Utterance to Text: The Bias of Language in Speech and Writing." *Harvard Educational Review* 47.3 (1977): 257–81.

Ong, Walter J. *Orality and Literacy: The Technologizing of the Word.* New York: Routledge, 1982.

Ortiz, Simon J. *After and Before the Lightning.* Tucson: U of Arizona P, 1994.

———. "Always the Stories: A Brief History and Thoughts on My Writing." Scholer 57–69.

———. Rev. of *Coyote Tales from the Indian Pueblos,* by Evelyn Dahl Reed and *The Other Side of Nowhere: Contemporary Coyote Tales,* by Peter Blue Cloud. *American Indian Quarterly* 16.4 (1992): 598–600.

———. *Song, Poetry and Language-Expression and Perception.* Tsaile, AZ: Navajo Community College, n.d.

———. "That's the Place Indians Talk About." *Wicazo Sa Review* 1.1 (spring 1985): 45–49.

———. "Towards a National Indian Literature: Cultural Authenticity in Nationalism." *MELUS* 8.2 (summer 1981): 7–12.

———. *Woven Stone.* Tucson: U of Arizona P, 1992.

Ossorio, Peter G. "An Overview of Descriptive Psychology." *The Social Construction of the Person.* Ed. Kenneth J. Gergen and Keith E. Davis. New York: Springer-Verlag, 1985. 19–40.

———. *Persons.* Whittier, CA: Linguistic Research Institute, 1996.

Owens, Louis. *Bone Game.* Norman: U of Oklahoma P, 1994.

———. *Other Destinies: Understanding the American Indian Novel.* Norman: U of Oklahoma P, 1992.

Paul, Doris A. *Navajo Code Talkers.* Philadelphia: Dorrance, 1973.

Perreault, Jeanne. "Notes from the Co-editors." *Ariel: A Review of International English Literature* 25.1 (1994): 9–11.

———, and Sylvia Vance, comps. and eds. *Writing the Circle: Native Women of Western Canada.* Edmonton: NeWest, 1990.

Petrone, Penny. *Native Literature in Canada: From the Oral Tradition to the Present.* Toronto: Oxford UP, 1990.

Polanyi, Livia. "Literary Complexity in Everyday Storytelling." Tannen, *Spoken* 155–70.

———. "The Nature of Meaning of Stories in Conversation." *Studies in Twentieth Century Literature* 6.1–2 (1981–82): 51–65.

———. "What Stories Can Tell Us About Their Teller's World." *Poetics Today* 2.2 (1981): 97–112.

Profeit-Leblanc, Louise. "Ancient Stories, Spiritual Legacies." *Telling It: Women and Language Across Cultures.* Ed. Telling It Book Collective: Sky Lee, Lee Maracle, Daphne Marlatt, and Betsy Warland. Vancouver: Press Gang, 1990.

Purdy, John Lloyd. "New Native American Fiction." Wiget, *Dictionary* 371–376.

Rabinow, Paul. "Representations Are Social Facts: Modernity and Post-Modernity in Anthropology." Clifford and Marcus 234–61.

Revard, Carter. *An Eagle Nation.* Tucson: U of Arizona P, 1993.

Roberts, Mary Kathleen. "Worlds and World Reconstruction." *Advances in Descriptive Psychology* 4 (1985): 17–43.

Roemer, Kenneth M., ed. *Approaches to Teaching Momaday's* The Way to Rainy Mountain. New York: MLA, 1988.

———. "Teaching Indian Literature." Wiget, *Dictionary* 347–52.

Rosenblatt, Louise M. "The Poem as Event." *College English* 26.2 (1964): 123–28.

Ruoff, A. LaVonne Brown. "Recent Native American Literary Criticism." *College English* 55.6 (Oct. 1993): 655–65.

———. "The Survival of Tradition: American Indian Oral and Written Narratives." *The Massachusetts Review* 27.2 (summer 1986): 274–93.

Ruppert, James. "Mediation and Multiple Narrative in Contemporary Native American Fiction." *Texas Studies in Literature and Language* 28.2 (summer 1982): 209–25.

———. *Mediation in Contemporary Native American Fiction.* Norman: U of Oklahoma P, 1995.

———. "The Uses of Oral Tradition in Six Contemporary Native American Poets." *American Indian Culture and Research Journal* 4.4 (1980): 87–110.

Sapir, Edward. "The Status of Linguistics as a Science." *Language* 5 (1929): 207–14.

Sarris, Greg. *Keeping Slug Woman Alive: A Holistic Approach to American Indian Texts.* Berkeley: U of California P, 1993.

——. "The Verbal Art of Mabel McKay: Talk as Culture, Contact and Cultural Critique." *MELUS* 16.1 (spring 1989–90): 95–112.

Saville-Troike, Muriel, ed. *Georgetown University Round Table on Languages and Linguistics 1977: Linguistics and Anthropology.* Washington, D. C.: Georgetown UP, 1977.

Scarberry-Garcia, Susan. *Landmarks of Healing: A Study of* House Made of Dawn. Albuquerque: U of New Mexico P, 1990.

Schipper, Mineke. "Culture, Identity, and Interdiscursivity." *Research in African Literatures* 24.4 (1993): 39–48.

Scholer, Bo, ed. *Coyote Was Here: Essays on Contemporary Native American Literary and Political Mobilization.* Aarhus, Den.: Seklos, 1984.

Schram, Peninnah. "One Generation Tells Another: The Transmission of Jewish Values Through Storytelling." *Literature in Performance* 4.2 (1984): 33–45.

Schwab, Gabriele. "Reader-Response and the Aesthetic Experience of Otherness." *Stanford Literature Review* 3 (1986): 107–36.

Sebeok, Thomas A. *American Signatures: Semiotic Inquiry and Method.* Ed. Iris Smith. Norman: U of Oklahoma P, 1991.

Sherzer, Joel, and Anthony C. Woodbury, eds. *Native American Discourse: Poetic and Rhetoric.* Cambridge: Cambridge UP, 1987.

Shuffelton, Frank, ed. *A Mixed Race: Ethnicity in Early America.* New York: Oxford UP, 1993.

Silko, Leslie Marmon. *Ceremony.* New York: Penguin, 1977.

——. "The Indian With a Camera." *A Circle of Nations: Voices and Visions of American Indians/North American Native Writers and Photographers.* Ed. John Gattuso. Hillsboro, OR: Beyond Words, 1993. 4–7.

——. "Landscape, History, and the Pueblo Imagination: From a High Arid Plateau in New Mexico." *On Nature: Nature, Landscape, and Natural History.* Ed. Daniel Halpern. San Francisco: North Point, 1987. 83–94.

——. "Language and Literature from a Pueblo Indian Perspective." *English Literature: Opening Up the Canon.* Ed. Leslie A. Fiedler and Houston A. Baker, Jr. Baltimore: Johns Hopkins UP, 1981. 54–72.

——. *Storyteller.* New York: Arcade, 1981.

——. *Yellow Woman and a Beauty of the Spirit: Essays on Native American Life Today.* New York: Simon, 1996.

——, and Dexter Fisher. "Stories and Their Tellers—A Conversation with Leslie Marmon Silko." *The Third Woman: Minority Women Writers of the United States.* Ed. Dexter Fisher. Boston: Houghton, 1980. 18–23.

Simard, Rodney. "American Indian Literatures, Authenticity, and the Canon." *World Literature Today* 66.2 (spring 1992): 243–48.

Sobol, Joseph D. "Innervision and Innertext: Oral and Interpretive Modes of Storytelling Performance." *Oral Tradition* 7.1 (1992): 66–86.

Spivak, Gayatri Chakravorty. Translator's Preface. *Of Grammatology.* By Jacques Derrida. Trans. Spivak. Baltimore: John Hopkins UP, 1976. 9–38.

Standing Bear, Luther. *Land of the Spotted Eagle.* Boston: Houghton, 1933.

Swearingen, C. Jan. "Oral Hermeneutics During the Transition to Literacy: The Contemporary Debate." *Cultural Anthropology* 1 (1986): 138–56.

Tannen, Deborah. "The Oral/Literate Continuum in Discourse." *Spoken.* 1–16.

——, ed. *Spoken and Written Language: Exploring Orality and Literacy.* Norwood, NJ: Ablex, 1982.

——. *Talking Voices: Repetition, Dialogue, and Imagery in Conversational Discourse.* New York: Cambridge UP, 1989.

Tapahonso, Luci. *Blue Horses Rush In: Poems & Stories.* Tucson: U of Arizona P, 1997.

——. *A Breeze Swept Through.* Albuquerque: West End, 1987.

——. *Sáanii Dahataał: The Women Are Singing.* Tucson: U of Arizona P, 1993.

——. *Seasonal Woman.* Santa Fe: Tooth of Time, 1981.

Tedlock, Dennis. *The Spoken Word and the Work of Interpretation.* Philadelphia: U of Pennsylvania P, 1983.

Tedlock, Dennis, and Bruce Mannheim. *The Dialogic Emergence of Culture.* Urbana: U of Illinois P, 1995.

Tedlock, Dennis, and Barbara Tedlock, eds. *Teachings from the American Earth: Indian Religion and Philosophy.* New York: Liveright, 1992.

Tirrell, Lynne. "Storytelling and Moral Agency." *The Journal of Aesthetics and Art Criticism* 48.2 (1990): 115–26.

Toelken, J. Barre. "The 'Pretty Language' of Yellowman: Genre, Mode, and Texture in Navaho Coyote Narratives." *Genre* 2.3 (1969): 211–35.

——. "Seeing with a Native Eye: How Many Sheep Will It Hold." *Seeing With a Native Eye: Essays on Native American Religion.* Ed. Walter Capps. New York: Harper, 1976.

——, and Tacheeni Scott. "Poetic Retranslation and the 'Pretty Languages' of Yellowman." *Traditional Literatures of the American Indian: Texts and Interpretations.* Comp. and ed. Karl Kroeber. Lincoln: U of Nebraska P, 1981. 65–116.

Tomm, Winnie. "Ethics and Self-knowing: The Satisfaction of Desire." *Explorations in Feminist Ethics: Theory and Practice.* Ed. Eve Browning Cole and Susan Coultrap-McQuin. Bloomington: Indiana UP, 1992. 101–10.

Tompkins, Jane P., ed. "An Introduction to Reader-Response Criticism." *Reader-Response Criticism: From Formalism to Post-Structuralism.* Baltimore: Johns Hopkins UP, 1980. ix–xxvi.

——. "The Reader in History: The Changing Shape of Literary Response." *Reader-Response Criticism.* 201–32.

Trinh T. Minh-ha. *Woman, Native, Other: Writing Postcoloniality and Feminism.* Bloomington: Indiana UP, 1989.

Tyler, Stephen A. "On Being Out of Words." *Cultural Anthropology* 1 (1986): 131–38.

Vangen, Kate Shanley. "The Devil's Domain: Leslie Silko's 'Storyteller.'" Scholer 116–17.

Vizenor, Gerald. *Manifest Manners: Postindian Warriors of Survivance.* Hanover, NH: UP of New England, 1994.

——, ed. *Narrative Chance: Postmodern Discourse on Native American Indian Literatures.* Albuquerque: U of New Mexico P, 1989.

——. "A Postmodern Introduction." *Narrative* 3–16.

Waldrop, Rosemarie. "Alarms & Excursions." *The Politics of Poetic Form: Poetry and Public Policy.* Ed. Charles Bernstein. New York: ROOF, 1990. 45–72.

Walters, Anna Lee. "American Indian Thought and Identity in American Fiction." Scholer 35–39.

——. *Ghost Singer.* Albuquerque: U of New Mexico P, 1988.

——. *Neon Pow-Wow: New Native American Voices of the Southwest.* Flagstaff, AZ: Northland, 1993.

——. *The Sun Is Not Merciful.* Ithaca: Firebrand, 1985.

——. *Talking Indian: Reflections on Survival and Writing.* Ithaca: Firebrand, 1992.

Walters, Gertrude. "Shimásání (Grandmother)." A. L. Walters, *Neon* 110.

Warrior, Robert Allan. "Reading American Indian Intellectual Traditions." *World Literature Today* 66.2 (spring 1992): 236–40.

——. *Tribal Secrets: Recovering American Intellectual Traditions* Minneapolis: U of Minnesota P, 1995.

Welch, James. *Winter in the Blood.* New York: Harper, 1974. New York: Penguin, 1986.

Wiget, Andrew, ed. *Dictionary of Native American Literature.* New York: Garland, 1994.

——. "Identity, Voice and Authority: Artist, Audience Relations in Native American Literature." *World Literature Today* 66.2 (spring 1992): 258–63.

——. "Native American Oral Literatures: A Critical Orientation." Wiget, *Dictionary* 3–18.

——. *Simon Ortiz.* Boise: Boise State UP, 1986.

Willard, William. "The Literary Stelae of Hidden Nations, The Question of Whether or Not Native American Literature Is a Minor Literature Depends on Who Asked the Question." *Wicazo Sa Review* 9.1 (spring 1995): 33–39.

Winters, Yvor. "The Indian in English" and "Open Letter to the Editors of This Quarter." Murphy 32–43.

Witherspoon, Gary. *Language and Art in the Navajo Universe.* Ann Arbor: U of Michigan P, 1977.

Wittgenstein, Ludwig. *Culture and Value.* Trans. Peter Winch. Ed. G. H. von Wright. Chicago: U of Chicago P, 1984.

——. *Lectures and Conversations on Aesthetics, Psychology and Religious Belief.* Comp. and ed. Cyril Barrett. Berkeley: U of California P, 1967.

——. *Philosophical Investigations.* Trans. G. E. M. Anscombe. 3rd ed. New York: Macmillan, 1958.

——. *Philosophical Investigations.* Oxford: Blackwell, 1984.

——. *Remarks on Colour.* Trans. Linda L. McAlister and Margarete Schattle. Ed. G. E. M. Anscombe. Berkeley: U of California P, 1977.

——. *Remarks on Frazer's* Golden Bough. Trans. A. C. Miles. Ed. Rush Rhees. S. Yorks, Eng.: Brynmill, 1979.

——. *Remarks on the Philosophy of Psychology.* Vol. 1. Ed. G. E. M. Anscombe and G. H. von Wright. Trans. Anscombe. Vol. 2. Ed. von Wright and Heikki Nyman. Trans. C. G. Luckhardt and M. A. E. Aue. Chicago: U of Chicago P, 1988.

——. *Tractatus Logico-Philosophicus.* Trans. C. K. Ogden. New York: Routledge, 1988.

Zeiger, Carolyn Allen. "The Miss Marple Model of Psychological Assessment." *Advances in Descriptive Psychology* 6 (1991): 151–83.

Zolbrod, Paul. "Navajo Poetry in a Changing World: What the Diné Can Teach Us." *Studies in American Indian Literatures* 6.4 (1994): 77–93.

INDEX

Abel (character), 52–64: disempowerment of, 54; identity of, 53, 62; and
language, 54–55, 58, 63; personhood
of, 53; running, 60; and the sacred, 52,
59–60, 62–63; silence of, 54–57, 59,
63
absence, 86, 106, 212, 214, 223, 226. *See
also* presence
absolutism, 70
accessibility, 79–80, 204
agency, 56, 119, 125, 140–141. *See also*
personhood
Alexie, Sherman, 155–156, 162: *First Indian on the Moon,* 190–198
Allen, Paula Gunn, 35, 87, 139–141,
159
American Indian literatures, 7, 51, 118–
119: canon of, 27; conversivity of, 209.
See also Native American literatures
animals, 117–126, 182–187, 223: horses,
76–81; Mountain Lion (character),
125; significance of, 121–122. *See also*
objectification; personification
audience, 74, 135: participatory, 72, 131–
134. *See also* listener-readers
autobiography. *See* ethnography

Baca, Lorenzo, 114
Bakhtin, Mikhail, 48, 69, 72–73, 170–
171
balance, 113, 127, 176, 216
Ballinger, Franchot, 182
Barnes, Kim, 23

Bataille, Gretchen, 4
Beck, Peggy, 96, 126, 214, 216, 219
Belin, Esther G., 82–85: "Bringing
Hannah Home," 83–85
Benally, Herbert John, 57, 126
Bird, Gloria, 14, 89, 91, 95, 205
Blaeser, Kimberly M., 113, 232n. 3: on
mixedblood Indians, 160; on Native
American literature, 197; on orality,
3, 13; on religion and spirituality, 79,
97–100, 115
boundaries, 110, 157, 195: complexity of,
92; conceptual, 139; of criticism and
theory, 10; interpretive, 26, 102; of our
worlds, 51, 211; perceptual, 30; Witt-
genstein on, 51, 92, 211. *See also* limits
Brown, Alanna Kathleen, 4, 128, 145
Bruchac, Joseph, 2

Campbell, Maria, 160–161
canon, 26–27, 49–51, 71
Castro, Michael, 108, 194
ceremonies, 53, 106, 109–110, 117, 129
change, 106, 110, 177, 203. *See also* transformation
Chinweizu, 9, 207–208, 210
Christianity, 79, 91, 97–104, 111–119
circularity, 64, 86–87, 178, 221: as conversive model, 47, 49, 86, 227
co-creativity, 156, 223: in conversive
scholarship, 10, 25; of stories, 111,
131, 217
colonization, 2, 50, 97, 217–218: effects

ABOUT THE AUTHOR

Susan Berry Brill de Ramírez is Associate Professor of English at Bradley University, where she has taught since completing her Ph.D. in English at the University of New Mexico in 1991. She has published widely in the areas of American Indian literatures, literary criticism and theory, women's literatures, and Bahá'í Studies. Her first book, *Wittgenstein and Critical Theory: Beyond Postmodern Criticism and Toward Descriptive Investigations* (Athens: Ohio UP, 1995), discusses the implications of Wittgensteinian philosophy for literary criticism and theory. She is currently researching the ethnographically constructed autobiographies of American Indian people and beginning work on an edited collection of essays on Native women writers.